SCIENCE AND RELIGION:
Fifty Years after Vatican II

SCIENCE AND RELIGION:
Fifty Years after Vatican II

A Time of Peace and Reconciliation

KENAN B. OSBORNE
and KI WOOK MIN

WIPF & STOCK · Eugene, Oregon

SCIENCE AND RELIGION: FIFTY YEARS AFTER VATICAN II
A Time of Peace and Reconciliation

Copyright © 2014 Kenan B. Osborne and Ki Wook Min. All rights reserved. Except for brief quotations in critical publications or reviews, no part of this book may be reproduced in any manner without prior written permission from the publisher. Write: Permissions, Wipf and Stock Publishers, 199 W. 8th Ave., Suite 3, Eugene, OR 97401.

Wipf & Stock
An imprint of Wipf and Stock Publishers
199 W. 8th Ave., Suite 3
Eugene, OR 97401

www.wipfandstock.com

ISBN 13: 978-1-62564-165-6

Manufactured in the U.S.A.

CONTENTS

	Introduction: A Time of Peace and Reconcilation	1
1	Science and Religion: An Identification of Terms	15
2	The Spiritual Beauty of Religion and Contemporary Scientific Issues	47
3	The Major Issues in Quantum Physics	81
4	Critical Alternatives: The Three Religions and Contemporary Science	98
5	Science and Religion: Frequent Forms of Challenge and Response	111
6	Two Major Intra-Religion Complications	131
7	Conclusions: A New Dimension in Science and Religion—A Time of Peace and Reconciliation	160
	Bibliography	179
	Index	189

INTRODUCTION
A Time of Peace and Reconciliation

PART ONE: THE MAJOR THEME OF THIS VOLUME

DURING THE PAST ONE hundred years, contemporary science has developed in a breathtaking way. Both the microcosm and the macrocosm of our universe have not only been studied in detail, but new findings and new theories have enriched our knowledge of the world in which we live out our lives. During this same period of time, communication has been computerized in both an immediate and a detailed way, and travel has included outstanding trips into space by humans themselves and by computerized instruments. The age of our universe is now computed in billions of years, and the multiple energies at work in the universe are breathtaking. The intense power of black holes as well as the unbelievable power of the miniscule neutrino leave the scientific community in wonderment. There is no doubt at all that contemporary science has changed the way contemporary women and men think, live, and plan.

During the same one hundred years, contemporary religions have experienced changes of which previous centuries of religious living had no inkling. These changes have opened the religions of the world to new vistas and new challenges. The leaders and scholars of the major religions have had to rethink the basic principles at work in their respective communities. Four major issues have complicated and challenged contemporary religion. These four issues are ecumenism, globalization, multiculturalism, and the enormous growth in contemporary human population. These four issues, along with the developments of science, have fundamentally changed the world in which we live physically, mentally, and religiously.

Ecumenism

The ecumenical movements that began in the early decades of the twentieth century have become a major part of today's religious world, not only in the Western world but throughout the entire gamut of religions on earth. The recent Lima Document (1982), with its presentation to all churches by the World Council of Churches and its petition for a response, has led to a multivolume publication of religious answers to the basic questions in the document.[1]

This alone has been a wake-up call for all religious denominations. Individual church denominations have had to face, in a serious way, the presence and validity of other denominations. In the past one hundred years, almost all religious denominations have responded, positively or negatively, to a new openness vis-à-vis alternative religious communities.

The academic interest in world religions has opened universities to departments of world religions, and not simply departments of a specific religion, such as Protestant religion, Catholic religion, and Jewish religion. In these new departments, Hinduism, Buddhism, Daoism, Islamic studies, and even native religions have attracted contemporary students in a strong way. In the past one hundred years, almost all religious denominations have responded, positively or negatively, to this openness to alternative religions.

In the United States, the Council of Centers on Jewish-Christian Relations (CCJR) includes in its membership scholars from fourteen academic programs, four affiliate memberships, and a host of liaison members. Another important research center is the National Resource Center on the Middle East, based at Georgetown University. Today, there are many resource centers that focus on the theological dialogue among Christians, Muslims, and Jews. These centers clearly emphasize that interreligious ecumenism has developed strongly and that this form of ecumenism has deeply influenced contemporary Christianity, Islam, and Judaism.

Globalization

Since the early decades of the twentieth century, the earth has become globalized in dimensions that could not and did not exist in earlier centuries. Globalization is now an intrinsic part of almost all human history and endeavor. It has profoundly affected one's daily life no matter where

---

1. World Council of Churches, "Lima Document."

one might live. The economical world has been globalized. Governmental structures operate in a globalized framework. The scientific world has also been globalized not only in view of our solar system but in a larger network, namely the entire universe.

In itself, some form of globalization has been part and parcel of human life from its origins onward. In the earliest data we have regarding human life, one notes how an early Paleolithic human family outgrew its "familial territory" and consequently the family began to take over some acres of the "familial territory" of its neighbor. This was done so that the first family could survive. In other words, the Paleolithic family, in its own limited way, globalized itself.

Five hundred years ago, a larger phenomenon of globalization began to take place. Ships belonging to European countries such as Spain and Portugal followed by England and France travelled to all areas of the earth, and commercial exchange began to take place in an unprecedented way. European settlers took over parts of East Asia and Sub-Saharan Africa, as well as the entire Western world from the Canadian north to Tierra del Fuego in the south. From those years onward, what happened in one continent affected other continents of the earth. Globalization was no longer a family affair; it had become an intercontinental affair.

Planet Earth has continued to become more and more globalized. Today, with Facebook and other similar forms of communication, even personal lives at times have become universally globalized. Human beings can no longer live in a neighborhood untouched by the happenings that take place throughout the continents of our world. People in Kansas can be deeply affected by the situations going on in Myanmar and Madagascar.

Through the processes of globalization, contemporary religions are also exposed more quickly to world events, and world events profoundly and more rapidly affect the theological patterns of each of these religions. There is now no comfort zone in which religions can live in isolation and maintain their centuries-long perspectives. Never before in human history—and for our purposes, religious history—has such an extensive form of globalization so intruded into people's daily existence. Religious beliefs that seemed untouchable are now touchable, for they are profoundly challenged in a globalized world.

Three fourths of the world population is non-Christian. This datum alone raises a question for all Christians, namely, why is the Christian religion superior to all other religions? If there are so many non-Christians, how can an all-loving Christian God who is the creator of all people dismiss the majority of human life as "unsaved"? In itself, this is not a new question for Christians, but it is now being asked in a globalized framework. All religions today, whether major or minor, have been challenged vis-à-vis any and every claim to superiority. Many Christian leaders and scholars have attempted to answer these challenges. Some answers have been arrogant and hostile; other answers are hesitant and tentative; still other answers include an opening to dialogue and mutual respect.[2]

Multiculturalism

A third major worldwide influence has taken place throughout planet earth. This issue is usually called *multiculturalism*. However, it might be more exact if the issue would be named *equi-culturalism*, since all cultures have positive validity and therefore smaller cultures cannot summarily be set to one side as secondary or even inferior. All cultures, including the major cultures and the minor cultures, have dimensions of little value, but they also have dimensions of tremendous value.

The linguistic, philosophical, and theological descriptions used by various religious groups are cultural. The common Euro-American philosophy, which is heavily based on the writings of Plato, Aristotle, and other Greek scholars, has dominated Christian theological endeavors for centuries. Postmodern philosophy, which is clearly a Euro-American form of thinking, is a contemporary Western philosophy, for it offers a more relational and more subjective form of thinking than the Platonic and Aristotelian format. In a strong way, postmodern philosophy in all its various forms has challenged Christian theologies of the twentieth and twenty-first centuries in ways that have reconstructed the standard theologies found in today's multidenominational Christianity. Nonetheless, postmodern thinking remains a Western form of communication, and therefore does not interconnect easily with Asian and Sub-Saharan forms of philosophy.

There is today a strong Western interest in Asian and Sub-Saharan African forms of thinking. Today, these Asian and African ways of thinking seriously challenge the Euro-American intellectual dominance. The Asian and African ways of thinking are in their very foundational roots radically different from the Euro-American ways of thinking, and this complicates

---

2. For further information on globalization, see The Globalization Website: http://sociology.emory.edu/faculty/globalization/index.html.

Introduction

any attempt to "baptize" these Asian or African philosophies. For instance, in many Asian cultures there was and is no native word for God as understood by the Western world. Early Christian missionaries had to coin some word or combination of characters to translate the Western term "God" into an Asian language. Moreover, the Western term "being" has no counterpart in many Asian and African philosophical worlds. The Western world cannot impose its understanding of being on major populations that have no corresponding term, since Asian and African thought patterns have their own integrity. This integrity needs to be respected by religious scholars.[3]

The Enormous Growth in Contemporary Human Population

Helmut Schmidt in his latest book, *Religion in der Verantwortung*, focuses on a fourth dimensions of today's world, namely, the enormous growth in world population from the mid-1800s to the beginning of the twenty-first century.[4] In the twenty-first century, he writes, we are faced with an enormous global population. Up to the end of the nineteenth century there were roughly 1,600 million people living on planet earth. During the twentieth century, this number increased to 6,000 million. Schmidt writes that by the end of 2050 there will be 9,000 million people inhabiting planet earth.[5]

About.com provides us with the following statistics: "The world population has grown tremendously over the past two thousand years. In 1999, the world population passed the six billion mark. The latest official current world population estimate, for mid-year 2011, is estimated at 6,928,198,253. The chart below shows past world population data back

---

3. Literature on multiculturalism is abundant. Some recent studies are: Cajes, *Anitism and Perichoresis*; Diaz, *Towards a Theology of the Chamoru*; Kato, *How Immigrant Christians*; Cheah, *Race and Religion in American Buddhism*. See also the series of books edited by Peter C. Phan, Theology in Global Perspective (Orbis, 2005–).

4. See Schmidt, *Religion in der Verantwortung*, 162–63: "In den Jahrtausenden bis zum Ende des 19. Jahrhunderts, als es 1600 Millionen Menschen gab, ist die Weltbevölkerung ziemlich langsam gewachsen. Aber im Verlauf des 20 Jahrhunderts hat sie sich vervierfacht, so dass es heute über 6000Millionen Erdbewohner gibt. . . . Und er wird weiter schrumpfen, weil in vier bis fünf Jahrzehntenten, sagen wir um das Jahr 2050 herum, 9000 Millionen Menschen auf der Erde leben werden." See also 151–55 and 195–96.

5. Ibid., 163.

to the year one thousand and future world population projections through the year 2083."[6]

World Population Growth[7]	
Year	population
1000	275 million
1500	450 million
1650	500 million
1750	700 million
1804	1 billion
1900	1.6 billion
1927	2 billion
1960	3 billion
1975	4 billion
1985	4.85 billion
1995	5.7 billion
1999	6 billion
2006	6.5 billion
2011	7 billion
2025	8 billion
2043	9 billion
2083	10 billion

The three Abrahamic religions began and developed during a time when the population of the world was numbered in the millions and this lasted, as seen above, to 1804. In 1804, the world population moved for the first time to the billions. In 1900 the world population totaled 1.6 billion, and in 2011 the world population had reached seven billion. The growth in population will, more than likely, move on to the ten-billion mark in 2083.

In the future, as in the immediate past, most of the population growth will take place in East Asia, particularly in China and India, but also in many other East Asian countries, such as Taiwan, Japan, Thailand, Cambodia, Laos, Myanmar, etc. In these areas, the growth will not involve to any major degree a population growth in Christianity, Islam, or Judaism.

6. Rosenberg, "Current World Population."
7. Ibid. Some dates have been omitted from the original table.

Introduction

In East Asia, Indonesia, Malaysia, Pakistan, and Bangladesh will, of course, experience strong Muslim growth and the Philippines will experience strong Christian growth. However, the growth of religion in the East Asian areas will double and perhaps triple, but the dominant religions will be Hinduism, Islam, Buddhism, and Daoism. The Christian populations in East Asia will grow in a very small way, and the Jewish populations in the same area will be minimal.

Besides the issue of numerical identity, the three major monotheistic religions will need to confront in a major way the following two issues:

a. **Religious superiority:** The claim of religious superiority, which is strong in the three Abrahamic religions, will not be tolerated in Hindu, Buddhist, and Daoist areas. As the percentage of world population tries to grow in these non-Christian and non-Jewish Asian areas, the claim of religious superiority by Christians and Jews will be ignored by the overwhelming Asian population. The Muslim population, as stated above, will benefit by the growth in population and this is primarily due to its presence in Indonesia, Pakistan, Afghanistan, Malaysia, etc.

b. **Salvation/redemption:** The claim that salvation or redemption is attainable only through a relationship to Christianity or Islam or Judaism will be a second major theme to be rejected by the many other religious communities in East Asia. For Christianity and Islam, this rejection will engender serious reconsideration of their salvific theologies. For conservative Orthodox Judaism, this rejection will probably not be discussed since conservative Orthodox Judaism rarely if ever moves beyond its own positions.

The positions on superiority and salvation by Christianity and Judaism will have little to no effect on the total population. The Asian religions will grow and at the same time they will give little to no attention to the Christian and Jewish views on superiority and salvation. The effect of world population on Sub-Saharan Africa is difficult to establish, since the death rate in Africa today is extremely high. Moreover, the various native religions are surviving and in some areas even thriving, but their impact on the many cultural areas of Africa remains to be seen.

In this volume, the above four agents of change are taken for granted, and the abundant academic resources on these issues are clearly endorsed. This volume, however, is deliberately focused in a very limited way. Since each of the Abrahamic religions, Christianity, Islam, and Judaism, professes a special form of superiority and yet remains mutually interrelated, this volume limits its religious focus to these three religions. In this volume their religious superiority is called into question today on the basis of two questions: Can a religion that professes one creator God (monotheism) be so superior that parts of God's creation might not be saved? Secondly, in today's third-millennial scientific world, can one say that the current position of contemporary Euro-American science is above any and all other religions? In the past fifty years, volumes have been published on the complicated issues between science and religion. In these volumes, scientists have at time belittled religion while at other times many scientists have reached out positively to the religious leadership in a dialogical way. Religious leaders have also moved in two directions. Some religious leaders decry the "secular" dimension of science, while other religious leaders have listened intently and willingly to the scientific presentations.

The title of this book is *Science and Religion: Fifty Years after Vatican II: A Time of Peace and Reconciliation*. In the interfacing of certain contemporary sciences and the three religions mentioned above, a distinct roster of serious questions has arisen and at times even serious challenges have arisen. The origins of these questions and challenges are bilocated. At times, the locus comes from contemporary scientists who question or challenge particular religious beliefs. At times, the locus comes from contemporary religious leaders and scholars who question or challenge particular scientific conclusions. The intensity of the questions and answers also varies: some *questions* have moved to the status of harsh *challenges*, while some differences have remained mere interrogations. The responses and reactions by both scientists and religious leaders have reflected this difference of gradation—a gradation between *question* and *challenge*.

No single volume can resolve all the science-religion issues. What we wish to accomplish by this present book is simply a matter of "laying out on the table" the main elements found in very specific issues in today's science-religion relationship. In this volume, therefore, the authors specify as clearly as possible the questions and challenges of four contemporary scientific fields: first of all, the findings of current Near Eastern archaeology, which affect the religious presentations of Abraham, his descendants, as also the historical issues in the Mosaic literature as presented in the Hebrew Scriptures, the Qur'an, and the New Testament.[8] The second sci-

---

8. For further information, see the Center for Jewish, Christian, and Islamic Studies

Introduction

entific issue focuses on the contemporary scientific writing of history. In the contemporary form of historical writing, historical verification is paramount. In the religious historical writings of the three religions, one finds that there are *histories of Israel*, on the one hand, and on the other hand there are *Jewish histories of Israel*. The same is equally true of the *histories of Christianity* and *Christian histories of the Christian world* as well as the *Histories of Islam* and *Islamic histories of the Muslim religion*. In current historical writing on these three religions, many scientific historians who have stressed historical verification have been labeled "minimalists." Likewise, some Christian, Islamic, and Jewish authors have merited the term "maximalists," since they tend to stretch historical verification to its outer limits.

The third and fourth scientific foci in this volume include two issues: quantum physics and the contemporary scientific age of the universe. Both of these physical sciences, each from a different basis, challenge the religious leaders and scholars of the three religions as regards their presentations of God's plan for the universe. Quantum physics, which focuses strongly on the microcosm, has found a plurality of various orders, plans, programs, procedures, etc. in the microscopic world. The microcosm, from the standpoint of quantum physics, is abundantly interrelational. In this richness of interrelational activity, no scientist has as yet discovered an overarching interrelational plan that governs all these orders, plans, programs, etc.

The same conclusion can be affirmed by the contemporary scientists who have researched the age of the universe. Today, the age of the universe is calculated in billions of years. Macrocosmic scientists, however, have as yet not discovered any overarching plan of our universe, but they have found an abundance of internal orders, plans, programs, and procedures within the historical formation of the universe—none of which, however, can be seen as an overarching plan for all finite reality. The lack of such an overarching plan at the both microcosmic and macrocosmic levels calls into question the overarching divine plans of the universe proposed by the three religions. Moreover, the multi-billion-year age of the universe can and should seriously cause us to question the validity of the "divine plan" for the finite universe as presented by the three religions. When one deals with billions of years, the issue of historical verification becomes extremely

at Chicago Theological Seminary (http://www.ctschicago.edu/academics/theological-centers), the Center for Judaic-Christian Studies at the University of California, Santa Barbara (http://www.jcstudies.com); and the Academy for Judaic, Christian and Islamic Studies at the University of California at Los Angeles (http://www.bpcusa.org/mission_partners/).

questionable. For the three religions, the claim for a historical divine plan for a multi-billion-year-old world becomes an unverifiable claim. Contemporary quantum mechanics and the current scientific age of the universe negate any simplistic presentation vis-à-vis the history of the universe. The three religions are now seriously challenged whenever they maintain the historical validity of a "divine plan for the created world."

PART TWO: THE HISTORICAL PROCESSES THAT UNITE OR DISUNITE CHRISTIANITY, ISLAM, AND JUDAISM

The focus of this present volume is on the interreligious situation *today*. The focus is not on the long history that restates the times when the three religions enjoyed moments of cooperation and the times when the three religions seriously acted against each other.

The Jewish community from its earliest times down to the first century C.E. went through many changes in its form of leadership, from Moses to prophets to kings to priests to Pharisees and scribes. For several centuries, the Jewish community was torn apart by its two kingdoms. The devastation of the Jerusalem temple in 70 C.E. gave rise to rabbinic Judaism, which is the primary form of Jewish communities today.

During the time of Herod, a new Jewish prophet became a major leader—Jesus. The community he formed was considered by some authors, at least in its earliest stage, as a sect within Judaism itself.[9] By the end of the first century C.E., this "sect" slowly but surely became a separate group and in time was called "church." In the first and early second century, these two groups, the Jewish community and the Jesus community, separated from each other, but the separation happened at different times depending on the locale. In the early part of the second century, one finds two differing religious communities: Judaism and the Christian church. The relationship between these two was more often than not divisive and depreciatory of each other. The subsequent history of the Jewish-Christian relationship is filled with tension and open warfare. None of this negative history can be overlooked.

In the beginning of the seventh century, a new prophet appeared—Mohammad. At first his followers came from his own tribe, the Quraysh. As his reputation developed, his relations with the leading families of

---

9. See Meier, "Jesus," 1321–22 n. 79. See also Brown, Osiek, and Perkins, "Early Church," 1339–43 n. 80.

Introduction

Quraysh became worse. In 622 C.E. he left Mecca, in which his position had become extremely difficult, and with his followers he settled in Yathrib (called Medina today). Mohammad's power in a slow but steady way became stronger. Jewish traders and their families lived in Medina during the seventh century and so there was some interaction between the two groups. At first, it was a positive relationship, but in time the relationship with the Jewish leaders in Medina became strained. The subsequent history of the Jewish-Muslim relationship is filled with tension and open warfare. None of this negative history can be overlooked.

Muslim-Christian relationships reflect this same process. In the beginning, there was a time of peace and openness, but as the Arab world became politically dominated by Muslim Caliphs the presence of Christians within the Caliphates more often than not became strained. This negative relationship between Muslims and Christians reached a negative and powerful disruption at the time of the Crusades. This lasted down to the Ottoman Empire's expansion from 1299 to the end of World War I. During many of those years, the Muslim expansion was far-reaching. The history of the Christian-Muslim relationship is filled with tension and open warfare. None of this negative history can be overlooked.

In more contemporary times, other situations arose which solidified the antipathy between the three religious groups. Rabbi Abraham Geiger (1810–1874), for instance, wrote several works that claimed that the Qur'an is based on Jewish sources.[10] In 1880 Edouard Sayous, in his volume *Jesus Christ d'apres Mahomet ou les notions et les doctrines musulmanes sur le Cristianisme*, defended a position in which he claimed that the basic ideas in the Qur'an came from three forms of Essenism. Tor Andrae, in his volume *Mohammed—The Man and his Faith*, claims that Mohammad's doctrines came from Ebionism, the pseudo-Clementine material, and Mani. George Windengren, in his volume *Mohammed, the Apostle of God and His Ascension*, claims that the sources of the Qur'an stem from Gnosticism and Manichaeism.

None of this historical material that indicates a rejection by one religion of another religion can be set to one side. In this volume, the authors do not negate these centuries of negative interaction, which at times reached a very brutal level. Rather, the authors, even with an acknowledgement of the history of brutal interaction, want to present *A Time of Peace*

---

10. Geiger, *Was hat Mohammed aus dem Judentum aufgenommen* (ET: *Judaism and Islam*); *Das Judenthum und seine Geschichte* (ET: *Judaism and Its History*).

and Reconciliation, which is profoundly needed today. The *history* of the three religions cannot be changed. But the *future* of the three religions can be changed. Our volume is a small step towards a more peaceful future of science and religion and of the three religions themselves. Our view is this: change can take place only if the scientific questions and challenges mentioned above are faced in a less defensive way and in a more receptive way. This does not mean that the three religions should simply "accept" the scientific data; rather, it means that the religious leaders and scholars of the three religions should enter into a more open-minded discussion with certain scientists who are also willing to enter in these discussions with open minds.[11]

However, the authors of this volume also realize that there are two major intra-religion issues that must be faced, again with an open mind, by the leaders and scholars of the three religions. The claim of monotheism by each of these three religions cannot be validated if only the monotheism of one religion is considered valid. How can there be three views of the one God? In the pages that follow the authors suggest that the notion of *glimpses* of God be seriously considered, since glimpses of God are, in our view, the only way that theologians and faith-filled men and women can believe in an infinite God. No religion has a total understanding of an infinite God, and no religion can place limits on an infinite God. Monotheism and divine infinity are not credible unless the monotheisms of the three religions are harmonized. This will be taken up in a special way in chapter 6.

The second intrareligious issue focuses on the three divine plans for creation, as expressed in the three Abrahamic religions. It is impossible for a monotheistic God to reveal three different historical plans of the created universe. The contemporary scientific age of the universe deeply complicates any explanation of a universe which is billions of years old. The three differing historical plans of God for the created universe need to be discussed and historically verified in a more solid way by the leaders and scholars of the three religions. This issue is also treated at length in chapter 6.

In chapter 8 one will find a series of conclusions that are not meant to be final statements. Rather, they are meant to provide clearer foci for the

---

11. Throughout this work, the phrase "leaders and scholars of the three religions" is used with great frequency. By this phrase the authors do not refer only to the top leaders, since these leaders have to be careful about what they say publicly. Rather, we refer to those scientists and religious experts who at an academic level can dialogue with each other in an open and non-hostile way.

Introduction

contemporary differences between certain scientific positions and certain religious positions of Christianity, Islam, and Judaism. Thus, the authors have kept the science-religion discussion within limited boundaries. The authors have not presented a solution to the situation; rather they have arrived at some serious "conclusions" that hopefully will bring about a better dialogue between certain scientists and certain religious leaders and scholars.

I would like to express my gratitude to the Franciscan Friars of the Province of St. Barbara. From age 14 onwards, the Franciscans have academically trained me and they have also provided me with the opportunity to gain my professional degrees. This volume speaks frequently of spirituality and over many years I have lived with many Friars who have in their own lives presented me with an example of deep spirituality.

I would also like to thank Ki Wook Min, who agreed to be a co-author of this volume. Ki Wook Min was a student of mine several years ago, and I have followed his academic journey through the master's degree and through his present endeavors to gain a doctoral degree. He, his wife, and their children have often visited me.

I would also like to express my gratitude to the publishers of Wipf & Stock. Over many years, the publishers have included four of my books in their listing. In the writing of this present volume, the editors and those who have read and corrected the ms. have all been extremely helpful and patient. Wipf & Stock has been a major publishing house for many authors over the past decades.

Authors

Kenan B. Osborne is a professor emeritus of the Graduate Theological Union / Franciscan School of Theology, in Berkeley, California. He received his doctorate in theology from Ludwig Maximilians Universität, Munich, Germany, in 1967. He is a former president of the Catholic Theological Society of America (1978–1979) and a member of the national board of the American Academy of Religion (1979–1981). Since 1990, he has traveled extensively throughout Eastern Asia and has lectured in many Chinese universities. He is the author of eighteen books.

Ki Wook Min is a scholar from Seoul, Korea. His major in college was the physical sciences, especially quantum mechanics. He was the valedictorian of his class and received a special honor from South Korea for his work in physics. He completed his master's thesis with honors, "God, Nature, and Quantum Theory," at the Graduate Theological Union, Berkeley, California. He is currently working on his doctoral thesis under the direction of Professors Robert J. Russell and Ted Peters at the Center for Theology and the Natural Sciences, which is in residence at the Graduate Theological Union.

1

SCIENCE AND RELIGION
An Identification of Terms

PART ONE: INTRODUCTORY CONSIDERATIONS
The Main Theme of This Chapter

THE MAIN THEME OF this chapter can be stated as follows. Over the past fifty years, many books, articles, and monographs have been written on various issues regarding contemporary science and its impact on the religious world. However, certain scientific developments have continued to raise major questions and even challenges to positions presented by today's religious world. This chapter provides a sharper specification of these science-religion questions/challenges.

The contextual focus of this entire volume centers almost exclusively on four scientific issues that continue to question and even challenge today's religious world. The four scientific issues involve the following:

1. **Archeological sciences:** Contemporary archeological findings in the mid-eastern Asian world continue to challenge the religious interpretation concerning the existence and life of Abraham, the lives of his descendants, and the entire history of Moses as presented in the sacred writings of Christianity, Islam, and Judaism.[1] Archeologists have

---

1. Most often, we will enumerate the three religions in the following sequence:

raised the *question of historical verification* as regards the historical format in which these themes are described and used in the sacred writings of the three religions.[2]

2. **Historical sciences:** Contemporary scientific historical methodology continues to challenge the historical veracity of these same themes regarding Abraham, his descendants, and the entire history of Moses as presented in the sacred writings of Christianity, Islam, and Judaism. Are the texts, as they are written, verifiable history or are they mythological narratives? Are they biased historical essays or are they presenting actual historical data? Contemporary historians continue to *question the historical verification* of the passages mentioned above.[3]

3. **Quantum physics:** Contemporary quantum physics challenges religious claims of a divine plan for all finite reality. Each of the three religions mentioned above has formulated a divine plan for creation that historically includes the passages on Abraham, his descendants, and the entire history of Moses. These three plans are central to the sacred writings of Christianity, Islam, and Judaism, since the three religions claim their validity on the basis of their respective divinely revealed plans for all creation. Quantum physics, which focuses on the microcosmic reality of the universe, has discovered many processes, systems, and plans, none of which provide any evidence of a fundamental plan for the entire universe, much less a divine plan for the entire universe. Quantum physics, in its own limited way, offers no scientific substantiation of an all-inclusive divine plan for the entire finite universe. Some physical scientists who specialize in quantum physics have raised the *issue of historical verification* as regards the format in which the sacred writings of the three religions present a divine plan of created reality.[4]

Christianity, Islam, and Judaism. The authors have decided on this alphabetical listing since alphabetizing generally has no overtone of superiority/inferiority. We do not wish to present material that would indicate one of these religions as superior over the other two.

2. See Woolley, *Abraham*; Kenyon, *Archaeology in the Holy Land*; North and King, "Biblical Archaeology"; Albright, *Archaeology of Palestine and the Bible*; Finkelstein and Silberman, *Bible Unearthed*.

3. Liverani, *Israel's History and the History of Israel*. See also Redford, *Egypt, Canaan and Israel*; Thompson, *Bible in History*.

4. See Omnès, *Philosophie de la science contemporaine* (ET: *Quantum Philosophy*). See also O'Murchu, *Quantum Theology*; Polkinghorne, *Serious Talk*; and Haught, *Christianity*

Science and Religion

4. **Physical sciences and the age of the universe:** Contemporary scientific data on the age of the universe also challenges the same issues as those mentioned above regarding quantum physics. Contemporary scientists who have studied the age of the entire universe are focused on the *macrocosmic* aspects of the universe, while quantum physics focuses on the *microcosmic* aspects of the same universe. Given the age of the universe, which scientists have posited from twelve to seventeen billion years, any and every pinpointing of an overarching timeline and plan is basically questioned. Scientists themselves, whenever they propose an exact dating of some physical development, need almost conclusive evidence in order to assign dates to certain physical developments that have occurred during the existence of the universe. Both scientists and religious scholars are profoundly challenged whenever they have proposed a "universal plan" for these billions of years.

Once again the question of *historical verification* is at stake, and any and all proposals of a detailed divine plan for a multi-billion-year-old universe can only be judged as valid if there is clear historical verification. Some physical scientists who specialize in the age of the universe have raised serious questions on the *issue of historical verification* as regards the formats in which the sacred writings of the three religions present a divine plan of created reality.[5]

These four scientific issues are centrally important to the main theme of this volume, for they are tightly interconnected to specific religious positions. For the sake of clarity, the religious issues in this volume have been limited to the three religious communities mentioned above, namely Christianity, Islam, and Judaism. These three religions have been selected since in their sacred writings the issues regarding Abraham, his descendants, and the Mosaic material are presented as historically intertwined. All three religions profess Abraham as their foundational patriarch. All three trace their histories through Abraham's descendants. All three present divinely revealed plans for creation.

The above material is dominant in the Hebrew Bible, which involves religious data regarding Abraham and his descendants as well as the entire Mosaic material as found and interpreted in the five books of the Torah. Major aspects of this material also appear in sections of the Qur'an, which

---

and Science.

5. See Peacocke, *Creation and the World of Science*; Prigogine, *From Being to Becoming*; Schloss, "Evolutionary Theory and Religious Belief"; and Ratzsch, *Battle of Beginnings*.

not only describe but also interpret the activity of Abraham, Ishamel, Isaac, Jacob, and Moses. In the Christian New Testament, the same main agents from Abraham and Moses are also mentioned as major forerunners of Jesus, and they are interpreted from the standpoint of Jesus as the fulfillment of the earlier Hebrew Scriptures.

It is the historical verification of the biblical material from Abraham to Moses as presented respectively in each of the three religions that has been questioned and challenged by contemporary science. Up until the present, many leaders and scholars from all three religious groups have addressed the four issues in one way or another.[6] However, none of their explanations can be considered adequate, as we shall see in later sections of this volume.

The Meaning of "Science" and "Religion" as Used in This Volume

In order to accomplish this goal, there is a need to provide a definition or at least a description of the terms "science" and "religion" as used throughout this volume. Recent literature on science and religion contains a wide diversity of meaning for these two terms. In these recent writings, the denotations and connotations of terms have not been employed in a univocal way.

An example of this diversity of meaning for the terms can be found in a recent volume, *The Oxford Handbook of Religion and Science*, edited by Philip Clayton and Zachary Simpson. In part 1 of this volume, the individual essays focus on the theme "Religion and Science Across the World's Traditions." In the first essay of this section, "Hinduism and Science," Sangeetha Menon begins with some fundamental religious issues. He writes:

> The fundamentals employed are acceptance of diverse views in metaphysics, faith, and belief systems; the ideal of *ahimsa*—nonviolence; the ideal of *satya*—Truth; the emphasis on ways of living guided by reflection, detachment (*sakshibhava*) and meditation.[7]

In this listing, the fundamentals are primarily fundamentals as understood within Hinduism. His use of the terms *ahimsa*, *satya*, and *sakshibhava*

---

6. A response to the questions and challenges of contemporary science has been made in a careful way by the following authors. For Judaism, see Finkelstein and Silberman, *Bible Unearthed*; Meyers, *Oxford Encyclopedia of Archaeology in the Near East*. For Islam, see Nasr, *Science and Civilization in Islam*; Hourani, *History of the Arab Peoples*. For Christianity, see North and King, "Biblical Archaeology"; Kenyon, *Digging Up Jericho* and *Digging Up Jerusalem*.

7. Menon, "Hinduism and Science," 8.

Science and Religion

clearly indicate a Hindu correspondence, just as the terms "hermeneutics," "phenomenology," and "structural analysis" might indicate a postmodern philosophical correspondence in a different essay.

Menon subsequently refers to other factors in the dialogue between Hinduism and contemporary science, namely: the fluid face of truth,[8] the issue of the one and the many,[9] the beginning and end of creation,[10] and also consciousness leading back to self.[11] In themselves, these terms are more cross-cultural, but his presentation of the meaning of these terms still bears a Hindu correlation. Truth is interpreted through the understanding of *satya*. The issue of the one and many is presented through the lens of the *Jaina* view, which is "many-sided." The beginning and ending of creation are described in terms of two Hindu hymns, the *Nasadiya Sukta* and the *Perushka Sukta*.

Menon is perfectly legitimate in his use of a Hindu construct. The point we wish to make is simply this: he is not focusing on religion-in-general, but on Hinduism, a theme which he had been asked to do. Nor is he truly focusing on contemporary science in general, but on a contemporary Hindu understanding of science. In the pages of his essay, the author engages Hindu positions with the physical sciences (creation), with psychology (neuroscience), and conflict (various sciences and Hindu belief). He notes that in Indian logic there is a fourfold preliminary for every dialogue, namely: elucidations of *vishaya* (the theme of the discourse), *prayojana* (its major goal), *sambandha* (the relation between the theme of the discourse and its goal), and *adhikari* (the qualified participant).[12]

In Menon's essay on religion and science, it is clear that Hinduism is the particular religion of the dialogue, and that this particular religion has certain parameters in which a dialogue with science needs to be maintained. Menon also limits the scope of science to certain Hindu themes and structures in which a particular science is presented. Thus, the precise

8. Ibid., 9–10.
9. Ibid., 10–11.
10. Ibid., 13–15.
11. Ibid., 15–21.
12. Ibid., 20. See also Sivaraman, *Hindu Spirituality*. Several essays in this volume present the manner in which Hindu scholars approach both thinking and being. See Sivaraman's "Introduction," xv–xl; and Bhattacharyya, "Vedanta as Philosophy of Spiritual Life," 231–58. Western scientists use a Western form of philosophy to speak about thinking and being; in the Hindu world, the Western terms "thinking and being" are expressed in a totally different form of *Weltanschauung*..

connotations and denotations of "science" and religion" in his essay are different from other essays on the same subject that are found in the same section of the *Oxford Handbook of Religion and Science*.

One finds this same pattern in the contribution of B. Allan Wallace, which centers on "Buddhism and Science." Likewise, the same pattern is evident in the contribution of Norbert Samuelson, whose essay focuses on "Judaism and Science." Seven of the authors for this section of the book use a particular denotation and connotation for both religion and science. Only in the final essay, "Atheism and Science," by Peter Atkins, does one find a more general focus on religion as well as on science. Because of its generality, Atkins' essay is often unclear as regards which religion or religions he is addressing or which particular aspect of science he is also addressing. For Atkins, the term "religion" is used in a wide denotative and connotative way and his use of the term "science" is equally broad in its denotations and connotations.

It is obvious that this entire section of the *Oxford Handbook of Religion and Science*, although entitled "Religion and Science," does not engender any univocal meaning of the terms "religion" "and science."

A similar diversity is found in section 2 of the *Oxford Handbook of Religion and Science*, which is entitled "Conceiving Religion in the Light of the Contemporary Sciences." In this second section the term "science," not "religion," dominates the material, but once again the term "science" in each essay has a particular denotation and connotation. There is no univocal denotation or connotation of the term "science" in this section. Bernard Carr focuses on cosmology, while Kirk Wegter-McNelly focuses on the contemporary physical sciences, especially the theory of relativity, as also on quantum theory, chaos theory, and the more recent string theory. Martinez Hewlett centers his contribution on molecular biology. In the remaining essays of section 2, other denotations and connotations of the term "science" have been selected by the respective authors. In these additional essays, science focuses on evolution, ecology, neurophenomenology, psychology, sociology, and anthropology. Not all "contemporary science" is the center of attention in the individual essays. Nor is the term "religion" univocal in these essays, for at times a given essay refers to religion in a very generic way, while at other times the term "religion" specifically connotes Western religions. Thus, when a given author in the volume refers to "religion and science," more often than not the references are to some specific aspect of either a specific religion or of a specific contemporary science.

Science and Religion

The *Oxford Handbook of Religion and Science* is a marvelous volume, and it rightfully joins many other superb books that, though described by the phrase "Religion and Science," center on many different religious issues as well as on many different aspects of the contemporary scientific world. In all of these essays, the reader must clearly understand which specific religious issue is center stage and which specific aspect of contemporary science is also center stage.

PART TWO: THE TERM "RELIGION" AS SPECIFICALLY USED IN THIS VOLUME

Part Two of this chapter presents a more lengthy description of two key aspects of our religion theme. First of all, there are major limitations on the term "religion." Secondly, there is an intrareligious challenge of the three religions regarding the divine plan for creation which complicates the specific meaning of religion as applied to Christianity, Islam, and Judaism. By and large, an attempt has been made throughout this volume to avoid using the phrase "religion and science" in either a univocal or in a generalized way.[13]

The Limitations on the Term "Religion"

The term "religion" in this book is, as mentioned, limited to three religions—Christianity, Islam, and Judaism—since these three religions maintain a common patriarchal base in Abraham. This common patriarchal base gives the three religions a certain form of mutuality and communality. More precisely, it is the revelation of a monotheistic God to Abraham that has united these three religions, and it is also the covenant and promise made to Abraham by God that has further united the three religions.

This common Abrahamic base for monotheism, however, is not simply presented spiritually. It is also presented *in a historical way* by each of the three religions, although in individualized and therefore different historical formats. In other words, when Christian, Islamic, and Judaic scholars and leaders over the centuries have described the *historical development* of this Abrahamic base, three different *histories* are offered. Each of these differing

---

13. At times, one cannot avoid using either the term "religion" or the term "science" in a generalized way. However, by and large the focus in this volume is on a specific centering of "religion" and on a specific centering of "science."

historical accounts, however, is claimed to be foundational for the respective religions. The veracity of the claim is more often than not validated by each of the three religions on the basis of divine revelation. We will see later in this volume, however, that there is a major problem if a monotheistic God makes three different revelatory statements describing the historical process of a divine plan for creation.

The *historicity* of the Abrahamic-Mosaic texts has been a central factor through which the followers of each of the three religions claim the validity of their respective religions. If the Abrahamic-Mosaic material is not historical, so it is stated, then the claims of each of the three religions to be the one correct religion are seriously questioned and even challenged. In the pages that follow, our focus is limited to the challenge of the historical validity of the Abrahamic-Mosaic material and its effects on the meaning and value of the three religions. The religious material is also limited, for the material on the Abrahamic-Mosaic passages, as used in these pages, is found primarily in the Jewish Scriptures, the Qur'an, and the New Testament. These three sources are *mutatis mutandis* the primary sources for each of the three religions. Secondary sources from each religion will also be used, but in an ancillary way.

All three religions have considered the revelation and covenant of God to Abraham as a continuation of the revelation and covenant of the same God to Noah. Some religious leaders also view the revelations to Abraham and Noah as continuations of the revelation and covenant that the same God made to Adam and Eve after their expulsion from the Garden of Eden. Because of this interconnection with Noah and Adam and Eve, each of the three religions has presented a divine plan for the entire historical universe, beginning with creation itself. However, each plan is presented in a differing way, since historically each plan provides the legitimacy of an individual religion. Judaism is the only superior religion since Judaism was central to all the divine revelations mentioned above. Islam is the only superior religion, since the divine revelations mentioned above are ultimately focused on the final revelation, which finds its expression in the Qur'an. Christianity is the only superior religion because Jesus is the final goal of all the revelations mentioned above.

In all three religions, the one God is clearly considered the creator of the entire universe. This creator God was active in and through Adam and Eve, in and through Noah, and in and through Abraham. In the three religions, the one creator God continues to be active in each respective religious

Science and Religion

entity, and God's historical activity is considered to indicate a divine plan for all creation. These plans begin with the first *moment of creation and are detailed in and through human history.* The centering on the divine plan for creation, which is part and parcel of the traditions of each of these three religions, is an integral part of the meaning of the term "religion" as used in this volume.

Some major contemporary scientific questions challenge these three different divine plans, since scientists have found no overarching plan for finite reality. These challenges stem primarily from quantum physics and the age of the universe, and in a secondary way from archaeology and contemporary scientific history. Thus, in this volume the term "religion" includes in a basic way the following elements in both its denotations and its connotations:

1. The term is *limited* to Christianity, Islam, and Judaism. No other religion is included in the presentation on religion in this volume.
2. The term *centers* on the Abrahamic monotheism of these three religions, that is, on the historical presentation of the life of Abraham and his descendants, and it also centers of the material that involves Moses.
3. The term *gravitates* around the historical way in which these three religions are not only centered on God's revelation to Abraham and but also on the historical ways in which the respective leaders and scholars of each religion have presented the development of their honoring of this monotheistic God.
4. The term *includes* the divine historical plans for creation that each of these three religions respectively has developed in detail.

Consequently, the term "religion" in this volume is defined in a limited way. The scientific questions and challenges that are apropos to this volume are also defined in a limited way, since they focus primarily on the four characteristics of science mentioned above.

The Intrareligious Challenge to the Three Religions Regarding the Divine Plan for Creation

There are intrareligious challenges to Christianity, Islam, and Judaism that do not come from the questions and challenges of contemporary science.

Rather, they come from the three religions themselves. In other words, the challenge of validity does not arise on the basis of science. Rather, the challenge comes from the theological stance of the three religions themselves. Belief in a "revelation" of God constitutes the *historical verification* of their respective plans for creation. However, a monotheistic God cannot reveal three differing historical plans for creation. The three religions may use the same material (Adam and Eve, Noah, Abraham, etc.), but the three religions use this material in three diverse ways. The historical plans for creation contain the same personages and divine actions, but the leaders and scholars have interpreted the material differently. It is the uniquely interpreted divine plan that provides each religion with its own historical validity.

To separate a divine plan from its individual religious and historical interpretation does not correspond to the belief system of the three religions. Members of the religions do not believe primarily in a generic divine plan for creation that can then be interpreted in three different ways. Rather, Christians believe in a divine plan for creation precisely because Jesus is the center of such a plan. Muslims believe in a divine plan for creation precisely because it is ultimately revealed in the Qur'an. Jewish people believe in a divine plan for creation precisely because of the Mosaic covenant and their selection by God to be the chosen people.

Three divine plans for creation, each with its own claim of God's revelation, constitute an intrareligious problem of profound dimensions. It is not the role of contemporary science to settle this diversity regarding a divine plan for finite reality. Whenever a scientist has denied the existence of a creator God or the existence of a divine plan for creation, religious scholars from all three religions have strongly challenged the views of the scientist. However, each religion in their complaint to the scientist maintains that there is a monotheistic creator God and that this God has a definite design for the created universe. When the religious leaders and scholars are asked to elaborate on this divine plan, the leaders and scholars of Christianity, Islam, and Judaism explain God's plan from their respective way. This leaves the scientist in a precarious position. If such a scientist allows that the Christian plan is the plan he has found in his scientific research, the leaders and scholars of Islam and Judaism cry foul since the scientist has not found verification for either the Islamic or Jewish divine plan for creation. If such a scientist allows that the Jewish plan is the plan he has found in his scientific research, the leaders and scholars of Islam and Christianity cry foul since the scientist has not found verification for either the Islamic or

Christian divine plan for creation. Finally, if such a scientist allows that the Islamic plan is the plan he has found in his scientific research, the leaders and scholars of Christianity and Judaism cry foul since the scientist has not found verification for either the Islamic or Jewish divine plan for creation.

When scientists claim that God did not create the universe and that there is no divine plan for the universe, the leaders and scholars of the three religions should not immediately center their responses on the scientists. Rather, they should settle the intrareligious challenges first, namely, the religious leaders and scholars should verify which God and which divine plan the scientists are disclaiming. Since there is no generic divine plan, the leaders and scholars of the three religions should come to grips with the as-yet-unresolved implication of their own problem: can a monotheistic God reveal three different historical plans for creation? Given this precarious intrareligious situation, many scientists simply leave the matter alone, for they do not want to get involved in a highly sensitive disagreement between Christians, Muslims, and Jews.

We want to stress that all three religions are to be honored and respected. Each religion has sacred texts, and the holiness of these texts is a major source for understanding the three religions. However, the sacred texts are only one part of the splendor of the three religions. Each religion is also honored by a long history in which sacred traditions have developed. Through its own text and traditions, each religion has provided special qualities to human history and these special qualities have increased the sacredness of human life. In no way at all do the following pages trivialize the beauty, honor, and holiness of the three religious movements. In the final chapter of this volume some positions are offered that might help the leaders and scholars of the three religions at least lessen the divisiveness of this internal disagreement.

PART THREE: THE TERM "SCIENCE" AS SPECIFICALLY USED IN THIS VOLUME

In Part Three of this chapter, our focus is on three issues: (a) the limitations of the term "science" as used in this volume; (b) contemporary archaeology of the Middle East from its earliest appearance B.C.E. down to the second century C.E.; and (c) contemporary biblical history on the role of religion in the Middle East from the sixth century B.C.E. down to the second century C.E.

The Limitations of the Term "Science" as Used in This Volume

The term "science" also needs to be specified as far as its denotations and connotations are concerned. In the pages that follow, the term "science" refers to the following four specific aspects of the contemporary scientific world:

1. Quantum physics
2. The contemporary scientific age of the universe
3. Contemporary archaeology of the Near East
4. Contemporary scientific historiography

These four aspects of contemporary science may seem to be disjointed for our volume, but it is our judgment that these four specific aspects of contemporary science have raised major questions and even challenges to the understanding of religion as it is defined above. In many ways, each of these four areas contributes scientific data that has called into question the *historical verification* of the Abraham-to-Moses data. Since the scientific aspects were presented above in a general way, there is need to specify how each of these four areas of science, each in its own distinctive manner, is apropos to the material in this volume. In other words, "quantum physics" is a general term; the way in which we are using it in the following pages is specific. Since the focus of our presentation of these four scientific programs is on the *historical verification* of the Abraham-Moses data, one must understand how each of the four scientific areas in a limited but specific way questions and even challenges the *historical verification* problem.

First Limitation: Quantum Physics

Quantum physics is a very recent part of contemporary science and its focus is primarily on the microcosm. In the microcosmic world, quantum physics has uncovered a number of processes, orders, and systems. Stuart Kauffman begins his volume *Origins of Order* with a section called "Themes."[14] In this brief introductory section he uses again and again the following words and phrases: natural selection, complex systems, spontaneous order, manifold varieties of symmetry for various organisms, complex coevolving systems, adaptive walks of certain orders, random sequences, parallel

---

14. Kauffman, *Origin of Order*, xiii–xviii.

processing, useful mutations, connected webs of metabolic transformations, and branching pathways of cell differentiation. The list could go on. Kauffman is indicating that the microcosm is replete with a variety of "plans" of historical development. Moreover, these microcosmic activities are also part of the macrocosm. In the macrocosm, microcosmic activity continues its "plans" of historical development.

Kauffman does not focus in any lengthy way on the issue of quantum physics and religion, but other authors do take up this theme. Roland Omnès, in his volume *Quantum Philosophy*, explores in a detailed way the relationship and non-relationship of quantum physics and various religious positions. John Polkinghorne has written several books that deal with the issue of quantum physics, such as *Serious Talk: Science and Religion in Dialogue* and *Quarks, Chaos, and Christianity: Questions to Science and Religion*. Robert Russell et al., in *Quantum Mechanics: Scientific Perspective and Divine Action*, consider in a focused way the connection of divine action to quantum physics. Many other books could also be cited on the issue of quantum physics vis-á-vis some aspects of religion.

The use of the term "quantum physics" in this volume centers on the religious issue of a divine plan for the universe. In quantum physics, scientists have uncovered many "plans," "processes," and "systems," but they have not found in the microcosmic world any comprehensive plan, process, or system, nor have they found a scientific, overarching plan that has remained constant since the beginning of the universe. This will become clearer as we describe the macrocosm as viewed by the contemporary scientists in their current study of the age of the universe.

Some religious leaders and scholars, as we shall see, have attempted to take quantum physics into account, but these religious leaders and scholars have not as yet provided an adequate response to the many challenges that quantum physics has raised. As of right now, the religious leaders need to face the challenges in a much more adequate way. In chapters 3 and 4 we will present in detail why quantum physics is central to the science-religion discussion, and why the challenges from certain aspects of quantum physics need to be honored more honestly by religious writers.

Second Limitation: *The Contemporary Scientific Age of the Universe*

The contemporary scientific understanding of the age of the universe is extremely complicated. Copernicus and Galileo in many ways began the process for re-evaluating the universe we live in, but in more recent times this re-evaluating process has moved into high gear.[15] Let us first determine to some extent what the term "universe" means in this context, and subsequently we will focus on the age of this universe.

The Term "Universe"

The term "universe" needs a careful description, since the scientific and the theological material on the meaning of the term is different. The following paragraphs do not attempt to present a detailed description of the term "universe" either from the standpoint of contemporary science or from the standpoint of contemporary religious studies. Rather, the following paragraphs highlight the key issues that have entered into a contemporary scientific understanding of the universe, on the one hand, and on the other hand the paragraphs highlight the key issues that have entered into a contemporary religious understanding of the universe.

Contemporary scientists use the term "universe," as also such similar terms as "world," "cosmos," etc., in several different ways, all of which are based on a complex set of scientific findings. Within the scientific perimeters, the term "universe" has several denotations and many connotations. However, these denotations and connotations do not result in a common scientific understanding of the universe. In the last 150 years, the term "universe" has had to be redefined again and again as additional information about the universe has been discovered. Consequently, in scientific usage the term "universe" is polyvalent.

Contemporary theologians and biblical scholars also use the term "universe" as also similar terms such as "world," "cosmos," etc., in a variety of ways. Contemporary religious investigations have also reinterpreted the term "universe" in a polyvalent way. Contemporary Christian, Islamic, and Jewish scholars offer three different plans of God for creation, each with its own denotations and connotations. The theological literature produced by contemporary scholars of these religions indicates, among other key items,

---

15. See the the November 10, 2011 issue of *Science*, in which there is mention of a new discovery by astronomers, namely, the data on the two immense clouds of gas that are pristine, free of metals fired out into the cosmos by stars. Dr. J. Xavier Prochaska notes, "Galaxies and stars really don't fill up much of the volume of the universe. We're rare. Our Milky Way is an island, if you will, in the vast expanse of the universe, so there's plenty of volume in the universe, which is far, far away from the galaxies." See Dunn, "Astronomers shed light on early stars in cosmos."

Science and Religion

that in crucial sections of their respective sacred writings one finds a high degree of influence stemming from classical Greek philosophy. Even today, Greek influence is a major factor for the religious interpretation of such terms as "cosmos," "world," "universe," "eon," and "material reality."

The term "universe" in its scientific usage generally means *our* universe. There are, as we shall indicate later, some scientific views that focus on a "multiverse" or even on "multiverses." The following paragraphs in this section do not include this focus, since the view of a multiverse is today only in its infancy.[16]

In contemporary science, our universe has its own space-time coordinates, its own laws, its own developments, etc. Since each world within a multiverse would have its own specific set of space-time coordinates, laws, developments, etc. Consequently, the term "universe" as used in the following pages refers only to *our* universe.[17] The realization that contemporary science focuses on our universe is one of today's constitutive elements when scientists begin to describe or define the term "universe."

As regards the origin of our universe, a large number of contemporary scientists, but by no means all contemporary scientists, refer to the "big bang theory."[18] In this theory, highly compressed hydrogen and helium within what scientists call a "singularity" exploded. The explosion from this singularity eventually produced the universe in which humans now live.[19]

The validity of the big bang theory remains controversial. Nonetheless, the manner in which it is argued rests on certain fundamental factors that contemporary science itself utilizes in a strong way. We can draw

---

16. See Rees, *Our Cosmic Habitat*. See also Smolin, *Life of the Cosmos*; and Carr, "Cosmology and Religion."

17. In the theological perspectives of Christianity, Islam, Hinduism, and Judaism, there has been an openness to other creatures beyond those of "our" universe, namely, the existence of creatures of an angelic nature and fallen angelic nature (devils). See Woods, "Angels." Woods presents the Christian theological history on angels in terms that clearly indicate that angels, in these historical documents, are seen as belonging to a different universe than "our" universe. Woods writes, "In Christian, as well as Jewish and Islamic belief, angels are immaterial spirits or pure intelligences created by God prior to human creation. . . . Strictly speaking, the existence of angels is not a matter of divine revelation, but is presupposed by both the biblical witness and Catholic Church teaching." Woods cites a statement from the fourth Lateran Council.

18. See Gibbs, "Profile: George F. R. Ellis," 55 n. 4.

19. The cosmologist Fred Hoyle first used the term "big bang" as a sarcastic approach to George LeMaitre's proposal that the universe originated from a physical speck. However, the name persists. See Ferris, *Coming of Age in the Milky Way*; Trinh, *Birth of the Universe*.

from today's contemporary science the following specific attributes of our universe.

Our Universe Had a Beginning

For many scientists, our universe is not durationally infinite. A durationally infinite universe was espoused by Aristotle and taken up by some medieval scholars. However, today a durationally infinite universe is no longer a common scientific approach.[20] This conclusion is based on the following data.

Hubble's Law

In our universe, galaxies today are moving away from planet Earth at speeds proportionate to their distance (Hubble's law). The expansion of the universe means that at one given time the galaxies were more compacted and dense and at other times they were less compacted and dense.[21] The physical interpretation of Hubble time allows us to run backward (but not forward) in order to gain an estimate of the age of the universe. The age of individual clusters in the universe establishes a limit on the age of the universe itself, since the total universe must be as old as the objects it contains. Typically, estimates based on Hubble's law range from fourteen to eighteen billion years.

There are two main parts to Hubble's law. First, there is the constant law, namely $v=Hd$, where V is velocity of recession, H is the Hubble constant, and D is distance. Hubble time, however, is the inverse of the Hubble constant: $T=1/H$. In actuality, the Hubble constant may not be constant, and therefore Hubble time is only a rough estimate of the age of the universe. Nonetheless, Hubble time, with all its calculations, does indicate in a solid way that the age of our universe needs to be estimated as somewhere between ten billion and twenty billion years.

Another aspect of the Hubble timeline is the current expansion of the universe. Will our universe continue to expand? There is at present no definitive answer. Scientists need to calculate more sharply not only how much mass the universe contains also whether this mass is below or above

---

20. Some scientists postulate the possibility of an infinite series of multiverses. No scientist claims that our universe is durationally infinite.

21. For Hubble's law, see Kutner, *Astronomy*.

Science and Religion

the critical amount. If it is above the critical amount, the universe will collapse on itself. As of this moment, scientists cannot and do not predict with any accuracy the continuation or the collapse of the universe. One can say that there is a process that will continue if the critical amount has not been attained, and that there is a process that will not continue if the critical amount has been reached. Is this process a divine plan for the universe? No scientist has as yet claimed that the process, which cannot be avoided, is indeed a sign of some divine plan.

Because of the ongoing differences in compaction and expansion of these galaxies, our universe exists in a spatiotemporal relativity. Scientists might describe our universe at one particular period of space-time, but their description needs to be reinterpreted in subsequent periods of space-time due to the ongoing expansion and contraction of galactic constructions. These changes indicate that *relativity* is an integral part of today's scientific description or definition of the universe.

Cosmic Microwave Background

The cosmic microwave background is a major scientific study that discriminates between the big bang model of the universe and the steady-state model of the universe. However, the CMB was first studied by scientists who were not involved in either model of the universe, and at the beginning these scientists had no inkling of the CMB's cosmological significance. Max Planck at the end of the nineteenth century was studying blackbody radiation, and scientists after him also focused on the unique character of a blackbody spectrum. In 1940 Andrew McKellar made the first observation of the CMB using interstellar molecules. Later, Robert Dicke began his study of atmospheric temperatures. In 1950 Fred Hoyle became another important scientist who took part in the CMB study. In 1965 two radio astronomers, Arno Penzias and Robert Wilson, discovered an excess radiation at 7.35 cm that was equivalent to a 3.5 +/-1 K blackbody. At first, they had no idea what this meant. They contacted Dicke and explained what they had found. Further papers then appeared by Penzias, Wilson, Dicke, Peebles, Roll, and Wilkinson.

The CMB pervades our universe, and Penzias and Wilson considered the CMB to be a remnant stemming from the big bang.[22] The discovery of

22. In 1978, Arno Penzias and Robert Wilson were awarded the Nobel Prize for Physics based on their discovery of the CMB in our universe. An Internet search of

the CMB and its subsequent investigation provided a scientific finding that establishes even more clearly a multi-billion-year age of our universe. Many scientists who have studied the CMB claim that it substantiates the big bang theory. Whether it accomplishes this substantiation is one issue; that it provides evidence of multi-billion-year-old universe is quite another issue, and it is this second issue that is important for our volume. Nonetheless, CMB and its actual ramifications are part and parcel of today's description/definition of the universe.

The CMB material is a challenge to the leaders and scholars of the three religions treated in this book. First of all, CMB studies have indicated again the multi-billion-year age of the universe. Secondly, at the very beginning of the big bang the singularity did not produce a uniform structure; if it had done so there would have been no structures that formed subsequently. Structures did develop, but in a variety of ways, and this diverse development is a situation that calls into question the existence of a divine plan for the created universe. Since one is dealing with a universe billions of years old, the question arises, what historical verification do we have, billions of years later, as to an initial plan? Moreover, since there were a variety of structures that moved in different directions, how can religious leaders and scholars present a well-organized multi-billion-year plan? How do these leaders and scholars provide historical verification for such a plan? These billions of years cannot be set aside by stating, "God revealed his plan." Each of these religions has developed a detailed historical plan that is meant to validate its religious teachings, but each religion does so basing its plan on an extremely precarious *historical verification*, namely, divine revelation. CMB seriously calls into question the *historical verification* of

---

"CMB" provides several explanations of CMB. Arthur Kosowsky states, "The radiation present today as a 2.7 K thermal background originated when the universe was denser by a factor of 10^9 and younger by a factor of around 5×10^4. The radiation provides the most distant direct image of the universe we can hope to see, at least until gravitational radiation becomes a useful astronomical data source. The microwave background radiation is extremely uniform, varying in temperature by only a few parts in 10^5 over the sky (apart from an overall dipole variation arising from our peculiar motion through the microwave background's rest frame); its departure from a perfect blackbody spectrum has yet to be detected.

The very existence of the microwave background provides crucial support for the Hot big bang cosmological model: the universe began in a very hot, dense state from which it expanded and cooled. The microwave background visible today was once in thermal equilibrium with the primordial plasma of the universe, and the universe at that time was highly uniform. Crucially, the universe could not have been perfectly uniform at that time or no structures would have formed subsequently."

Science and Religion

all three divine plans that have been presented respectively by the three religions.

Atmospheric Percentage of Hydrogen and Helium

The amount of hydrogen and helium found in the atmosphere of today's universe, although not abundant (helium registers at 5.4 percent and hydrogen at 0.5 percent), is enough to support the big bang theory. Some scientists go so far as to use this finding to establish the big bang theory. For our purposes, the composition of the atmosphere, in so far as it contains both hydrogen and helium, may not necessarily lead one to verify the big bang theory, but it does lead to a multi-billion-year-old universe, since the earth's atmosphere has never been elementally constant and it has taken billions of year to bring about the present molecular consistency of the earth's atmosphere. One also sees in this development of atmospheric elements another indication of the relativity of the universe. Our universe is clearly a changing universe, and during some of these changes life forms, including humans, were impossible due to the lack of a certain percentage of atmospheric elements, such as helium, hydrogen, and oxygen.

This scientific issue is important for our discussion, since scientific studies of the universe both currently and historically do not find that the universe developed with the formation of our solar system as the key solar system, or with the development of Earth and life forms (dependent as these are on certain percentage of atmospheric hydrogen, helium, and oxygen) as the goal of the universe. Teleologically, the planet Earth and human life itself are not the centering reason for the multi-billion-year-old universe. The precise formation of Earth and the development of life, including human life, took place due to many factors, especially chemical factors, which cannot be described as "necessary" processes. They simply happened and there is at least some form of relativity to these occurrences in nature.

Space-Time Coordinates

The studies of Steven Hawking, George Ellis, and Roger Penrose in the early 1970s concluded that both space and time had a finite beginning with the singularity of the big bang. Our precise coordinates of space-time did not exist prior to the big bang.[23] In other words, our form of space-time did not exist prior to the inception of our universe. Consequently, the particular space-time coordinates of our universe are an integral part of the meaning of the phrase "our universe." Space-time coordinates in a different universe would not and could not be identical to the space-time coordinates of our universe. There may be other universes, but they would differ radically from ours. Just as the coordinate of time is in a continuous process of change, so too, according to the scientists mentioned above, is the coordinate of space. The limits of outer space are continuously changing, so that our universe has at times more space and at times less space. In this we see another basis of why the term "universe" is highly relative and polyvalent. The respective plans for creation of the three religions are not presented by their religious leaders in a relative or polyvalent way; they are presented in an absolute and unchanging way. The issue of space-time coordinates challenges the *historical verification* of the three religious plans of the universe.

Origin of the Universe

Even on the basis of the big bang theory (or the multiverse theory as well), we do not have today any scientific proposals that adequately answer the questions, where did our universe come from, and why did our universe suddenly begin? Contemporary science is deeply focused on the forces, powers, and structures within our universe. The origin of our universe is, at times, a scientific focus as one can see from the big bang theory and the implications of CMB, but originistic knowledge is not the primary reason why contemporary science exists. For contemporary science, *how* the universe began is one issue; *what* is the composition and constitution of our universe is a totally different issue. It is this second issue that provides the major centering of contemporary science. When scientists study our universe they are more interested in its internal forces and less concerned about a theory of its origins.

The above five issues present major aspects concerning our universe in so far as contemporary science is concerned. Even though detailed issues for each issue are not formulated, major conclusions regarding the definition of the universe for contemporary science can be summarized as follows:

23. See Hawking, *Brief History of Time*. See also Hawking, *On the Big Bang and Black Holes*; Ellis and Hawking, *Large Scale Structure of Space-Time*; Penrose, *Cycles of Time*.

- The universe we are talking about is *our* universe.
- Our universe is *constantly changing*.
- Our universe is *fundamentally relational* and *not absolute*.
- Our universe is *coterminous with our space-time coordinates*.
- Our universe, therefore, is a *polyvalent universe*.

These contemporary scientific issues regarding our universe are intelligible within a scientific framework. In this scientific framework, religious issues do not play any pivotal role. Scientists do not need any recourse to divine help when they consider Hubble's law, CMB, the multivalence of space-time coordinates, and the relativity of the universe. This does not mean that contemporary science is against religion or against belief in God. Rather, it means that contemporary science remains valid both in its findings and in its projections, while at the same time it can remain neutral vis-à-vis the issue of religion. Scientists can be theistic or atheistic, religious or non-religious.

The Age of Our Universe

The age of the universe has become a matter of great importance since this age is now calculated in billions of years. Roughly, contemporary scientists move from a twelve-billion-year-old universe to a fifteen-billion-year-old universe and for some scientists to a seventeen-billion-year-old universe. A few scientists even go beyond seventeen billion years. However, since many billions of years are involved in these calculations, the issue of verification for almost all data is restricted. Scientists present differing ages since they see that time is inevitable for certain kinds of formation to occur. For some scientists, the age of the universe is calculated at twelve billion years. For the majority of scientists, the age of the universe is calculated at around fifteen billion years. For another smaller group of scientists, the age of the universe is calculated at seventeen to twenty billion years. This differentiation among scientists is based on the number of years needed for the development of a certain microcosmic or macrocosmic process. The emergence of a process takes time, and scientists calculate how much time was needed to arrive at a certain complex involved in the process.

Other scientists have calculated the age of many stars. On the basis of the oldest stars, these same scientists have calculated the age of the universe. The globular cluster of such stars varies, and scientists using this calculation estimate that the range for the age of the universe is somewhere between fourteen and eighteen billion years.

No matter how the time of the universe is calculated, the age of the universe is calculated in billions of years. As such, historical verification of details within the development of the universe must be carefully analyzed. Neither a scientist nor a religious theologian is working with a simplistic framework; rather, they are both working with a multi-billion-year complex.

Physical scientists who have developed these calculations regarding the age of the universe not only question the conclusions of the religious leaders and scholars of all three religions who tend to claim knowledge of the distant past; they also challenge these same leaders as to the legitimacy of the historical claims they make as they trace creation through Adam and Eve to Noah, to Abraham, to Moses, to Jesus, and to Mohammad. Historical verification is difficult for those who want to calculate the origin of the universe itself; but historical verification is also difficult when one focuses on the origin of human life. In both instances, there are several different proposals. To the foundational question "When did the universe itself begin?" there are differing answers, all of which lack absolute historical verification. To the more relative question "When did human life begin?" there are also differing answers all of which lack absolute historical verification. The three religious plans for the universe and the appearance of human beings are not exempt from the issue of historical verification. Contemporary sciences not only *question* these religious plans; they *challenge* these religious plans in a serious way. This is not a new challenge, but at the beginning of the twenty-first century theologians from all three religions have as yet not adequately measured up to the challenges presented by these scientists.

Third Limitation: Contemporary Archaeology of the Middle East from Its Earliest Appearance B.C.E. to the Second Century C.E.

Since the late eighteen hundreds, contemporary archaeology throughout the Middle East has gradually raised questions for the religious scholars who have written on the historical origins of the three Abrahamic religions.[24] The data of these archeologists has become a major factor for anyone who wishes to discuss the early history of Christianity, Islam, and

---

24. See Williams, *Archaeology in Biblical Research*, 23–35.

Science and Religion

Judaism. In the contemporary Middle East, the archeological endeavors have often followed a certain guideline, namely, what can be learned about the sacred texts of all three religions outside these texts themselves?

By itself, archaeology is limited, for to understand an artifact dating it is crucial. But the dating is only a beginning, since one must then ask, how does one describe the culture that gave rise to the artifact? Cultures more often than not are the basic reasons why such an artifact had been produced and retained, while other objects are not remembered at all. Cultural studies include a review of what each culture considered valuable as far as preserving certain details and artifacts. If someone is going to write a description of a learned person at a given time in history, why is this person selectable as someone who should be remembered? The person is, of course, important, but culturally and historically she or he is important for other reasons than simply personal value. Culturally, he or she is important. Another person at the same period of time and in the same cultural milieu may have done something, but there is no archaeological data about such a person, since culturally what he or she did had little to no social value.

Many other issues are involved with archaeology, and as a result one cannot jump to conclusions by simply finding an artifact. Nonetheless, contemporary archaeology has revolutionized our appreciation of biblical historical traditions. On the one hand, archaeology does not and cannot prove the historicity of the Bible. On the other hand, archaeology by itself cannot disprove aspects of the biblical material. In its best moments, archaeology can raise serious questions, and it can also provide major elements that can resolve serious questions. Ernest Wright makes the statement:

> A previous generation of scholars was inclined to make skepticism an important element in historical method, an almost primary ingredient in the conclusions drawn from use of the [archaeological] method. Today most of us take a far more positive line, and are inclined to give a tradition the benefit of the doubt unless there is evidence to the contrary; this is a basic and all-important scholarly shift in viewpoint, and archaeology is its cause.[25]

Let us consider some examples of this interplay of archaeology, culture, and history. Leonard Woolley was a major archeologist on the city of Ur in the early part of the twentieth century. The book of Genesis states, "After Teran was seventy, he had three sons: Abram, Nahor, and Haran. . . . Teran's sons were born in the city of Ur in Chaldea" (Gen 11:26–28). However,

25. Wright, "Biblical Archaeology Today," 151.

Woolley writes, "At Ur, no concrete memorial of Abraham was brought to light. That was only to be expected. . . . The chances that there should have been tablets bearing the name of Abraham, that any one of them should have been preserved and finally that this one [tablet] should have happened to be within the limits of our narrow field were indeed infinitesimal."[26]

A second and more contemporary example is taken from the work of Kathleen Kenyon. In her volume *Archaeology in the Holy Land*, she develops the questionability of the Abraham story even further. She challenges the historicity of certain biblical historical data when she writes:

> It is certain that one cannot build up a chronology on the spans of years attributed to the Patriarchs, nor regard it as factual that Abraham was seventy-five years old when he left Harran and a hundred when Isaac was born, or that Isaac was sixty when Jacob was born and that Jacob was a hundred and thirty when he went into Egypt, for the evidence from the skeletons in the Jericho tombs shows that the expectation of life at this period was short. Many individuals seem to have died before they were thirty-five and few seem to have reached the age of fifty.[27]

Israel Finkelstein and Neil Asher Silberman, in their book *The Bible Unearthed: Archaeology's New Vision of Ancient Israel and the Origin of Its Sacred Texts*, present in a fairly forthright way the results of contemporary archaeology vis-à-vis the Mosaic material. They indicate on several occasions that archaeological evidence is totally lacking for certain Mosaic themes. For instance, they focus on the exodus account in the Sinai desert, and at the end of their presentation they conclude:

> Repeated archaeological surveys in all regions of the peninsula, including the mountainous area around the tradition site of Mount Sinai, near St. Catherine's Monastery, have yielded only negative evidence: not even a single shard, no structure, not a single house, no trace of an ancient encampment.[28]

These two authors acknowledge that there are far too many contradictions between the archaeological findings and the historical biblical narratives. They conclude that these contradictions indicate that the Bible does

---

26. Wooley, *Abraham*, 9–10.
27. Kenyon, *Archaeology in the Holy Land*, 194.
28. Finkelstein and Silberman, *Bible Unearthed*, 62–63.

Science and Religion

not provide a precise description of what actually occurred.[29] The authors also state that Egypt in the Mosaic age closely controlled its borders. However, a major exodus of Jewish people finds no mention in contemporary Egyptian writings.

> If a great mass of fleeing Israelites had passed through the border fortifications of the pharaonic regime, a record should exist. Yet in the abundant Egyptian sources describing the time of the New Kingdom in general and the thirteenth century in particular, there is no reference to the Israelites, not even a single clue.[30]

The Merneptah stele, which dates from the end of the thirteenth century B.C.E., makes mention of a group called Israel who were already living in Canaan. Finkelstein and Silberman immediately add that there is "no clue, not even a single word, about early Israelites in Egypt: neither in monumental inscriptions on walls of temples, nor in tomb inscriptions, nor in papyri."[31] The one and only mention of Israel at this early date (the Merneptah stele) cannot be exploited beyond the stele. Any and all further implications are for the most part conjectures. The mention of Israel on the Merneptah stele remains disputed. Some scholars say that there is no reference at all to Israel; other scholars allow a reference to a wandering tribe or small village.[32]

Many other contemporary archeologists of the Middle East could be cited who have made archaeological conclusions similar to those of Woolley, Kenyon, Finkelstein, and Silberman.[33] In many ways, these archeologists have not only questioned biblical data as historically true; they have also challenged biblical commentators from all three religions.

Walter G. Williams has provided us with a comprehensive overview of biblically related archaeology down to 1965. His book *Archaeology in Biblical Research* recounts archaeological interest from the royal library of Nineveh under Tiglath-Pileser III (744–727 B.C.E.) down to the middle of the twentieth century Walter G. Williams is clearly indebted to William F. Albright, who today remains a respected biblical archaeologist, but many major contemporary archaeologists see in his work a biased approach.

29. Ibid., 21.
30. Ibid., 59.
31. Ibid., 60.

32. References on the Internet to "Merneptah Stele" range from doubt and even denial about its reference to Israel to overstatements of its value for Israelitic history.

33. See Mangalith, "On the Origin and Antiquity of the Name Israel."

Albright, they state, was looking for data that would verify biblical texts. Consequently, Albright seems to have reached conclusions vis-à-vis archaeological data that, in his view, benefited biblical data. Kenyon, along with many others, is by no means a follower of Albright's view.[34]

In 1969, David Noel Freedman and Jonas Greenfield were the editors of the book *New Directions in Biblical Archaeology*. This volume includes the presentations given at a symposium on biblical archaeology held in the San Francisco Bay Area in 1966.[35] The quality of both the presenters/writers and also the depth and breadth of their archaeological endeavors indicate that biblical archaeology is a multifaceted undertaking.

Biblically oriented archaeologists have tended to move in various directions. These men and women are not united as far as the results of their findings are concerned. Eilat Mazar, for instance, maintains that in 2005 she discovered the palace of David in Jerusalem. However, David Ilam of Hebrew Union College and also a well-known archaeologist believes that the ruins were built in the eighth or ninth century B.C.E., long after the lifetime of King David. Israel Finkelstein, a so-called "low-chronology archaeologist," has attempted to demolish the views of Mazar. Thomas Levy, Yosef Garfinkle, Amihai Mazar, and Ygael Madin have also written essays that criticize Mazar's claims. These are all Jewish anthropologists who are studying the Jewish roots of the Palestinian area. As one can see, the Jewish archaeologists are not all of one mind.

There are also other archaeologists who disagree with one another. William Albright, Walter Williams, and G. Ernest Wright have already been mentioned. David Noel Freedman, Jonas Greenfield, Frank Moore Cross, Robert Boling, Patrick Skehan, Floyd Filson, Roland de Vaux, and Yohanan Aharoni could also be cited.

This variety of archaeological interpretations by experts is of major importance today. However, the material in the sacred texts that centers on the details concerning Abraham, his descendants, and the entire Moses episode has, in the last fifty years, become center stage. In the first place, the Abraham-to-Moses material remains questionable since almost all data referring to these people and events are found only in the sacred texts

---

34. See Albright, "Impact of Archaeology on Biblical Research—1966." A more recent and more lengthy presentation of biblical archaeology is the essay by Robert North and Philip J. King, "Biblical Archaeology." For a survey, see *Biblical Archaeologist* 48 (1982), 73–107 and 201–28.

35. The editors included seven articles on the Dead Sea Scrolls which had appeared in *McCormick Quarterly*, March 1968.

themselves. Secondly, archaeological data has in no way proved what these scriptural texts describe about Abraham to Moses.

Even with these sacred texts, one can ask a deeper question, since scriptural scholars and archaeologists can be and are Christian, Islamic, and Jewish. Based on their religious background, one can legitimately inquire: which Abraham, which Isaac, which Jacob, which sons of Jacob, and which Moses is one talking about? If one is speaking about an Abraham whose religious development culminates in Jesus, then both Islamic and Jewish scholars disown such an Abraham. If one is speaking about an Abraham whose religious development culminates in Ishmael, Mohammad, and the Qur'an, then both Christian and Jewish scholars disown such an Abraham. Finally, if the Abraham in question is the Jewish Abraham, then Christian and Islamic leaders disown such an Abraham. There is no neutral Abraham, nor is there a neutral Ishmael, Isaac, Jacob, the sons of Jacob, nor is the Moses material neutral. Archaeology is not the only source of this disowning, for the religious leaders and scholars of a given religion are the ones who primarily disown the interpretations given to these figures by the religious leaders and scholars of the other two religions.

This issue of a religious stance is major, since no archeologist of any solid standing wants to claim validity for his or her efforts solely on the basis of a religious stance. Part of the questioning of contemporary archaeologists, however, is based on the fundamental disagreement of the Christian, Islamic, and Jewish leaders themselves. As long as there is a religious disagreement over Abraham, his descendants, etc., archaeologists are not anxious to claim historical validity for a Christian Abraham, an Islamic Abraham, or a Jewish Abraham. The internal lack of neutrality by religious leaders is a major element that confronts the question of historical verification by archaeologists. The conclusions of archaeologists on issues involving Abraham, his descendants, and Moses cannot be interpreted in a way that favors one of the three religions. Such a goal is not the goal of archaeologists. The objections and questioning of archaeologists today vis-à-vis the three religions and their positions on Abraham, his descendants, and Moses involve a request for the three religions themselves to get together more carefully, if they wish to claim legitimacy for the role of Abraham, his descendants, and Moses.

The intrareligious issue once again surfaces in a strong and unavoidable way. Prior to any conclusions on archaeological data, the intrareligious questions need to be faced by the leaders and scholars of the three religions.

Three religious views on the history of Abraham, his descendants, and the Moses material remain theologically intolerable and historically impossible.

4. Fourth Limitation: Contemporary Biblical History on the Role of Religion in the Middle East from the Sixth Century BC.E. Down to the Second Century C.E.

The fourth major factor that has questioned and even challenged the three Abrahamic religions is the emergence of modern historical analyses. This historically oriented interpretation of sacred texts includes many interlacing issues. One begins with the development of critical texts and versions of the sacred writings. On the basis of a critical text, biblical scholars have moved into what is called Old and New Testament criticism. Pre-critical interpretation of the sacred writings came to end around 1650 with the work of Richard Simon (1638–1712). His work became popular and was translated into English and German.[36] The development of historical biblical criticism from 1650 onward was extensive.[37] To date, there is no common acceptance on the meaning of historiographical writing, for the meaning of history, whether religious or non-religious, was also developed in a variety of ways throughout the nineteenth and twentieth centuries.

In 2011, Garret Galvin's volume *Egypt as a Place of Refuge* appeared. In this volume numerous authors are cited who have raised serious doubts about the historical veracity of many biblical texts. His bibliography is thorough and indicative of the widespread hesitation by contemporary historical scholars to accept the material in the sacred writings as verifiable.[38] Over and over again, many biblical historians have accepted the literary nature of a story form in the sacred writings, and therefore their positions oppose the interpretation of the sacred texts as historical facts.[39] Galvin writes:

---

36. Auvray, *Richard Simon*; Steinmann, *Richard Simon et les origenes de l'exégèse biblique*.

37. Other biblical scholars who continued this historical orientation of biblical literature from the eighteenth century onward include: J. Morinus, L. Capellus, H. Grotius, J. Leclerc, B. F. Kennicott, W. McKane, and A. Schultens. W. Schröder, J. D. Michaelis, J. Astruc, J. S. Semler, J. G. Hamann, J. G. Herder, J. G. Eichhorn, W. M. L. de Wette, W. Vatke, H. Ewald, J. Wellhausen, B. Duhm, S. R. Driver, W. Robertson Smith.

38. Galvin, *Egypt as a Place of Refuge*, 189–209.

39. Examples of this focus on story form can be found in Sweeney, "Reassessment of the Masoretic and Septuagint Versions," 189; Willis, "Text of I Kings 11:43—12:3," 43.

I will pay more explicit attention to the question of genre. I believe much work remains to be done on incorporating insights from literary criticism into the overall picture of Israel's relationship to Egypt.[40]

In contemporary biblical criticism, hermeneutics plays a major role. Biblical hermeneutics, however, moves in several directions. There is today a major discussion on the meaning of the *literal sense* of scriptural passages. There is also a "fundamentalistic" sense for the reading of the sacred texts, namely, the that texts themselves are always literally factual. There is a typological hermeneutic, which stresses that there is a deeper meaning than the literal meaning of a sacred text. The deeper meaning was and is intended by God, even though it was not necessarily intended by the author. This further typological sense is due, so some scholars argue, either to further divine revelations or to a development in the understanding of revelation itself.[41]

Other forms of hermeneutics include the New Heideggerian hermeneutics, furthered by Rudolph Bultmann, Emile Fuchs, Hans-Georg Gadamer, and Gerhardt Ebeling. Another form of contemporary hermeneutics is literary criticism, which has its own proponents, such as A. N. Wilder, Norman Perrin, Robert W. Funk, Dominic Crossan, and others. Other forms of appeal have also been utilized.[42]

Another group of contemporary biblical historiographers have recently appeared. These writers have been labeled "minimalists." In the area of biblical history, they include the Assyriologist Mario Liverani, whose book *Israel's History and the History of Israel* has created a major stir among scriptural scholars. Another scholar, Donald Redford, has contributed to this way of thinking as found in his volume *Egypt, Canaan and Israel in Ancient Times*. Other "minimalist" scholars include Thomas L. Thompson, whose book is entitled *The Bible in History*, and John Van Seters, whose recent book is *The Edited Bible: The Curious History of the "Editor" in Biblical Criticism*.

From the beginning of public debate over these last volumes, the term "minimalism" has been used in a pejorative way.[43] In his book, Liverani

---

40. Galvin, *Egypt as a Place of Refuge*, 6.
41. Brown and Schneiders, "Hermeneutics," 1157.
42. Ibid., 1159–65.

43. In the case of Mario Liverani, see the review of Liverani's book by Claude Marriotini, at http://doctor.claudemariottini.com/2008/01/mario-liverani-and-history-of-israel.html.

questions the contemporary Christian, Islamic, and Jewish scholars who maintain the historicity of the Abrahamic-Mosaic literature. The focus of his arguments is on the historical verification of these sections in the sacred writings. Liverani as well as the other "minimalists" portray in a detailed way the differences between some Jewish historians who construct a Jewish history based on the data that is verified only on the basis of the Torah, and other scholars who strive to remain religiously neutral as they write books on the history of Judaism.

A similar distinction has been made for scholars who write on the history of Christianity or the history of Islam. There are scholars who will verify the historicity of the Abrahamic-Mosaic material only if historical material outside the sacred writings verifies the religious text. They are negatively referred to as "minimalists." Religious scholars who accept data simply because the data is referred to in the sacred texts are negatively referred to as "maximalists."

Religious historians are deeply concerned about the historical verification, but there are some Christian, Islamic, and Jewish writers who maintain that the Pentateuch can be in itself a source of historical verification. There are other religious historians who require historical verification outside of major sacred scriptures.

Often a literal hermeneutic of the Pentateuch shows itself when a scholar writes a "history of Israel" or a "history of Islam" or a "history of Christianity." In all of these histories, the authors favor an overarching view of Pentateuchal history that benefits Christianity, Islam, or Judaism. In some ways, these writers could be called "maximalists," for they clearly present many historical issues in the Pentateuch as verifiably historical, and this position stretches the validity of historical verification into many gray areas. Historical data is not verified by "faith," but by acceptable sources based on data.

The contemporary scientific historians raise major questions and challenges. These can be summarized as follows:

- Are religious leaders and scholars of the three religions able to set aside their religious "prejudice" (if one can use that word in a non-confrontational way) and on the basis of historical evidence respond to the questions that scientific historians have raised?
- If an author who is a "maximalist" or at least, more often than not, tends to accept scriptural data as historically true, is not rejected in

Science and Religion

an outright way by his or her peers, why are the minimalists of the scriptural writings disallowed an equal voice?

The rejection of minimalist historians is rightly questioned today. Many current historians, the minimalists included, have questioned and challenged the leaders and scholars of the three religions on the issue of scriptural history. The response of some leaders and scholars of the three religions has been, in an intensive and extensive way, fairly negative to any and all minimalistic presentations. In their rejection, the leaders and scholars have tended to uphold the historical verification of many issues in the Pentateuch on the basis of the sacredness of the writing. However, from a growing number of sources today, as we have seen in the three issues above—archaeology, quantum physics, and the age of the universe—key factors in the Pentateuch and other religious writings are today seriously questioned and even challenged as regards their historical verification. In some cases, there does not seem to be any verification of the historicity of these issues at all. Not only minimalists but also many middle-of-the-road historians claim that scripture alone does not offer adequate historical verification. These voices should not be dismissed. Rather their views should be included in contemporary religion-science discussions.

•••

The material in this chapter indicates in a fairly precise way what the term "science" entails in this volume and what the term "religion" entails. Since our focus is limited, many of the major issues as found in the contemporary religion-science dialogues are not central to this volume.

The material in The material in chapter two sets the sets the stage for the remainder of this volume. It focuses on the beauty and value of the three religions. This material is meant to show that the three religions have today and in the past a strong centering that has drawn millions of people over the years to find the presence of God in their day-to-day lives. This volume in no way wants to diminish the value of the three religions. Chapter also contains a final section indicating the struggle by religious leaders and scholars to find answers to contemporary scientific issues. In chapter 3, the development of quantum physics is presented in detail. At the end of Chapter three there is a series of questions and challenges that quantum physics presents to the religious focus of this volume. In chapter 4, there is a more thorough consideration of the scientific issues that have given rise to the questions and challenges made by contemporary scientists and the major religious answers. Various responses and alternatives are likewise discussed in that chapter. In chapter 5, the focus is on various forms of response that both scientists and leaders and scholars of religion have made. Chapter 7 moves away from a scientific consideration to the intrareligious issues that need to be considered honestly. Until these issues are clarified the struggles between science and religion cannot be dealt with. The final chapter offers a series of conclusions and implications.

2

THE SPIRITUAL BEAUTY OF RELIGION AND CONTEMPORARY SCIENTIFIC ISSUES

CHAPTER 3 CENTERS ON the ultimate spiritual beauty found in all three religions, Christianity, Islam, and Judaism. In each of these religious communities the "religion" itself is not the ultimate source of sublimity and holiness. Rather, each religion offers a small but important spiritual glimpse of an infinite all-powerful God, and it is precisely this small glimpse of the divine that has over the centuries made each religion an awesome, honored, and profound source of holiness. It is this divine presence that ultimately provides each religion with its beauty, aura, and power to draw individuals into the respective community. In other words, spirituality—not dogma, not theology, and not hierarchy—is the sacred core that makes a religion effective.

PART ONE: THE MEANING OF SPIRITUALITY

Allabahkhsh K. Brohi, at the beginning of his essay "The Spiritual Significance of the Quran," describes spirituality in a very careful way. He writes:

> Spirituality means many things to many minds and is undeniably a term that is used in varying contexts with different shades of meanings. Many have used this term to designate a special mark

of spiritual disposition, and others have employed it to mark off a higher and final development of life itself. In the way the present writer understands it, it will be appropriate to say that anyone who reflects God or the Holy Spirit as the vital determining norm or principle of his or her life could validly be called "spiritual."[1]

In this citation, Brohi uses the phrase "anyone who reflects God or the Holy Spirit" is "spiritual." The same conclusion could easily be said about every religious community that has ever existed. Each religious community by reflecting God or the Holy Spirit is spiritual. One could also conclude that the depth and breadth of a community's reflection of God is precisely the main reason why people want to join a given community. Religions are ultimately God centered; they are not self centered.[2] Why do many people want to join Christian communities, Islamic communities, or Jewish communities? The fundamental answer is clear: what ultimately draws them is the beauty of God.

Spirituality is God centered and, as we shall see throughout this volume, the relationship of one's spiritual life to a God-centered life has been and remains a major complication for monotheistic belief. If God is the spiritual center of all religions, and if God is one, how can there be three religions that claim to be monotheistic? In reality these religions move from monotheism to "propriotheism," namely, to "our understanding of God" as Trinity, or Allah, or Yahweh. If there is only one God and if this one God is the center of spirituality, then some aspect of monotheism must be common to each of the three religions, for the members of each religion have been touched by the one and only transcendent and infinite God. It is not enough for the members of a given religion to say, "We believe in one God and this one God is Trinity, Allah, or Yahweh." Rather, monotheism means that one and the same God is basically the spiritual center of each and every claim of a centering monotheistic belief. If this were not correct, the infinity of a monotheistic God would be denied.

God is beyond all description, for God is eternal and therefore timeless. God is infinite and therefore unlimited. God is also omnipotent and therefore utterly free. God is omniscient and therefore utterly wise. God is omnipresent and therefore everywhere. If this description of God is accepted by a religion—and it is accepted by Christianity, Islam, and

---

1. Brohi, "Spiritual Significance of the Quran," 11.
2. Even religions that do not believe in a "personal God" are spiritual in and through the ways in which they (such as Buddhism) reflect transcendence.

The Spiritual Beauty of Religion and Contemporary Scientific Issues

Judaism—then no human being can put into words what God truly is. In our limited lives, however, each spiritual Christian, Muslim, and Jew has come to know at least something about this one and infinite God, and it is precisely this "something about God" that continues to draw us into our religious spirituality and into a given religious community.

Over many centuries, the leaders and scholars of each of the three religions have given us glimpses of this transcendent God through their wisdom, their writings, and their example. The mystics and the saints of each of the three religions have also provided us with insights into the holiness of God through their own wisdom, writings, and example. Nonetheless, when all is said and done by any and all of these important religious predecessors, God remains a mystery.

Still—and this is a major "still"—the way in which each of the three religions presents this glimpse of God is the issue that draws people to the three religions. One is a true Christian when he or she has fallen deeply in love with God after meditating on the Christian *glimpse* of God. One is a true Muslim when he or she has fallen deeply in love with God after meditating on the Islamic *glimpse* of Allah. One is a true Jewish believer when he or she has fallen deeply in love with God after meditating on the Jewish *glimpse* of Yahweh.

However, this approach gives rise to an inevitable question, namely, in what ways have the three religions presented this unveiling of the mystery of God? This question is formidable, since only in the presentations by each religion of God's mystery can one find the basic reason why one is and remains a religious Christian, a religious Muslim, or a religious Jew. People are not religious within a given community because they can philosophically conclude that God exists. Rather, people are religious and remain religious because of their deep and holy belief in a God who is one and who is unlimited in love and compassion. One's belief is based on the grace or gift of God, for it is God who first reveals his own self to an individual. Only then do individuals respond to this gifting of God. This does not mean that one knows everything about God; rather, God's gift can be best described as a "glimpse of God," or a "glimpse of divine love and compassion."

Each of the three religions has developed a theological expression of its own glimpse of God, and they have done this in two ways. First, each religion presents the way in which its main leaders and scholars over many centuries have *theologically* described God. Secondly, each religion has expressed, again over many centuries, its *spiritual understanding* of its own glimpse of God, and they have done this through its adherents' prayer life, its public worship, and its religious stories and symbols. The technical or theological presentation of God that each religion rightfully formulates has its place, but the majority of adherents of a given religion do not find their spiritual understanding of God in technical theology. Rather, they begin to understand God through prayer and devotion, through worship and celebration, and through helping others and being helped by others. God is not found only in a given religion's technical description of God, its theology, but also and most often in and through the ways in which a religion on a daily basis touches the deepest aspects of a person's life. Theological presentations of God have their place, but by no means do they totally express how the members of a given religion see and love the divinely willed unveiling of God. Even with profound theological studies on the meaning of God as found in their respective histories, no religion has a complete grasp of either who God is or what God is. Consequently, the term "glimpse" has been used deliberately to highlight this limitation.

In Part One of this chapter, the focus is on the major aspects of the "glimpse of God" that the leaders and scholars as well as the mystics and saints of the three traditions have imparted to us. In Part Two of this chapter the focus changes. Contemporary science has raised both questions and challenges about the existence of God. These scientific questions and challenges present contemporary religious leaders, scholars, and general adherents, even with the ultimate beauty of their glimpses of God, with a bothersome question: has there as yet been an adequate religious response to the scientific questions and challenges that contemporary scientists have developed?

The questions and challenges raised by contemporary scientists vis-à-vis particular issues in Christianity, Islam, and Judaism do not center on the divine core of these religions. Scientists, by and large, are questioning/challenging the historical verification of certain details which the three religions present. In this volume, the details that we are considering refer to Abraham and his descendants, as well as to the Mosaic material as found in the sacred scriptures of the three religions.

Scientific questions do not and will not shape the material of this chapter, for this chapter focuses on the transcendent beauty in each of the three religions. The transcendent beauty of God as reflected in each religion is the core of this chapter, for here we stand before the reflection of an

The Spiritual Beauty of Religion and Contemporary Scientific Issues

infinite God and we entrust ourselves to this God even though we have only a small glimpse of the infinite Creator.

PART TWO: THE TRANSCENDENT BEAUTY OF GOD THAT IS PRESENT IN EACH OF THE THREE RELIGIOUS TRADITIONS

The Transcendent Beauty of God That Is Present in Christianity

The New Testament is the basic text for all Christians, and in the New Testament the authors describe, each in his own way, something about the life of Jesus. For Christians, Jesus is central, since Jesus has revealed in a distinctive way the love and beauty of God. Jesus did this in a straightforward way through the style of his life and through his message. He did this through the way he lived, through the way he died, and through his risen presence after death. The only way to understand the Christian approach to the transcendent beauty of God is through the revelation that Jesus has made of his Father-God.

Mohammad and Moses are not considered the center of Islamic or Jewish faith. They are key prophets and leaders, but in the Islamic religion it is Allah who has revealed himself in the Qur'an, and in the Jewish religion the focus is on Yahweh who is revealed in the Torah.

One might follow this pattern and say that the Christian religion focuses on God as revealed in the New Testament Gospels. However, in Christianity it is the person of Jesus who is the center of Christian faith, and consequently the Gospels are not quite the same as the Qur'an and the Torah. The incarnation of the Logos in the humanity of Jesus is the center of Christian faith. Let us consider this Jesus-Gospel issue in some depth.

The writers of each Gospel composed their work with a particular group or groups of people in mind. In other words, they were writing for specific audiences or readerships.[3] The Gospels were meant to be read

---

3. In the first century C.E., most Mediterranean people were illiterate. Young people from aristocratic and wealthy families did attend universities in which a major focus was on rhetoric. In the rhetoric departments, one was not taught primarily on how to read and write; rather, they were specifically taught how to speak publicly in ways in which people would remember what they had said. The gospels and the letters of the New Testament were primarily composed by writers who knew that the material would be read

aloud to the Jesus community to which the authors themselves belonged. Moreover, the author of each Gospel intended to put in writing the way that his particular Jesus community believed in Jesus. This written form of their belief in Jesus would then be reread to the next generation of this same Jesus community and then to the next generation, etc. In this way, the goal of the author of each Gospel was to maintain a common belief in Jesus and his message. With this goal in mind, one can see how and why each Gospel is somewhat different from the others. Each was written for a distinct and specific Jesus community, and therefore the authors took into account certain issues that needed to be emphasized and clarified because of their own community's needs.

A secondary goal was to explain to others who were not members of the author's community but who were challenging the home community's belief about Jesus. These others challenged the ways in which the Christians presented the presence and message of Jesus as the fulfillment of the Torah and the Prophets. Through this goal, each individual Gospel provided a source of unity for a given Jesus community as they struggled against the outsiders who opposed them. In the early part of the first century C.E., some of these outsiders were Jewish people who felt that the Jesus community, which at that time was a sect or a special community within Judaism, had moved beyond the normal boundaries of Jewish thought.[4]

In the Gospel of Matthew, some scholars have found passages that evidence a defense by the author against Jewish critics. After the destruction of the Jewish temple in 70 C.E., it seems that many Jewish scholars fled from Jerusalem to Jamnia.[5] In the latter part of the first century, Jewish scholars from Jamnia often traveled to the port city of Caesarea Maritima, in which many biblical scholars place the author of the Gospel of Matthew.[6] The Jamnian scholars evidently complained publicly against the "false Judaism" that the Jesus communities in Caesarea Maritima were maintaining. The author of Matthew's Gospel had these Jewish leaders in mind as he was writing.

---

publicly before the intended communities.

4. For the view that the early Jesus-community was similar to a sect within Judaism, see Neusner, "Varieties of Judaism in the Formative Age," especially 189–90.

5. See "Jamnia" in the *Jewish Encyclopedia*, online: http://www.jewishencyclopedia.com/articles/8510-jamnia.

6. For the authorship, date, and place of Matthew's Gospel, see Viviano, "Gospel According to Matthew," 630–32. See also Kilpatrick, *Origin of the Gospel According to St. Matthew*.

The Spiritual Beauty of Religion and Contemporary Scientific Issues

In Caesarea, the Jesus community had become a fairly strong and well-known group, and many of these followers continued to consider themselves Jewish even though they believed in Jesus. Benedict Viviano, in his analysis of Matthew's Gospel, argues as follows. The author of the Gospel of Matthew defends the position that the Jesus community is not only a true Jewish community, but *the only true Jewish community*, since Jesus is the "royal son of God and Immanuel, God with us." Jesus was "given all [divine] authority as Son of Man over the kingdom of God in heaven and on earth." Jesus is a "Son of David. . . . With this title Jesus is seen as a new Solomon, with connotations as healer and wise man. Jesus speaks a wisdom incarnate" (see Mathew, 11:25-30 and 23:37-39). "Equally, if not more important is the non-confessional but public title of Jesus as the Son of Man which runs through the Gospel, culminating in the grand finale in 28:18-20." This title is based on Daniel 7:13-14, and it indicates that Jesus is the one who fulfills Daniel's prophecy for Jesus is the Messiah who announced the end of the world.[7]

Moreover, the three Synoptic Gospels, each in its own way, focus at least to some extent on a non-Jewish mission. The Jesus communities as presented in these three Gospels include non-Jewish people, namely Greeks, who were by the end of the first century able to be part of Jewish Jesus communities. Some followers of Jesus who were deeply rooted in Judaism questioned this openness to non-Jews, and the issue became a major point of division in the early Jesus communities (Acts 9:26-31). In an unspoken but realistic way, the question of the acceptance of non-Jews into the Jesus communities includes a God question: is the God of the Jewish Jesus communities only a God for the Jews or is this God a God of all men and women?

This God issue reveals part of the glimpse of God that the followers of Jesus had to confront. By the end of the first century, the Jesus communities by and large had accepted a God who is a "God for all."[8] This is a major be-

---

7. Viviano, "Gospel According to Matthew," 631-32.

8. In later centuries, the Roman Catholic Church restricted the openness of God, for in many official writings one reads, "Outside the [Roman Catholic] Church there is no salvation" ("Extra ecclesiam nulla salus"). The fourth Lateran Council expressed this teaching as follows: "Una vero est fidelium universalis Ecclesia, extra quam nullus omnino salvatur." Denzinger and Schönmetzer, *Enchiridion Symbolorum*, n. 802. The Second Vatican Council in its *Declaration on the Relation of the Church to Non-Christian Religions* attempted to express the Catholic position in a much more welcoming way. See also Knitter, "Bridge or Boundary?"

lief of the first-century followers of Jesus, and this openness of the Christian communities to non-Jewish people was and remains a major aspect of the New Testament presentation of God.[9]

Contemporary scholars are not unified in the terminology that best describes the earliest followers of Jesus. First-century followers of Jesus are described and categorized today in different ways.[10] The overriding judgment of contemporary scholars is that Jesus did not establish a "Christian church." Rather, he established a group of followers who in one way or another could be considered as: (1) a new Jewish sect; (2) a Jewish millenarian movement; (3) a Jewish charismatic religious movement; or (4) a new community similar to other contemporary Jewish communities. The development of the Jewish followers of Jesus into a "church" took place slowly and occurred at different times and in different areas of the Mediterranean world. The Johannine community remained part of the Jewish synagogue structure until roughly 85 C.E., when there was a Jewish ban that disallowed the followers of Jesus to be part of the synagogue community. It was after this period of time that the Johannine community or communities can be referred to as part of a "Christian church."[11] The exact time when the followers of Jesus can be called the "church" has been an issue of historical discussion for the past 150 years.

The standard position of the Vatican leaders of the Catholic Church is that Jesus himself founded a "church" and Peter was put in charge of this church. In the scholarly world, this view cannot be verified. The Catholic bishops at Vatican II deliberately avoided the twentieth-century historical material on the "foundation" of the church. They continued to express the "standard" approach, which today is seen by many Catholic biblical scholars as unhistorical. However, one can legitimately argue that the first-century Christian communities were basically not a "church" in the technical

---

9. When Constantine made Christianity the major religion of the Roman Empire, Christian leaders began to persecute in a strong way those who were not Christians. In other words, God was no longer a God open to others, but a God open only to the Christian community. A recent book, *Jesus Wars*, by Philip Jensen, provides an enormous amount of historical material through which we can see a closing of doors and windows to those who do not accept a given intellectual approach to Christian theology.

10 See Osborne, *Theology of Church for the Third Millennium*. In this volume, the details of the four approaches concerning first-century Christians are described in detail (284–320).

11. For the separation of the Johannine communities from the synagogue, see Perkins, "Gospel According to John"; see also Maloney, "Johannine Theology."

The Spiritual Beauty of Religion and Contemporary Scientific Issues

meaning of the term; rather they were God-oriented communities that struggled to include both Jews and non-Jews.

In the New Testament as a whole there is indeed a focus on Jesus, but more importantly there is a focus on what Jesus stood for, what he preached, and what kind of belief in Yahweh-God he was urging. The human Jesus would have had no lasting value if he had only preached himself. Rather, Jesus was urging his followers to view Yahweh in a different way from the view of some major Jewish leaders of his time. In this basic sense, Jesus was fundamentally a revealer of Yahweh.

There have been many attempts to state succinctly the central message of Jesus that he himself preached during his lifetime. In the last fifty years such scholars as Leonardo Boff, Jean Francois Bonnefoy, Günther Bornkamm, Oscar Cullmann, and Joachim Jeremias have offered a particular description of Jesus' message.[12] Perhaps such a task may never be accomplished in a satisfying way, but all of these authors, as well as many others, have gravitated around several key themes, so that at least the general parameters of Jesus' basic message can be fairly well established.

Jeremias centers his structure of Jesus' message—both the message of his life and the message of his preaching—on four themes:

a. The return of the quenched Spirit

b. Overcoming the rule of Satan

c. The dawn of the kingdom of God

d. The poor have the good news preached to them[13]

Jeremias mentions that in late Jewish history (200 B.C.E. onward) no prophets had appeared, and yet many Jews believed that the prophets would once again appear and the situation of the Jews under the Romans would be rectified and the end of the world would take place.[14] In the Gospels and in many other writings of the New Testament, Jesus was seen as the return of the prophet, and this meant that the Spirit of God had returned to the chosen people.[15] Jesus may not have preached that he was a prophet and

---

12. See for instance Boff, *Passion of Christ*; Bonnefoy, *Christ and the Cosmos*; Bornkamm, *Jesus of Nazareth*; Jeremias, *New Testament Theology*.

13. Jeremias, *New Testament Theology*, 76–121.

14. See Meier, "Jesus," 1323–25. Meier notes that an eschatological prophet is mentioned in the Qumran material.

15. From the time of Daniel onward, the Jewish people had had no prophet. Among the ordinary Jewish populace, a belief had developed that when a new prophet was sent by Yahweh then the spirit of God would indeed return and the end of the world would be

therefore that he was filled with the Spirit of God, but many Jewish followers of Jesus at that time believed that Jesus was a prophet and therefore "the quenched Spirit" had returned in and through Jesus. This was truly good news.

If the Spirit had returned and Jewish life was again moving forward to the end time as Yahweh had planned, then Satan and his demons were slated for extinction. Evil was as yet not totally overcome, but evil was on its way out of human life and therefore on its way to extinction. Evil, therefore, is not the final answer, and this was truly good news.[16]

Central to Jesus' teaching is the kingdom of God. Notice that it is not the kingdom of Jesus, nor is it the kingdom of the church. In the Gospels, the kingdom of God is not a political, economic, or social entity. Rather, it is a "kingdom" of the Spirit, and its "king" is, of course, God. This kingdom, however, was not established as a finished entity. Rather, through Jesus' life, death, and resurrection the final kingdom had its beginning and only at the end time would it be complete. This too was truly good news.[17]

The major leaders of the Jewish establishment at the time of Jesus might have dickered about these three themes, but the three themes were to some extent tolerable for the majority of Jews. After all, Jesus was claiming that the Spirit of God had returned and was with Jesus and therefore with the Jewish people. Jesus also claimed that the presence of evil (Satan) was on its way out, but not yet gone. Thirdly, God's kingdom had begun to take root in the chosen people. None of these three issues caused the major Jewish leaders of that period of time to call for Jesus' death.

It is the fourth theme that created the deadly situation. This fourth theme is that the poor have the good news preached to them.[18] God's message was meant for the poor—not only those who were materially poor but also those who were socially rejected, such as tax collectors, prostitutes, lepers, etc. In taking this stance, Jesus publicly defied the major Jewish leadership of his day. The poor, taken in the broader sense, were often those who had been "excommunicated" by the major Jewish leaders. Such people were not to be welcomed in the synagogues. In many instances, they were

---

at hand. The "quenched spirit" would then return. See Jeremias, *New Testament Theology*, 76–85.

16. Ibid., 85–96.

17. Ibid., 96–108.

18. Ibid., 108–21. Jeremias brings the four issues together in ch. 4, "The Period of Grace," (122–58), and he takes up the theme of Jesus' death in ch. 6, "Jesus' Testimony to his Mission" (250–99).

thrown out of the synagogues. Since they were not observant of the Law as the Jewish leaders understood it, they were excluded from any rights of Jewish propriety. Jesus not only stated publicly that these poor would be chosen by God for his kingdom, but he also stated that they would get to heaven before the major Jewish leaders. He even stated, according to the Gospels, that the major Jewish leaders would not be accepted into the kingdom of God at all because they had rejected the poor.

On this issue of the poor, Jesus openly challenged the central religious leaders of his time. These challenges played a major role for his arrest. Jesus was publicly defying the authority of the major Jewish leaders. Jesus was claiming that God did not accept what the Jewish leaders had formulated vis-à-vis who belongs to God and who does not belong to God. Because of this, the main Jewish leaders wanted Jesus to be silenced.

When these same leaders took Jesus to Pilate, the Roman governor, the charges were, however, changed. Instead of charging that Jesus had defied Jewish leadership, the Gospels indicate that the Jewish leaders charged that Jesus had defied Roman rule. Jesus, they said, wanted to establish a messianic kingdom that challenged the role of the Roman kingdom. Pilate would have dismissed the case if the charges were only about Jewish leadership. However, Pilate was unable to dismiss the case once the charges became political and against Roman rule.

The resurrection of Jesus throughout the New Testament indicates that the Spirit has returned and continues to be with us, that Satan with his evil bent is headed for final meaninglessness, that the kingdom of God will attain its fulfillment, and that the poor will be the exalted members in the kingdom of Yahweh.

It is in this last theme—the poor have the good news preached to them—that the message of Jesus shows us the beauty of God in an incomprehensible way. God is compassionate without limits. God is caring and loving in spite of our shortcomings. God is forgiving in an endless way. It is precisely this understanding of God that keeps Christians within the many forms of the Christian church today. Fundamentally, Christians are not church people. Fundamentally, they are people who love God because God has first loved them. It is in the community called the Christian church that they find others who also believe in God in a similar way. In the Christian community, one finds the encouragement to keep believing in such a compassionate and good God.

The questions and challenges of contemporary science are not focused on this Christian position of belief. We will see in the second part of this chapter that the scientific questions and challenges focus on certain ways that Christian leaders and Christian people describe specific secondary aspects of their belief.

Through Jesus, a revelation of God took place. Jesus preached the kingdom of God, and the God who is the lord of the kingdom is infinitely compassionate, loving, and relational. One can describe the New Testament God as unending goodness, infinite love, fontal fullness, and relationally gifting.[19] Since God is transcendent, any and all descriptions of God are limited by their very nature. Since God is infinite, no one can limit God, and this applies to God's compassion, forgiveness, love, and presence. However, since God is infinite, all of our finite descriptions of God are limited by their very nature.

In the Gospels, Jesus again and again presents us with a God who is unlimited. In the opening chapter of Mark's Gospel (1:21–45), Jesus cures a demoniac. He then cures Simon's mother-in-law and this is followed by the cure of "all who were ill or possessed by demons" and "many who were sick with various diseases." Jesus even "drove out many demons." The second chapter of Mark begins with another cure, namely, the cure of a paralytic (2:1–12). Through the healing Jesus, one perceives the healing God.

In the Gospels we read that certain Jewish leaders of high rank rebuked Jesus for such cures, since those he cured were sinners and outcasts. Jesus openly confronted these Jewish leaders time and time again, indicating that the leaders were placing limits on God's love, care, and mercy. The Gospels clearly indicate that the elders of the Jewish faith restricted the mercy of God, and they did so because of their interpretation of the Torah. Jesus openly challenged them, presenting a God who is far above the law. In Luke's Gospel, we hear the same thing, for the author presents Jesus as a person who, in his ministry to outcasts, is boundary breaking (5:12–16).[20]

God, in the Christian presentation, has no boundaries. Neither church leadership nor church administration can put boundaries on God. Christian churches are truly spiritual when individual Christians and the Christian communities reflect a God without boundaries. However, these

---

19. This description of God is found throughout Christian literature. In my analysis of the Trinity in the writings of St. Bonaventure, I have found an abundant use of these words to described God; see Osborne, *Ecclesiology for the Twenty-First Century*, 293–320.

20. Karris, "Gospel According to Luke," 692.

The Spiritual Beauty of Religion and Contemporary Scientific Issues

individuals and communities have never reflected God totally, for God is beyond all limits. What attracts people to join these Christian groups? Fundamentally and basically, people are attracted when they catch a glimpse of a holy and infinitely compassionate God. God-centeredness is or at least should be the spiritual beauty of each and every Christian and of each and every Christian community.

To explain the core of Christian life, Bonaventure Kloppenburg uses the phrase "The Church as mystery of the moon." He bases his position on the dogmatic constitution on the church, *Lumen gentium*, promulgated by the bishops at Vatican II.

> The Council begins its Dogmatic Constitution on the Church with the words, *Lumen gentium*. But this "light of the nations" is not the Church: "Christ is the light of all nations"! (LG 1/14). From its very opening words, therefore, Vatican II seeks to give a completely Christocentric and thus relativized idea of the Church. We can understand the Church only if we relate it to Christ, the glorified Lord.[21]

Kloppenburg goes on to say that whenever the church itself is absolutized, separated from Christ and considered only in its structures, it ceases to be a mystery and becomes simply another religious society or organization. It ceases to deserve special attention. He continues:

> Only Christ is the light of the world. He is the Sun, sole source of light. At the side of the Sun, which is Christ, stands the Church like the moon which receives all its light, brilliance and warmth from the sun.[22]

Kloppenburg continues this imagery. He writes that Christian communities have a "borrowed" light, which waxes and wanes. The light of the Christian communities is no more than a "pale shimmer" or a "dark radiance." The witnessing to God by the Christian communities can often become obscured. Even though the Christian communities have been called the "salt of the earth," they can become tasteless. Even more, Christian communities can be excessively human. Only when they draw intimately near to Christ do they reflect him. The human Jesus, however, reflects God. Ultimately, then, God is the unending Light, reflected in and through Jesus and from Jesus into the Christian communities. It is the light of God that draws

---

21. Kloppenburg, *Ecclesiology of Vatican*, 19.
22. Ibid., 21.

people to Jesus and to the Christian communities. However, the reflection of God in both the human Jesus and in the Christian communities is limited. We can catch only a glimpse or glimmer of God who is infinite Light. The divine Light goes beyond all boundaries and has no limits whatsoever.

In the above paragraphs, we can catch only a small glimpse of the spiritual beauty of the Christian religion. Ultimately, the spiritual beauty is the transcendent God, and the Christian communities share in that beauty when, like the moon, which has no light of its own, they reflect the human Jesus.

The Transcendent Beauty of God That Is present in Islam

In the volume entitled *Islamic Spirituality: Foundations*, edited by Seyyed Hossein Nasr, there are several essays that present the spirituality of the Islamic religion in a powerful way.[23] In his introductory essay, Nasr notes that the term "spirituality" as used in the English language has a strong Christian connotation. Thus, he asks a different question: what does spirituality mean in the context of the Islamic tradition? He turns to the major languages of the Islamic tradition: Arabic, Persian, and Turkish. In the Arabic language, a term that is often used is *rūhāniyyah*, and in the Persian language, a term that is used with frequency is *ma'nawiyyat*. The word, *rūh*, which means "spirit," is described in the Qur'an as follows: "The Spirit is from the command of my Lord" (XVII, 85). The second term comes from is *ma'nā*, which connotes inwardness as real and not just apparent. It also connotes "spirit" with a focus on a higher level of reality, namely the reality of Allah. Nasr concludes:

> In summary, these terms refer to that which is related to the world of the Spirit, is in Divine Proximity, possesses inwardness and interiority and is identified with the real—and therefore also from the Islamic point of view—permanent and abiding rather than transient and passing.[24]

Nasr then explains that there is yet another dimension for spirituality as used in the Islamic languages, namely the sense of presence, *barakah*, "or that grace which flows in the vein of the universe and within the life of

23. In this volume, see Ashraf, "Inner Meaning of the Islamic Rites"; Chishti, "Female Spirituality in Islam." Other essays that also express Islamic spirituality in a strong and careful way are cited in the pages of this volume.

24. Nasr, "Introduction," in *Islamic Spirituality*, xvii.

man to the extent that he dedicates himself to God."[25] In this understanding of spiritual life, both moral perfection and beauty of the soul are also a referent. In all of this, the term "spirituality" evokes in the Islamic mind a proximity both to Allah and to the world of spirit.

Allahbakhsh K. Brohi, in his essay "The Spiritual Significance of the Quran," mentions that the titles to various sections of his essay indicate his focus. These titles include: "Spirituality and Human Growth," "The Human Predicament," "The Love of God," "To Please God," "Meeting the Lord," and "The Qur'an and the Problems of Life." The beginning of spirituality is, of course, Allah. Allah is present throughout the world to every human being. In chapter 30 of the Qur'an we read:

> So set thy face steadily and truly to the Faith: (establish) Allah's handiwork according to the pattern on which He has made mankind; no change (let there be) in the work (wrought) by Allah: that is the standard Religion: but most among mankind understand not. (Sūrah XXX, 30).[26]

The opening words of the Qur'an, in many ways, move in this direction, and these opening lines are the basis of Islamic spirituality.

**IN THE NAME OF ALLAH,
MOST GRACIOUS, MOST MERCIFUL.**

Praise be to Allah,
The Cherisher and Sustainer of the Worlds,
Most Gracious, Most Merciful;
Master of the Day of Judgement.
Thee do we worship,
and Thine aid we seek.

Show us the straight way,
The way of those on whom
Thou hast bestowed Thy grace,
Those whose (portion)
Is not wrath,
And who go not astray.[27]

---

25. Ibid., xvii.
26. This translation is taken from Ali, *Meaning of the Holy Qur'ān*, 1015–16.
27. From ibid., 14–15.

Thomas Cleary indicates that this opening passage of the Qur'an has at times been compared to the Lord's Prayer of Jesus in terms of its popularity.[28] He also writes:

> "The Compassionate, the Merciful" (*ar Rahmaan ar Rahiim*): These names of God are intensive derivatives of the root R-H-M, which suggests compassion and mercy. I have translated the definite article as indicating God to be characterized by the epitome of these qualities, whose intensive forms refer to the exaltation of God infinitely beyond corresponding human qualities.[29]

Mohammad himself often noted that chapter 1 (Sūrah I), *The Opening*: Al Fātihah, is the best of all chapters, and the material in the chapter is frequently repeated or referred to throughout the Qur'an. Cleary states, "All praise belongs to [the] God (*al 'amdu li Laah*)." The definite article is used, Cleary writes, since Allah alone is ultimately worthy of praise.[30]

Al-Ghazali speaks of praise as an aspect of gratitude and considers praise as half of the straight way to Allah.[31] The compassionate Allah is Lord of all the worlds, that is, any and every cosmos, but it is especially focused on the world that we humans, often subjectively, describe. The Sufi giant Muhiyuddin Ibn al Arabi speaks of the cosmos that we humans describe and analyze as "imagination." For him, human understanding of the cosmos is not exact, since only Allah understands the meaning of our cosmos.[32]

Cleary goes on to say that the descriptive terms "The Compassionate" and "The Merciful" are central for Islamic spirituality. In the Islamic approach to spirituality, it is not Allah's power or judgment that is central; rather the very center of Allah is compassion and mercy. Cleary strengthens his position by citing Al-Ghazali, who sees the two attributes of Allah, compassionate and merciful, as the deepest meaning of who Allah truly is. They inherently contain all other divine attributes. Compassion is the reason why a created world exists; mercy is the revelation of Allah's bounty of the source of being.[33] Cleary moves on to describe the phrase "show us the straight way" (*ihdinaa as siraat al mustaqiim*). The Arabic word for

28. Cleary, *Essential Koran*, 165–166.
29. Ibid. 165
30. Ibid. 165.
31. Ibid.165
32. Ibid. 165.
33. Ibid. 165–66.

"straight" is *mustaqiim*. Originally, *mustaqiim* meant standing erect and being one who accomplishes his or her goals. However, *mustaqiim* acquired other meanings: upright, correct, sound, in order, even, regular, symmetrical, proportionate, harmonious, honest, straightforward, righteous, and honorable. "All of these senses," Cleary concludes, "should be read into the expression 'straight way' as used in the Qur'an."[34]

In 1991, Albert Hourani published his major work, *A History of the Arab Peoples*.[35] In chapter 2, "The Formation of an Empire," and in chapter 3, "The Articulation of Islam," he offers us a historical picture not only of the growth of Islam but also the growth of its articulation in and through Islamic political leadership as also in and through Islamic mystic and philosophical leadership. Hourani focuses on Allah as found in the Qur'an:

> The God of the Qur'an is transcendent and one, but the Qur'an speaks of Him as having attributes—will, knowledge, hearing, sight and speech; and in some sense the Qur'an is His Word. How can the possession of attributes be reconciled with God? How, in particular, can those attributes which are also those of human beings be described in terms which preserve the infinite distance between God and man?[36]

He continues:

> God is all-powerful and his justice is not like human justice. If the Qur'an ascribes attributes to him, they must be accepted as divine attributes, not on the analogy of human ones, and without asking how they inhere in Him. Among these attributes is the Qur'an. It is His speech, because the Qur'an itself says so; and it is uncreated since "nothing of God is created and the Qur'an is of God." Man should respond to God's will by acts as well as faith.[37]

Francis E. Peters, in his volume *Islam: A Guide for Jews and Christians*, describes the beauty of God which is heard in the "music" of the Qur'an.[38]

---

34. Ibid. 166.

35. Hourani's book can be considered as "scientific history" since he presents both the successes and failures of Islam. By contrast, Efraim Karsh's book *Islamic Imperialism* is a one-sided approach to the history of Islam.

36. Hourani, *History of the Arab Peoples*, 62.

37. Ibid., 64.

38. At times, Peters seems to unite Christian, Jewish, and Islamic thought in ways that may be pushing the issue of unity too far. On the whole, however, the book is worth reading since it provides many historical details in which there are connections between Islamic thought and Judaeo-Christian thought.

It is precisely in the recitation of the Qur'an, he writes, that there is beauty. The Qur'an was meant to be recited and sung, not simply read. Early on, the Sūras were sung or "cantilated." In the singing, people heard poetry, and then they wept for joy. Peters notes that Christians and Jews may hear the lyrics but too often we do not hear the music; ye it is in and through the "music" that the beauty of God is perceived.[39]

Over several centuries, people from many parts of the world have heard the "music" of the Qur'an and have perceived the beauty of Allah. The Qur'an, however, notes that what these followers of Allah hear is only a faint sound, a taste or a glimpse as mentioned above, of what Allah truly is. Nonetheless, be it a faint musical sound, a slight taste, or an enchanting glimpse, Islamic followers have reached out to this beauty of God. This spiritual beauty is the very heart of Islamic spirituality.

Seyyed Hossein Nasr, in his essay on "God" in the volume *Islamic Spirituality: Foundations*, clearly unites Allah and beauty. He writes that Allah is first and foremost One, and "it is the Oneness of God that lies at the center of both the Qur'anic doctrine of God and Islamic spirituality. The first Islamic testimony (*Shahādah*), which contains all metaphysics and which also possesses the power to operate the transformation of the human soul in the direction of its primordial perfection is *Lā ilāha illa'Llāh* [there is no divinity but God, but Allah]."[40] Nasr continues:

> This supreme synthesis of Islamic doctrine is, first of all, a statement about the Divine Nature as being One, beyond all duality and otherness and, second, as being the Source of all reality, beauty, and goodness, of all that is positive in the universe. The testimony means also that "there is no reality but the Divine Reality," "There is no beauty but the Divine Beauty," etc. Finally, the testimony is the means of integration of the human being in the light of the Oneness which belongs to God alone.[41]

In the Islamic approach to prayer, the highest level is called *ihsān*, which literally means "beauty" or "virtue."[42] Once again, we hear how God's beauty is the center of one's spirituality and religion. Jean-Louis Michon emphasizes that the first pillar of Islamic faith is the affirmation that God is One and without equal. "God is All-Powerful, that He created the world,

39. Peters, *Islam*, 116–17.
40. Nasr, "God," 312.
41. Ibid.
42. Brohi, "Spiritual Dimension of Prayer," 138.

The Spiritual Beauty of Religion and Contemporary Scientific Issues

that to Him all things return, that nothing occurs without His Will and that everything except Him is doomed to disappear."[43] Michon goes on to a further question:

> Between this all-powerful, transcendent, infinite God and the ephemeral, imperfect, and limited creature is there a possible connection? All religions have provided an answer to this fundamental question, and it is affirmative, seeing, as the word religion itself implies, the existence of a bond between the creature and the Creator, religion being that which "binds" (*religat*) man to God. From one religion to another that which varies is not, therefore, the existence of a liaison between heaven and hearth, which is universally recognized, but the modalities through which this bond is realized, actualized.[44]

Michon states that a bond between God and creature is univocal for all religions; the difference is only in its modality. If one described the univocal connection as "God-creature," and claims that this is univocal, then it means that the reality of God is the same for all religions. If this divine univocity were true, many issues separating the three religions would be meaningless.

However, it is the view of the authors of this present volume that God, for the three religions, is *not univocal*. The characteristics of Trinity, Allah, and Yahweh are not simply "modalities" of a univocal God. Monotheism may mean that there is one God and only one God, but the term "monotheism" as used in the three religions does not state that there are several descriptions of God and that they are univocal. The difference appears to be more than modality as Michon describes it.

Nonetheless, Michon in his essay provides us with an image of Sufism, which is deeply spiritual. In this form of Islamic spirituality, one sees the Qur'an lived out on a day-to-day basis in a very profound way. Michon clearly sees in Sufism elements that are likewise present in Neoplatonic Hellenism, Byzantine Christianity, Mazdeism of ancient Persia, Hinduism, and Buddhism.[45] In Sufi literature, Francis of Assisi is called the *poverello* and

---

43. Michon, "Spiritual Practices of Sufism," 265.

44. Ibid.: "All religions," he writes, "move in this fundamental manner. Religions vary only in a modal way." From 284 to his conclusion in 290–291, Michon indicates that the "final stage," the "perfect mystical" stage" of the several variants of Sufism, lead to a union with God, and this union with God is the common goal of all religions.

45. Ibid., 268.

similarly the Sufis are called *al-fuqayr*.[46] Both terms mean "the little poor one." *Al-fuqayr* and *poverello* indicate a common thread between Islam and Christianity, but it is only a small thread, yet an important one.

The writings of Frithjof Schuon also emphasize a universal mystical quest in all religions.[47] In his approach, monotheism is transformed into mono-spirituality. If there is a place where monotheistic diversity begins to be seriously questioned, it lies in the area of univocal spirituality. In the area of univocal spirituality, religions truly become porous to one another. The beauty of univocal spirituality outshines the beauty of religious identity and difference or the beauty of differing theologies. Even the Qur'an makes mention of cosmic and univocal prayer:

> The seven heavens and the earth,
> And all beings therein,
> Declare his glory;
> There is not a thing
> But celebrates his praise. (Surah 17:44)[48]

However, one must note that a univocal spirituality does not mean that the three religions are spiritually the same. Once again, the different meanings of God, Trinity, Allah, and Yahweh enter into the discussion, since fundamentally spirituality is God centered. The theological question remains: which God are we talking about? Fortunately, univocal spirituality helps each of the three religions to be profoundly open to each other. In many ways, univocal spirituality might engender an openness among the three religions in today's ecumenical approach. We will return to univocal spirituality in the final chapter.

The Transcendent Beauty of God That Is Present in Judaism

The beauty of the Jewish religion can be found in its long history, in its historical writings, and in its present importance. In some foundational ways, however, the beauty of the Jewish faith differs from the beauty of the Christian faith and the Islamic faith. First of all, Judaism is far more genetically centered than Christianity or Islam. If one is born into a Jewish family, that person generally also practices his or her Jewish faith. If one is

---

46. Ibid., 267.
47. For details on Schuon, see ibid., 291 n. 3.
48. From Ali, *Meaning of the Holy Qur'ān*, 686.

not born into a Jewish family, he or she might become a person who accepts the Jewish faith and is welcomed into a Jewish community, but he or she is never fully Jewish. Marriages between a Jewish man or woman and a non-Jewish partner are, even today, not fully acceptable, nor have Jewish leaders over the centuries strongly engaged in a movement of conversion to Judaism. The Jewish religion, by and large, has tended to be a religion of and for Jewish people, while Islam and Christianity have engaged in a conversion approach.

A second complication that indicates that the Jewish religion differs from the Christian and Islamic religions is the more recent history of European Judaism. Arnold Eisen begins his book *Rethinking Modern Judaism* with a description of the powerful changes that modern Judaism has experienced.

> Most scholars of Judaism in the modern period, myself included, understand their subject to be the massive transformation of Jewish religious belief and practice that has occurred over the past two hundred years or so, a change that came in the wake of the awesome double shock that first convulsed the Jews of western and central Europe at the end of the eighteenth century and has since gone on to affect the lives of all Jews everywhere.[49]

Eisen lists these two "shocks" under the titles "Emancipation" and "Enlightenment." His understanding of emancipation is "the opening of doors long closed to Jews, the reality or promise of political and economic opportunities of which earlier generations could not even dream, and the pursuit of new and multiple options by individuals suddenly cut loose from the integral communities which had long anchored Jews and constrained them."[50] The newness of these experiences can only be understood when emancipation is connected to enlightenment. Eisen describes enlightenment as follows:

> Enlightenment, the second shock, was no less overwhelming. It entailed a new language on the lips, a new set of furniture for the mind, and a radical questioning of truths long held to be self-evident.[51]

---

49. Eisen, *Rethinking Modern Judaism*, 1.
50. Ibid.
51. Ibid.

Science and Religion: Fifty Years after Vatican II

The primacy of emancipation over enlightenment is based on the fact that the vast majority of European Jews prior to emancipation were not intellectuals. Prior to emancipation, they were basically unaware of enlightenment ideas on history, science, and psychology. The Eastern European Jews lived both physically and intellectually in a ghetto world. When they were allowed to move westward into the mainstream of Europe, they arrived in a world that intellectually was new to them.

In time, the younger generation of emancipated European Jews became intellectually enlightened in virtue of contemporary scholarship. For many historians of this period of time, the Jewish intelligentsia was simply secularized. Eisen's volume is a major effort to show that this view is too simplistic. Jewish intellectuals did indeed revise their thinking on beliefs and practices. Many developed new forms of Judaism with which they might live more comfortably. These revisions affected ritual, *mitzvah* (commandment), ethical obligations, language, philosophical thought, and interreligious diversity.[52]

In his conclusion, Eisen presents a summation of his views on modern Judaism. Major factors are involved: the creation of the state of Israel, the ascent of American Jewry to a position of affluence, and the remembrance of the Holocaust. Contemporary Judaism is found in multiple life-worlds and yet it also contains local narratives. He mentions how Seder is now seen as a multifaceted and newly described ceremony. Passover has become a holiday of freedom and liberation that involves no social isolation. For many, Seder is a Jewish alternative to other forms of political and cultural ceremony. Seder is now child centered, but it also puts strict limits on the boundaries between Jews and Gentiles which it helps to sustain.[53]

Eisen has attempted to explain to his own Jewish confreres and to those who are not Jewish that something different is happening in modern Judaism. To call this happening "secularization" is a misleading and a misunderstood approach. Contemporary Judaism remains Jewish even with a newly understood religious contour.[54] In all of this, Eisen tends towards a genetic understanding of Judaism.

---

52. Ibid., 1–20.

53. Ibid., 242–63.

54. It is also true that Eisen centers heavily on "nostalgia." The nostalgia, however, is not on religious issues but on familial nostalgia such as the Seder meal. See ibid., 156–87. Further references are in his index.

The Spiritual Beauty of Religion and Contemporary Scientific Issues

A second major issue that has separated the beauty of the Jewish faith from the beauty of the Christian faith and Islamic faith is the issue that Jews are seen as God's chosen people. In the history of Judaism, this notion of chosen people has often been an alienating factor vis-à-vis Jews and others, but it has also been a self-sustaining factor vis-à-vis the internal understanding of Jewish people. In the Jewish Scriptures one often reads that the Jewish people are God's "chosen ones." At times, these same sacred writings imply that the Jewish people are the chosen ones, and therefore they also have a certain form of superiority. This is seen in the scriptural description of the end time, when Jerusalem will be at peace, Yahweh will be worshipped in an honorable way, and other nations will respect the Jewish presence and authority over Jerusalem.

This status of chosen people is complicated in the sacred writings by the presentation of the end of the world. Only at the time of Daniel and, shortly later, the time of the Maccabees do we find mention of an "afterlife." For thousands of years, the wide majority of Jewish people did not believe that there was any form of a personal afterlife. The end of the world, therefore, is not a new life in heaven. Rather, the Hebrew Bible indicates that at the end time the city of Jerusalem would be a place of ultimate peace. Jewish leaders would be in charge. Many non-Jewish groups would accept this social and religious hierarchy of Jewish leadership. Non-Jewish groups who challenged the Jewish rule of Palestine would be weakened or even destroyed by Yahweh. This form of end time is described in earthly terms, not heavenly terms. It is also described in political and social terms besides its basic religious existence.

In the Hebrew Bible, therefore, Jewish spirituality is presented as a spirituality within human history and as a spirituality that sees the culmination of earthly life under the guidance of a chosen people. What one finds in the Hebrew Bible is one approach. Today, as is evident in entries on the Internet, a different hermeneutic is presented when one looks for material on "Jewish eschatology" and "Jewish people as the chosen people." In these Internet references, statements are made that Jewish people have *always* believed in a personal afterlife. Statements are also made that modify the meaning of "chosen people," even though a claim is made that this new understanding is the *traditional* understanding.[55]

55. There is an abundance of material on the Internet when one enters "Jewish chosen people." It is clear that today there is not a single approach to the meaning of "chosen people" either in its exegetical form for the biblical texts or for the secondary literature on this issue. That the phrase has been historically divisive is all that this essay is stating. This

A spirituality that does not include a personal afterlife and includes a form of superiority based on genetics tend to make our study of Jewish spirituality different from our study of Christian or Islamic spirituality. We simply need to keep these issues in mind as we look more deeply into the beauty of Jewish spirituality, for they have not yet been settled in any uniform way by Jewish leaders themselves.

In the introduction to the volume *Jewish Spirituality from the Bible Through the Middle Ages*, Arthur Green focuses on the core of Jewish spirituality. He writes:

> Seeking the face of God, striving to live in His presence and to fashion the life of holiness appropriate to God's presence—these have been the core of that religious civilization known to the world as Judaism, the collective religious expression of the people of Israel. . . . Life in the presence of God—or the cultivation of a life in the ordinary world bearing the holiness once associated with sacred space and time, with Temple and with holy days—is perhaps as close as one can come to a definition of "spirituality" that is native to the Jewish tradition and indeed faithful to its Semitic roots.[56]

Green openly states that God is the ultimate centering of spirituality. As with Christianity and Islam, the religion itself is not the center. Only God truly centers every form of spirituality.[57] Green moves on to show that in Judaism the term "spirituality" is a latecomer. The ideas behind the English term are Hellenic in origin, since the word is based on an understanding of a human person as a union of body and spirit. In a later part of Jewish history, the term "spirituality" was taken over by the Kabbalists and pietists to describe a religious ideal that by the early Middle Ages was an amalgam of Graeco-Jewish perspectives. The same can be said of the term "mysticism," which is not present in classical Jewish sources. Instead of using the

---

same diversity is found in the material on the Internet brought up by searching "Jewish belief in life after death."

56. Green, "Introduction," xiii.

57. Once again, it should be noted that in non-personal religions, e.g., Buddhism, a personal God is not what is intended by this statement regarding God as the ultimate center of spirituality. In Buddhism there is a transcendence that is its centering. In Daoism, the Dao is the centering, but it too cannot be named for if it is named it is seen immediately as not the Dao. See the opening lines of the *Tao Te Ching*.

The Spiritual Beauty of Religion and Contemporary Scientific Issues

term "spirituality," Green suggests the phrase "Israel's striving for life in the presence of God."[58]

David Sperling, in his essay, "Israel's Religion in the Ancient Near East," offers a carefully constructed historical analysis of the way in which Israelite faith became Judaism. The faith of the earliest Israelites was deeply influenced by Near Eastern religions of that time. Only gradually did this Israelite faith become a more defined reality which is today called Judaism.

Jon Levenson's essay "The Jerusalem Temple in Devotional and Visionary Experience" is a profound analysis of the historical passage from early Israelite faith to Judaism. Even though the term "temple" is used in his title, Levenson wants to say that the enduring reality of "temple" within Jewish spirituality also includes the temple's forefather, namely, the "tent of meeting." In Psalm 26:8 one reads, "O Lord, I love your temple abode, the dwelling place [*meqom, mishkan*] of Your glory." The issue of a "place of meeting" can refer to the temple but also to the earlier tent of meeting. Other words about a building are also found in the sacred Jewish scriptures. For instance, in Psalm 27:4–5 the poet says, "I long to live in the house [*beyt*] of the Lord," and "he shall hide me in his pavilion [*sukkoh*]; in the secret of his tabernacle ['*oholo*] shall he hide me."[59] In Psalm 74 a similar approach is taken. This psalm was written after the destruction of the first temple in 587 B.C.E. In this hymn, we find words that describe a meeting place: a "sanctuary" (*miqdash*), a "tent" (*mishkan*) and a "tabernacle" (*mo'adely-'El*).[60] In all of these meeting places, it is Yahweh who is meeting his people. Yahweh's presence is the basis of Jewish spirituality, and his "presence" (*kavod*, which is often translated as "glory") is the basis of the beauty of Jewish spirituality.

Levenson also writes of a second element that centralizes Jewish spirituality. This second perspective finds the climax at the point at which God graciously signals the *acceptability* of the complex and elaborate system of worship mandated and executed at Sinai. He cites a passage from Leviticus (9:23–24).[61]

These two climactic movements (*kavod* and *acceptability*), Levenson concludes, define two poles not only of the Torah but of biblical spirituality, and, he adds, they also seem to define the Jewish world view itself. The

---

58. Green., "Introduction," xv.
59. Levenson, "Jerusalem Temple," 77.
60. Ibid., 34.
61. Ibid., 35.

presence of God is the core of spiritual meaning.[62] He goes on to state that the goal of the exodus from Egypt is "not so much the promised land but intimacy with YHWH made available to Israel in the Tabernacle."[63] The goal of the temple and the exodus is the blessing of Yahweh. Psalm 134, with the superscription "A song ascending degrees," expresses this in a hymnic way.

> Now bless the Lord, all you servants of the Lord who stand nightly in the house of the Lord. Lift your hands toward the sanctuary and bless the Lord. May the Lord, maker of heaven and earth, bless you from Zion.

The "tent of meeting," whether temple, sanctuary, tabernacle, pavilion, etc., is a "holy place" (*heykhal qodsho*). God's earthly presence in a tent of meeting does not diminish his presence in the heavens, for there is a relationship between the earthly tent of meeting and the heavenly temple. Yahweh is simultaneously otherness and omnipresence.[64]

Joel Rosenberg, who was mentioned above, ends his essay "Biblical Tradition: Literature and Spirit in Ancient Israel" in a way similar to that of Levenson. Rosenberg concludes:

> [Israel's] devotional life was appropriately familial and communal, and her evolving task collectively assumed: the gradual elaboration of the name and essence of the tradition's ultimate source, the Sovereign, whose majesty the world has not yet fully come to know.[65]

One could also summarize the essay of James Kugel, "Topics in the History of the Spirituality of the Psalms," in a similar way, for he writes: "No book of the Bible seems to summon up the concerns of spirituality in the biblical period more than the book of Psalms."[66] Kugel, however, ends his essay with a question: if the Hebrew psalms sum up Jewish spirituality, why did others, such as the inhabitants of Qumran, continue to create their own psalm-like compositions? He calls this historical process of further Jewish hymns, canticles, and songs the "scripturalization of the Psalms." The psalms did indeed become a part of a sacred book that was to be read, but they also became part of liturgical life. Levenson notes that "psalms as texts

---

62. Ibid., 37.
63. Ibid., 37.
64. Ibid., 39.
65. Rosenberg, "Biblical Tradition," 107.
66. Kugel, "Topics," 113.

for teaching" are not totally corresponding to "psalms as texts for worship." In this process of tension and development we see that "the psalms were not to serve as the prayers and praises of every heart, at least not primarily; new hands were put to work setting the praise of God in words."[67] Jewish spirituality is an ongoing process.

The second volume, *Jewish Spirituality from the Sixteenth-Century Revival to the Present*, describes in great detail the historical ups and downs of Jewish spirituality. Many of the contributors of this volume of essays are hesitant to claim a complete revival or renewal of Jewish spirituality. There have been major historical factors that have challenged Judaism itself and left enormous divisions and doubts regarding the meaning and validity of certain forms of Jewish spirituality. What is amazing throughout this volume is the depth and breadth of the many voices of deeply spiritual men who analyzed and sought to transform contemporary Judaism. The names include Martin Buber, Abraham Joshua Heschel, Gershom Sholem, Marshall Sklare, Joseph Greenblum, Mordecai Kaplan, Jack Kugelmass, and many more.

The writings of these men bear witness to a major problem in contemporary Judaism, a problem that Eisen in his writings has documented in great detail. This problem arose when the Eastern European Jews left their ghetto existence and came into Western Europe. They were, as Eisen stated above, emancipated and intellectualized. The result of this Jewish situation was the staggering growth of secularized Jews. The sacred writings of Judaism do indeed present a transcendent beauty of Yahweh. For the growing number of secularized Jews, such a transcendent beauty of Yahweh became marginal. The Jewish authors mentioned above attempted to renew religious Judaism and Jewish spirituality. This secularization has made it difficult for Jewish authors to present a contemporary and acceptable form of the transcendent beauty of Yahweh. Today there are, of course, many dedicated and religiously focused Jewish people, but the majority of the Jewish population seems to remain within the secularized ambit.

Eisen ends his own volume with a section that helps unite the contemporary struggles in Jewish spirituality with similar struggles in other religious communities. He writes, "If Protestants and Catholics, too, are in search of meaning and community, and are locating it through a renewed relationship to tradition, their quest satisfies an ever-present Jewish need for reassurance that they are a *part of* and not only *apart from* the larger

---

67. Ibid., 136.

society."⁶⁸ "Modern Judaism, then, with its rethinking, thankfully remains very much a work in progress."⁶⁹ Eisen's judgments fit in very well with the focus of this chapter on today's spiritualties of Christianity, Islam, and Judaism.

***

In all three religions, there exists a form of multi-denominationalism. The denominations within Christianity, Islam, and Judaism range from very conservative groups to more openly ecumenical groups. In reality, Christianity, Islam, and Judaism are each a title for a group of believers who basically have a common identity but in actuality offer differing approaches to that common identity. Nonetheless, each group can be classified as Christianity, Islam, and Judaism.[70] Thus, there is an internal strain within Christianity, within Islam, and within Judaism. Each denomination claims to be its own, that is, Christian, Islamic, or Jewish. Some members of these three religious groups even claim to be the normative form of Christianity, or of Islam, or of Judaism. In reality, however, none of the denominational forms has ever been accepted as normative except by its own members.[71]

In the center of each of the three religions, and in each denominational group of the three religions, one finds that it is God's presence that is the spiritual beauty that draws people into the groups and keeps them there. As long as the divine spiritual beauty of God centralizes a Christian gathering,

---

68. Eisen, *Rethinking Modern Judaism*, 258.

69. Ibid., 263.

70. In Christianity, Islam, and Judaism there are some fringe groups that are considered by some as "beyond the pale" and by others as "on the fringe." Within these three religions, there are a few groups that consider themselves as the central group. This usually means that the "central group" is the normative group for all others. However, such central and normative groups do not have in reality the acclaim of all Christians, of all Muslims, or of all religious Jews. It is one thing to claim such a position; it is quite another thing to actualize it.

71. In the Christian tradition, the Roman Catholic Church has maintained that it is the "normative form" of the Christian faith. The Eastern Orthodox churches reject such a claim, as do the Anglican Church and the Reformation churches. Roman Catholics, internally, are required to acknowledge that the Roman Catholic Church is the only true church. Beyond this internal requirement, the Roman Catholic Church is accepted as merely one form of the Christian community. Some forms of the Jewish religion also claim that they alone are the true expression of Judaism, and some forms of the Islamic religion also make such a claim. In reality, however, these claims are not universally accepted by either the Jewish communities or by the Islamic communities.

The Spiritual Beauty of Religion and Contemporary Scientific Issues

an Islamic gathering, or a Jewish gathering, one can perceive a holy reality within the respective group. In these groups, from ultra-conservative to ultra-liberal, it is the "glimpse of God" that maintains the integrity of the community. At times, however, even the leaders of these communities do not understand the centrality of the Divine. These leaders indicate that the center of *their* Christianity, of *their* Islam, or of *their* Judaism is *their own* ultra-conservative or ultra-liberal status. In these instances, the beauty of God is not the center, nor is God the centering power in each of these groups. Rather, the centering power is the acceptance of a conservative or of a liberal position. By no means does this mean that the middle position is the center, for middle-position Christians, Muslims, and Jews can also lose sight of the true center, namely, the beauty of God.

However, this God, as stated above is not univocal, but this is not a totally negative description of God. Leaders and scholars in each of the three religions have expressed again and again that it is God, whether Trinity, Allah, and Yahweh, who has revealed himself or who has revealed divine beauty and holiness. In all three religions, the origin is in God's action of revelation. Revelation, however, is a relational word, since one reveals *something* to *someone*. Consequently, revelation is not only a self-revelation of someone or something to another; it is also a reception by another of whom or of what is revealed.

In the twelfth century, Peter Lombard wrote his *Libri IV Sententiarum*.[72] The first book is entitled *De Deo Uno et Trino* (*On God Who Is One and Three*). In this book Lombard discusses the way in which God reveals himself. He argues that there are two issues involved in a divine revelation, namely, a mission (*missio*) and a manifestation (*manifestatio*). In other words, in revelation there is not only an action on the part of God (*missio*); there is also an action on the part of those who receive this revelation (*manifestatio*). A manifestation (*manifestatio*) is always twofold: something "manifests" the mission (*missio*) but this *missio* is meaningless unless it is experienced, that is, the *missio* is understood only when it is made manifest to someone else. At times what one says is misunderstood by the person to whom one speaks. The same situation applies to a manifestation. A creative reality can manifest something, but the one who sees the manifestation might interpret the manifestation differently.

---

72. Lombard, *Summa Theologica—Libri IV Sententiarum*, Tomus I, Inquisitio Secunda, Quaestio II (pp. 697–751).

Moreover, God's self-manifestation is never complete, since God is infinite. The manifestation of God is always a partial manifestation. This is important for the issue of ecumenism. Each religious group manifests something of God, but never the totality of God. Because of this limitedness, the three religions can lean on each other for clarification and support. The manifestation of God is always a glimpse of God, never a total manifestation of God.

This manifestation indicates that we humans are able to perceive something of God's revelation (*missio*). In other words, a divine revelation includes some form of manifestation (*missio*) that we humans are able to comprehend. If a man or woman would come up to you and say, "I am revealing. I am revealing," you might ask, "What are you revealing and to whom are you revealing it?" Revealing is a relational term. There is one who reveals and there is also one who is able to understand what is being revealed; there is both a *missio* and a *manifestatio*. In other words, there is a God who reveals and there is someone or there are some people who are able to see and understand God's manifestation at least to some degree. Divine revelation is a two-sided event: on the one hand, there is God who is revealing (a *missio*), and on the other hand, there is someone or some group who are able to understand (a *manifestatio*). However, the manifestation of God is only a glimpse of the infinite God. It is never a full picture of the spiritual beauty of God, which is infinite and endless.

The centering of God in Christianity, for instance, is the union (which means a relation) of God to the humanity of Jesus. The humanity of Jesus is in Christianity the fundamental and most exhaustive manifestation (*manifestatio*) of God as understood by the Christian church. The human Jesus centers all denominations of the Christian religion. In the *Catechism of the Catholic Church*, for instance, there is a section entitled "The Revelation of God." And this divine revelation takes place in an ultimate way through Jesus. We read:

> It pleased God, in his goodness and wisdom, to reveal himself and to make known the mystery of his will. His will was that men should have access to the Father, through Christ, the Word made flesh, in the Holy Spirit, and thus become sharers in the divine nature.[73]

---

73. See *Catechism of the Catholic Church*, n. 51, available online at http://www.vatican.va/archive/ENG0015/_INDEX.HTM. This same interconnection of divine revelation to a centering in Jesus is basic for Anglican, Protestant, evangelical, and free churches.

The Spiritual Beauty of Religion and Contemporary Scientific Issues

Although this is a Roman Catholic form of expressing the relationship of divine revelation and Jesus, it is a statement that has parallel expressions throughout all the denominations of Christianity. Jesus is the center of Christianity. In his humanness God is revealed to us. Jesus is the fundamental manifestation of God's self-revelation, but Jesus in his humanity does not and cannot manifest the totality of God.

In Islam, the centering of Allah in Islam is the union of Allah to the Qur'an. The centering is not Allah's relationship to Mohammad, but to the Qur'an. In the opening chapter of the Qur'an, as cited above, we read, "All praise belongs to God" (*al hamdu li Laah*). Cleary comments, "The definite article here is understood to make a categorical statement; as the source of all there is, God alone is ultimately worthy of praise."[74] In Islam, the glimpse of God is in many ways an overpowering and beautiful event.

In Judaism, the centering of Yahweh is the union of Yahweh to his people. At the conclusion of his essay "Biblical Tradition: Literature and Spirit in Ancient Israel," Joel Rosenberg makes the following statement, which in many ways describes the centering of Yahweh in each and every Jewish person and Jewish community:

> The quotational and dialogic rhythms of her lore and learning attest to the seriousness with which she [Judaism] undertook the Hebrew Bible's mandate for survival and continuity. Her devotional life was appropriately familial and communal, and her evolving task collectively assumed: the gradual elaboration of the name and essence of the tradition's ultimate source, the Sovereign whose majesty the world has not yet fully come to know. The labor of the anonymous tradents of the earliest traditions and that of its latter-day interpreters are in this sense one and continuous.[75]

In each of these citations there is a fundamental relational interconnection between God on the one hand and a group of religious people on the other. Because of the issue of relationship there cannot be a univocal understanding of God. In other words, the term "God" within the framework of human life is a term used differently by three different groups of people. Each of these communities has a relationship to God. The God of Christians is a God who is related to the human nature of Jesus and through Jesus to his community. The Islamic Allah is a divine being who is related to

---

74. Cleary, *Essential Koran*, 165.
75. Rosenberg, "Biblical Tradition," 107.

the Qur'an and all who honor the Qur'an. The Jewish God is Yahweh who covenanted with Jews through Moses.

When we speak about different terminologies for God, we do not mean that there are three different natures of God. God, in God's own self, is indeed a unique unity. It is only when God relates to us that we are able to speak about God-in-relation-to-us. Consequently, God-in-relation-to-Christianity is one glimpse of God; God-in-relation-to-Islam is another glimpse of God; and God-in-relation-to-Israel is yet another glimpse of God. Given the three different relationships of God to Christianity, Islam, and Judaism, God-in-relation cannot be univocal, since each perception of God is only a glimpse of an infinite God. Each relationship of God to a spiritual community is special, and it is special because of a mission and a manifestation. These are not generic words. The mission is clearly from God to us, and the manifestation is clearly a manifestation of God to us, but this manifestation is only a glimpse, beautiful as it might be. Once more, a danger is present, namely, the danger of claiming one form of God to be the only form of God. Since God is infinite, no religion can put limits on God.

One needs to begin with the reality: God reveals, but to whom? The "to whom" is profoundly important, since the fundamental "to whom" for Christians is Jesus himself united to those who accept him. The fundamental "to whom" for Muslims is Allah united to those who accept his words and even his presence in the Qur'an. The fundamental "to whom" for the Jewish people is Yahweh united to those people who were and are God's anonymous tradents and the latter-day interpreters.

The spiritual beauty of God is central to all three religions, but this central revelation of the beauty of God is manifested in different ways in and through each religion. The spirituality of the three religions might be open to some form of univocal spirituality, but because of the relational issues involved in the spiritualties of the three religions, neither an insistence on the univocal nature of God nor an insistence on a univocal spirituality can be affirmed. When one uses the term "divine revelation," he or she is describing a two-faceted action: a mission and a manifestation. The way in which we humans are able to catch a glimpse of God determines how we honor God in practical life and in our places of worship. Since we humans see only a glimpse of God, no one religious group can claim superiority. God is greater than any human expression, theology, and spirituality involving God. God remains infinite, far surpassing anything that we might claim about who and what God is.

The Spiritual Beauty of Religion and Contemporary Scientific Issues

A major issue that complicates the three views of God's spiritual beauty in each religion is precisely the *infinitude of God*. Christianity, Islam, and Judaism, each in their own way, make a claim that their respective religious positions truly honor God in a most profound way. Were it not for the Jewish faith, some Jewish authors have stated, there would be no Islamic or Christian faith. Such a view gives a pre-eminence to the Jewish faith. Christians believe that in Jesus all the covenants and promises of the Jewish tradition have reached a final dimension. Jesus is the center and goal of God's plan for the created world. Such a view gives a pre-eminence to the Christian faith. Islamic leaders and scholars reverence the Qur'an as Allah's final revelation prior to the end of the world. In other words, the Qur'an is God's ultimate revelation for the entire human race. Such a view gives a pre-eminence to the Islamic faith.

All three religions honor God (the Trinity, Allah, and Yahweh) as infinite, and yet all three religions put a limit (in Latin *finis*) on God. For example, Judaism is often touted as the ultimate foundation for the three religions. One cannot move beyond the *finis* of this ultimate foundation. In Christianity, Jesus is the *finis* of all creation. One cannot move beyond this *finis* of an ultimate end of all creation. In Islam, the Qur'an is the final divine revelation for all humanity. One cannot move beyond this *finis* of a final revelation. The problematic issue is not the word *finis*, but God's own infinitude. The infinitude of God disallows any religious *finis* on the existence of an infinite God.

In chapter 7, we will return to this issue of finality and its relationship to an infinite God. There we will see that there are major problems for the three religions that rise from their non-acceptance of the infinitude of God. These problems become evident when the leaders, scholars, and even the members of a given religion profess that God is infinite but then claim that God is limited to the contours of their own particular faith.

In the first part of this chapter, the focus has been on the spiritual beauty found in each of the three religions. We have seen that the foundational beauty of Christianity, Islam, and Judaism is the infinite beauty of God. Each religion has at its center a beauty that is not its own, for the beauty is that of God, which each religion reflects in its own way. Individuals have been attracted to one of these religions because in the sacred writings, the theological writings, the mystical aspects, the liturgical aspects, and the pastoral aspects of each religion there are brilliant reflections and glimpses of the infinite beauty of God. Each of the three religions has a beauty that no scientific questioning or challenging can contradict, for science itself is not a religiously oriented field of knowledge. Even though contemporary science has raised legitimate questions and challenges, these questions and challenges do not center on the heart of each religion; rather, they focus on secondary issues such as historical verification and clarity of expression.

PART TWO: THE RELATIONSHIP OF REVEALED RELIGION TO CONTEMPORARY SCIENCE

Even though all three religions present profound glimpses of the infinite beauty of God, there are still difficulties that the three religions encounter when responding to the questions and challenges that contemporary scientists have expressed. The basis for these difficulties is, however, totally distinct from what has been described in part one on this chapter.

Some contemporary scientists, such as Paul Davis, J. D. Barrow and Frank Tipler, Edward O. Wilson, Richard Dawkins, and Peter Atkins, have spoken out strongly against religion.[76] However, all of these authors seem to have moved beyond their competence as scientists for they have expressed themselves in terms of their own personal philosophies and not in terms of the scientific community. Most contemporary scientists move in a different direction. These women and men honor science by staying within the limits of science. Personally, some scientists may be religious, and most often these women and men know when the scientific borders are being crossed.

The four scientific issues that are central to this volume—namely, current archaeological study of the Near East, scientific writing of history, quantum mechanics, and contemporary scientific studies on the age of the universe—do not question or challenge the above material on "The Spiritual Beauty of the Three Religions." Rather, contemporary scientific questions and challenges focus on other specific factors presented by the three religions.

However, before we move into the scientific challenges on the historical verification of certain religious issues, it is necessary to present in a more detailed way the radically changed horizons of contemporary science.

---

76. See Davies, *Superforce*; Barrows and Tipler, *Anthropic Cosmological Principle*; Wilson, *Consilience*; Dawkins, *Blind Watchmaker*; Atkins, "Atheism and Science."

3

THE MAJOR ISSUES IN QUANTUM PHYSICS

Two of the most significant scientific issues in modern times that have affected the theology and faith of the three religions are quantum physics and the scientific age of the universe. In this chapter we focus on quantum physics.[1] All three Abrahamic religions base their presentation on God and God's relationship to creation within an unchangeable framework. In all three religions, certain beliefs are presented as immutable positions. For example, in Christian belief, Jesus is the ultimate center of all creation. In Islamic belief, the Qur'an is the final revelation of Allah prior to the end of the world. In Jewish belief, the covenants with Abraham and with Moses are unbreakable.

Quantum physics has studied intently the microcosmic universe and to date has found no position that is unchangeable. Planet Earth and human life are not the center of the microcosmic or macrocosmic universe. This brings into question the role of Jesus as the center of all creation, the role of the Qur'an as the final revelation of God, and the immutability of God's covenants with Abraham and Moses. Relationality, not immutability, is present throughout the quantum universe.

As a result, there are two foci: immutability and relationality. The contemporary quantum universe and the longstanding immutable universe of the Abrahamic religions seem to be moving in opposite ways. In many ways

---

1. Ki Wook Min is the major author of this chapter.

today, the issues of quantum physics seem to be the most difficult when it comes to the science-religion discussion.[2]

PART ONE: A BRIEF HISTORY OF QUANTUM PHYSICS

The term "quantum" means "a quantity or a discrete amount."[3] We have become accustomed to this idea concerning the size, weight, temperature, movement, and disposition of objects in our daily lives, regardless of the type of object under consideration. However, these aspects are largely changed when we scale down to the atomic level. The motion, energy, and spins of particles consisting of atoms can be described in discrete amounts. The continuity of material property as a basic concept of Newtonian classical physics is not applied to the atomic world. In the early twentieth century, many scientists were responsible for the formation of quantum physics. The theory of relativity was strongly established by one individual, Albert Einstein, whereas quantum physics was achieved by many scientists who interacted with one another. Consequently, quantum physics can be said to have a communal characteristic.

The discovery of quantum physics was completed through two directions.[4] The first direction began from an experiment of heat radiation. In October 1900, Max Planck announced a formula that fit the experimental results perfectly, yet he had no explanation for the formula. It just happened to fit. He tried to find an explanation through the late fall of 1900 and finally he was able to derive his formula by assuming that the atoms could not take on any possible energy, but only certain special "allowed" values. After his announcement, quantum physics was developed by Neils Bohr's theory about the hydrogen atom. Finally, Werner Heisenberg completed quantum physics by discovering the matrix formulation of it.

The second direction began with Einstein, who determined the duality of light. However, he criticized in an extreme way the idea of quantum physics, even though he had played a big role in its development. After Einstein's work, Louis de Broglie extended the wave-particle duality to material reality itself, and Erwin Schrödinger established the wave equation, that is, the Schrödinger equation. Finally, Max Born interpreted the

---

2. This section on quantum physics is basically the work of Ki Wook Min, who will receive his doctoral degree in science and religion in the academic year 2014–2015.

3. Davies and Brown, *Ghost in the Atom*, 1.

4. See Goswami, *Quantum Mechanics*, chapter one.

The Major Issues in Quantum Physics

de Broglie-Schrödinger wave as a probability wave and completed the formulation of wave physics.

What is the origin of quantum theory? We can see its origin of change in philosophical thought as well as in its historical development when we review the process of the historical development of quantum theory.[5] Planck attempted a scientific proposition on radiating particles, and found that these radiating particles were emitted as a discontinuous quantum of energy. The result was very different from classical physics. The thought that energy emits and absorbs discontinuous energy quanta was a way of thinking that jolted the traditional physics system.

As a result, another and different attempt was made by Einstein. He developed his new idea through two methods. The first was the *photoelectric effect*. In 1905, Einstein's mathematical description of how the photoelectric effect was caused by absorption of quanta of light (now called photons) appeared in the article entitled, "On a Heuristic Viewpoint Concerning the Production and Transformation of Light."[6] This paper proposed the simple description of photons, and showed how photons explained the phenomena of the photoelectric effect. Einstein's position proved Philipp Lenard's 1920 observation of the variation in electron energy with light frequency.

Einstein's second method was about the *specific heat capacity* of solids. The previous theory could explain this issue in high temperatures, but it could not be adapted to low temperatures. Under such circumstances, Einstein proposed the possibility that the low-temperature state of matter can be solved by his application of the quantum theory about the elastic vibration of solid particles.[7] In 1906, he assumed that specific heat capacity is a consequence of the vibrations of the atoms within the lattice of a given solid. Also, his simplifying approximation was improved upon by taking into account the fact that the frequencies of lattice vibrations can have a range of values. Nonetheless, he did not opt for a complete contradiction between the wave theory and the photon concept. He thought that the contradictions could be understood in the future.

Meanwhile, in 1913 Bohr described the unusual stability of atoms using Planck's quantum theory.[8] He explained the stability of atoms by applying quantum theory to the atomic model, and he formulated the theoretical

---

5. Heisenberg, *Physics and Philosophy*, 30–43.
6. See Einstein, "Über einen die Erzeugung."
7. See Goswami, *Quantum Mechanics*, ch. 1.
8. Heisenberg, *Physics and Philosophy*, 34–35.

interpretation about the line spectrum from the atoms emitting electrons. Bohr's theory was based on an interpretation-methodology that combined both the classical physics of electron motion and the quantum condition of quantum physics. Therefore, we can say that Bohr did not abandon the classical way.[9] Moreover, in France in 1924, Louis de Broglie showed the solution on duality between waves and particles through electrons. His position is called the "correspondence principle." In other words, just as light quanta correspond to light waves, electrons correspond to the matter waves. He interpreted the matter wave through Bohr's quantum condition. In other words, the relationship between particles and waves was unified through the quantum condition by de Broglie. Heisenberg created a mathematical framework for quantum physics in 1925, and Newtonian dynamics was replaced by the matrix equation. It was revolutionary that many classical results of Newtonian dynamics, like energy conservation law, could be re-described into the new system.

Another direction is the Schrödinger equation, which comes from the theory of matter wave by de Broglie. In early 1926, Schrödinger was successful in describing the energy value of the stop state of a hydrogen atom as *Eigenvalue* in his wave equation, and he further generalized the method of corresponding the classical dynamics equation with the wave dynamics equation.[10] In 1924, the development of the fundamental understanding of quantum theory was started by Bohr with help of his assistant Hendrik Kramers and through his consultation with a young American visiting scholar, John Slater.[11] They made important theoretical proposals regarding the interaction of light and matter that rejected the photon. Although the proposals were the wrong way forward, they stimulated important experimental work, especially the work on the concept of the probability wave, which was a revolutionary moment vis-à-vis Newtonian physics as evaluated by Heisenberg.[12] The concept of the probability wave created a bridge between an indeterministic physical phenomenon and a concrete physical phenomenon.

The contradiction between particles and waves was solved by an unexpected method challenging the "reality" concept. That is, matter in

9. Popper and Bartley, *Quantum Theory and the Schism in Physics*, 8–10.

10. Heisenberg, *Physics and Philosophy*, 43.

11. For details on Bohr's struggle with the Compton effect, see Kumar, *Quantum*, 141–42.

12 Heisenberg, *Physics and Philosophy*, 37–38.

The Major Issues in Quantum Physics

a subatomic level does not exist in a certain limited place, but represents "the tendency of being." Atomic events do not happen as certain facts, but only occur with "the tendency of happening." This tendency in the formulation of quantum theory is represented by probability, and is associated with the mathematical amount that has the form of waves. The probability function includes two sides: the objective fact, on the one hand, and the observer's perceiving process in observing the fact, on the other hand. When we observe the position and velocity of an electron, this observation has accuracy only in the situation of the experiment at the time. The error from the process of the experiment is not due to the electron itself, but due to the fact that the observer's perception about the electron is not complete. Quantum physicists tried to represent such incompleteness of perception or subjectivity of perception into a probability function. The concept of the probability distribution in classical physics is similar to the probability function in quantum physics. However, the degree of uncertainty from the uncertainty principle could not be discovered in classical physics. The probability function made through the law of quantum theory can explain the state change following the time change after being given an initial condition. The probability function has both an objective element-like tendency and a subjective element-like tendency, namely the fact that it is functioning, but also the fact the scientist is perceiving only a moment of this functioning.[13]

Unlike Newtonian classical physics, the probability function does not represent an event, but instead the situation represents the entire combination of probable conditions from the process of observation. Through observation itself, the probability function does bring about discrete change. The observation is the realization of the probable condition. An observer's recognition about the target system with observance is also discrete. Also, the mathematical equation including it has a discrete form. "The quantum jump" is an example. Heisenberg said that the transition from the probability state to the reality state happens and we are able to observe this transition. The process of transition stems from the exact causality law.[14]

---

13. Exactly speaking, the probability distribution function or the probability density function is a better statement than the probability function. See the Wikipedia article on the probability function.

14. Heisenberg, *Physics and Philosophy*, 41–42. See also Kumar's lengthy discussion of Heisenberg's process of discernment, in *Quantum*, 183–97.

Science and Religion: Fifty Years after Vatican II

PART TWO: THREE SIGNIFICANT ISSUES PERTINENT TO QUANTUM PHYSICS

In Part One, we have reviewed a brief history of how quantum physics has been discovered and developed. We have also reviewed its physical meaning. We will consider the philosophical and theological meanings and issues regarding quantum theory in the next chapter. At this point, our focus on three significant issues with quantum physics: the Heisenberg uncertainty principle, Bohr's complementarity, and quantum non-locality.

Heisenberg's Uncertainty Principle

What is the uncertainty principle? We should first understand what "certainty" is before contemplating the meaning of the uncertainty principle. Generally speaking, "certainty" in this respect means that we can determine the future through current knowledge about the movement of an object. According to Newton's law of motion, the movement of an object is based on certain laws. Therefore, if we observe a moving object and the movement of its position and velocity, which can be accurately quantified at the same time, we can calculate the object's orbit and its velocity at any point in the orbit. For example, if we can accurately measure the position and velocity of Earth and its moon at any time, we will be able to know where an eclipse can be seen on the planet in advance. In contrast, we cannot know in advance the exact future path of a storm through the current weather forecast because we cannot determine the several measurements required to make the decision. In this case, we cannot say there is certainty about the course of the storm. Likewise, when a coin is thrown up, it appears not to be known in advance whether it will be heads or tails. Or when a dice is thrown, one might think that we can never be certain of the dice number. However, in the case where we know the status of motion, the acting force, the direction, and the distance—all of these just prior to the downfall itself—we are able to know what can take place in advance. Thus, the above-mentioned actions are examples of certainty. We come to know certainty through our experiences as well as through Newton's physics. That is, our certainty has been based on our common sense and on the physicists' common sense. Heisenberg's uncertainty principle has destroyed this form of common sense and it has also eliminated our reliance on Newtonian common sense.

The Major Issues in Quantum Physics

So, how did the Heisenberg uncertainty principle break down our common sense? It had been a precondition that we can accurately measure the exact location and velocity of an object at the same time, if we would like to predict the future of the object's movement. This can be calculated by Newton's physics. However, according to the Heisenberg uncertainty principle, it is a mistake to think that the position and velocity of an object can be measured accurately at the same time; it is impossible to measure accurately both the position and velocity simultaneously. Therefore, the future of the movement of objects cannot be known. That is "uncertainty." Heisenberg objects to certainty as mentioned above. Since Newton, people have considered the exact location and velocity as easy scientific facts. In addition, since the physics of Newton, it has been the premise to determine the exact location and speed at the same time. But physics is a study based on experimental facts. Therefore, if nature itself is uncertain in principle, it is incorrect to think that location and velocity can be known accurately and can be quantified at the same time. What can we do in this case? Physicists have given up the methods and thoughts they have used and believed in the past. They have given up the adherence to old concepts in order to create new concepts.

Can we think that limitations exist? Heisenberg abandoned the concept of accuracy of both location and velocity. Instead, he thought that location and velocity have the limitation of accuracy. In that perspective, he found that there is an inverse relationship between the degree of inaccuracy in the location and the degree of inaccuracy in the velocity. This relationship expresses Heisenberg's uncertainty principle:

(uncertainty range of location) · (uncertainty range of velocity) ≥ (constant)

Let us look more closely at the Heisenberg uncertainty principle. Even though we have explained that we cannot measure position and velocity accurately at the same time, a more correct representation is "position and momentum." The momentum is the product of the mass and velocity of a particle. If the momentum of a particle is small, the uncertainty principle greatly affects the movement of it. That is why, in the case of large momentum, even if there is uncertainty of momentum, the ratio of uncertainty about the momentum of the particle is less. Think of the following example. When we measure the position of a particle, the momentum is bigger and the disturbance is smaller. And if the momentum is larger, the wavelength is shorter, and therefore it is difficult to detect the nature of the wave. In short, the particle having large momentum has weak uncertainty. Also, if the nature of the wave is weaker, the nature of the particles is stronger. The nature of the particles as common sense can be considered clearly. In layman's terms: when we observe a baseball flying through the air, although the baseball receives the light, there is neither disturbance nor the nature of a wave. Because the momentum is very large, the wavelength is very short. The wavelength of a baseball flying through the air is about 1/100,000,000,000,000,000 of the diameter of the nucleus.

So what is the true meaning of the Heisenberg uncertainty principle? The uncertainty principle, as mentioned above, is simply a description of the expression, and it is used simply for convenience. The following is the actual formal use:

(uncertainty range of location) · (uncertainty range of momentum) ≥ (Planck constant)

The Plank constant in this formula is called "quantum of action" or "quantum" and is usually written as h.

We cannot apply Newton's physics to the microscopic world. Instead, we are using quantum physics that has modified Newton's physics to meet the condition of the uncertainty principle. The Planck constant is used frequently in quantum physics, but what is the Planck constant? If Planck's constant is a value of 0, as we look at the formula of the uncertainty principle, we can see that the uncertainty range of both the position and the momentum becomes 0. That means when we measure both position and momentum at the same time precisely, the duality of particles and waves disappears and the particles exist as particles only, and the wave exists as the wave only. As such, quantum physics returns to Newton dynamics. The microscopic world becomes just a thumbnail of everyday life we experience.

However, the Planck constant is really bizarre, causing the phenomenon of uncertainty. We can think the physical meaning of the Planck constant is like that. The universe gives us the limitation of both the quantity indicating the location of the particle and the quantity indicating the amount of momentum representing the status of movement of the same particle. This limitation is completely original; one cannot find it anywhere. The universe does not limit each of the two amounts, but the product of the

The Major Issues in Quantum Physics

two amounts is banned under any attempt at valuation. This is the value of the Planck constant.

Until now, the nature of natural sciences has focused on *when* and *where*. It is a description of the "objective world." However, it is known that it is impossible to know the quantum world completely and accurately. This fact may not be easily accepted. Einstein had opposed Heisenberg and Bohr, who had completed the uncertainty principle. He did not object to using the method of probability itself. Probability can be used when the number of particles is great. However, in that case, knowing the position and momentum of each particle is limited. Einstein proposed a difficult question to Bohr and Heisenberg in order to prove that there is a mistake in the uncertainty principle after the "thought experiment."[15] However, physicists could always resolve the problem that Einstein had posed, for Einstein, to the moment of his death, said repeatedly, "God does not like gambling and dice throwing." By saying this, he disallowed quantum theory. After the uncertainty principle was publicized in 1927, despite the many subsequent attempts of physicists, there is no fact or theory to reverse it. Today, the quantum physics completed by Heisenberg is recognized as the right method. Also, it has been accepted as an indispensable part of the scientific community supporting modern civilization.

Bohr's Complementarity

Alister E. McGrath, in his book *Science & Religion*, reviewed how analogies serve an important role in both science and religion.[16] In chapter 7, he explains in detail the use of the concept of "complementarity."

> [But] what happens if two apparently contradictory analogies seem to be required, on the basis of the evidence available? For example, let us define two models, A and A^{-1}, which are linked by the logical condition that the two are mutually exclusive. This immediately raises the question of the ontological status of the thing which is being modeled. Can we say that it "is" A, when the associated suggestion that it is also A^{-1} would lead to a blatant logical contradiction?[17]

---

15 Jammer, *Philosophy of Quantum Mechanics*, 121–23.
16 See also Palakeel, *Use of Analogy in Theological Discourse*.
17. McGrath, *Science & Religion*, 165.

McGrath's question brings us to the core of the complementarity theory. One could say that Bohr's complementarity theory helps us to see how we can use and understand the model analogy found in theology. If so, what is the complementarity principle? Einstein's theoretical account for his experiment of the photoelectric effect suggested that the nature of light should be considered as if it is behaving like particles. However, his idea of particles behaving as a wave of light was met with intense opposition. By the 1920s it was clear that the nature of light needed to be explained on the basis of a wave model, at least in some respects. Consequently, there has been chaos. As far as Newtonian physics is concerned, one had to abandon either wave or particle when thinking about the nature of light. Light could be a wave or a particle, but not both. This chaos led Bohr to develop his notion of the complementarity theory.[18]

It was Bohr who first introduced the complementarity concept. In 1927 he introduced it as the framework for an interpretation of quantum physics. It is the concept that presented the epistemological foundation to understand the phenomena of the atomic particle-wave duality and the Heisenberg uncertainty principle: the location—velocity measurement. For Bohr, the classical models of "waves" and "particles" were both required to explain the nature of light. But when we think of "complementarity," we might make a mistake. What is the mistake? McGrath, in his book "*Science & Religion: An Introduction*," explains our mistake as the following:

> This does not mean that electrons "are" particles or that they "are" waves: it means that, whatever they ultimately are, their behavior may be described on the basis of wave or particle models, and that a complete description of that behavior rests upon the bringing together of what are, in effect, mutually exclusive ways of representing them.[19]

Bohr had stressed his complementarity theory as an inevitable outcome of his interpretation of contemporary theories and experiments: light as wave or light as particle. Subsequently, this principle was not limited to the physical symptoms, and thus it could be applied widely to life phenomena and social symptoms. Let us explain this in more detail.

On September 16, 1927, in the Italian town of Como, at a conference to mark the centenary of the death of the Italian physicist Alessandro Volta, Bohr explained the concept of complementarity in his lecture *The Quantum*

18 Ibid., 167.
19 Ibid.

Postulate and the Recent Development of Atomic Theory. His lecture was philosophical as well as physical.

> The very nature of the quantum theory . . . forces us to regard the space-time coordination and the claim of causality, the union of which characterizes the classical theories, as complementary but exclusive feature of the description . . . as complementary pictures of the phenomena . . . only together [do they] offer a natural generalization of the classical mode of description.[20]

However, this concept had very conflictive aspects. Many people thought that certainty as the foundation of science was collapsing. The debate between certainty and probability in the interpretation of quantum physics was not completely resolved until the present day. In short, the complementarity principle states that in the atomic world, two kinds of contradictory propositions that we experience in everyday life can be established at the same time. Only when two contradictory views are used and combined with each other complementarily can we understand the atomic phenomenon. By themselves, they cannot be explained. If only one of the so-called "mutually contradictory" two elements—wave or particle—is right, then the other is wrong. That is the logic of everyday life. However, this way is no longer acceptable. Therefore, the logic in our knowledge seems to have crashed to the ground.

Bohr insisted that even if the concept of particles and waves are mutually contradictory, we can still understand the strange truth of the atomic world if and when we use all models. Specifically, waves and particles are not mutually exclusive but mutually complementary. Even though, at first glance, the characteristics of particles and the characteristics of waves may seem to contrast with each other, we should realize that we need to use both in order to fully comprehend all the information about the atomic world without ambiguity.[21]

The Heisenberg uncertainty principle could be said to be a mathematical statement, whereas the complementarity principle could be said to be a philosophical statement. For the Heisenberg uncertainty principle, it is impossible to measure the exact location and the exact velocity of the particles at the same time because the two activities interfere with each other. However, the two activities can only be complete when there is adequate information of each other. Therefore, wave particles have a complementary relationship.

20 Niels Bohr, "Quantum Postulate," 580–90.
21 Ibid.

Both the location and velocity information are complementary to each other. The new framework of understanding the atomic world was introduced by putting wave and particle, position and velocity, together. This brought about a major innovation of our knowledge system about what nature can be. Bohr discovered that the complementarity principle is an indispensable logical and philosophical tool required in the natural law.[22]

According to Bohr, it is meaningless to ask what the "reality" of electrons is. Physics can provide only our view of nature; it cannot explain what the "reality" of nature truly is. In particular, given the status of an experiment in detail, when we perform an experiment on the system of quantum physics, physics gives us meaningful predictions with already well-known language, a language one's colleagues understand.[23]

With the development of the principle of complementarity, Western philosophical thought on parts and wholes and on the macro- and micro-world has changed dramatically. Bohr insisted that we must design what we wish to observe, or describe how to arrange the experimental apparatus before we can know what an electron does. It is Bohr's important philosophical notion that uncertainty and ambiguity do not result from our incomplete knowledge of nature, but that they are both something indispensable in the quantum world itself.

Quantum Non-Locality: The Einstein-Podolsky-Rosen Experiment

In the quantum world, there are correlations between the properties of distant systems. A famous example of such correlations is provided by the Einstein-Podolsky-Rosen (EPR) experiment. The correlations in the EPR experiment suggest that there are non-local influences between distant systems, particularly systems between which no light signal can travel. Orthodox quantum physics and its various interpretations postulate the existence of such non-locality systems. The question of whether the EPR correlations imply non-locality and the exact nature of this non-locality is a matter of ongoing controversy.

In this section, we will briefly review quantum non-locality and we will do this with the help of Raymond Y. Chiao's essay, "Quantum Non-Localities: Experimental Evidence." Chiao identifies quantum non-locality with quantum actions-at-a-distance. He states:

22 Jammer, *Philosophy of Quantum Mechanics*, 86–94.
23 Bohr, "Quantum Postulate," 580–90.

The Major Issues in Quantum Physics

By "actions-at-a-distance," I shall mean physical effects, events, or conditions, or more precisely, the correlations between such effects, events, or conditions that are separated by a space-like interval from each other, i.e., so that a light signal could not have passed between them.[24]

He presents three explicit kinds of quantum non-localities as experimental evidences: the Aharonov-Bohm effect, the Einstein-Podolsky-Rosen effect, and the tunnel effect. We can say that these non-local effects stem from the supposition of the principle of quantum physics. The Aharonov-Bohm effect and the tunnel effect involve single-particle interference,[25] but the Einstein-Podolsky-Rosen effect involves a two-particle interference, that is, an entangled state of two particles. However, in his essay Chiao does not distinguish between them.[26]

1. *The Aharonov-Bohm Effect*

Briefly physically speaking, the Aharonov-Bohm effect presents the predicted effect of an electromagnetic vector or scalar potential in electronic interference phenomena in the absence of electric or magnetic fields on the electrons.

The fundamental equations of motion for a charged object are usually expressed in terms of the magnetic field and the electric field. The force on a charged particle can be conveniently written as in the equations below.

$$\vec{F} = q\vec{E} \quad \vec{F} = q\vec{v} \times \vec{B}$$ [27]

q is the particle's charge, v is its velocity, and the symbol x represents the vector product. Associated with it is a scalar potential, V, defined at any point as the work, W, necessary to move a charge from minus infinity to that point, $V = W/q$. Generally, there is only the difference in potentials between two points in classical physics, and this potential difference can be used in computing the electric field. A vector potential is also associated

24. Chiao, "Quantum Nonlocalities," 17.
25. Ibid., 17–18.
26. Ibid. 17.

27. Chiao states in his essay: "The Lorentz force law comes out from the Aharonov-Bohm effect." The formulation in the text above is an elementary equation of the electric field and the magnetic field in order to understand Chiao's explanation.

with it, for it is a convenient mathematical aid for calculating the magnetic field. In quantum physics, however, the basic equations that describe the motion of all objects contain V directly, and they cannot be simply eliminated. Nonetheless, it was initially believed that these potentials had no independent significance.

In 1959, Y. Aharonov and D. Bohm discovered that both the scalar and vector potentials should play a major role in quantum physics. They proposed two electron interference experiments in which some of the electron properties would be sensitive to changes in V, even when there were no electric or magnetic fields present on the charged particles. The absence of an electric field means that, classically, there are no forces acting on the particles; but in quantum physics it is still possible to change the properties of the electron. These counterintuitive predictions are known as the Aharonov-Bohm effect.[28]

The Aharonov-Bohm effect plays an important role in understanding the properties of electrical circuits whose wires or transistors are smaller than a few micrometers. The electrical resistance in a wire loop oscillates periodically as the magnetic flux threading the loop is increased with a period of h/e (in which h is Planck's constant and e is the charge of the electron), which is called the normal-metal flux quantum. In single wires, the electrical resistance fluctuates randomly as a function of magnetic flux. Both these observations, which were made possible by advances in technology for fabricating small samples, reflect the Aharonov-Bohm effect. Accordingly, Chiao mentions that we can gain a deeper understanding of the world through non-local quantum effects than through local classical effects. He adds, "From this example, we can see underneath the local effects of classical physics to the deeper, nonlocal effects of quantum physics from which they spring."[29]

2. The Einstein-Podolsky-Rosen Effect

In order to understand the Einstein-Podolsky-Rosen effect, let us trace the historical background of the effect or experiment. Historically, after the discovery of the Heisenberg uncertainty principle, the EPR experiment was introduced by Einstein, Podolsky and Rosen. It was a kind of thought experiment that challenged long-held ideas concerning the relationship

---

28 Ibid., 18–20.
29 Ibid., 21.

between the observed values of physical quantities and the values that can be accounted for by a physical theory. The EPR paper was designed to argue that quantum physics is not a complete physical theory.[30]

According to its authors, the EPR experiment yields a dichotomy. The two sides of the dichotomy are the following: either 1) the result of a measurement performed on one part A of a quantum system has a non-local effect on the physical reality of another distant part B, in the sense that quantum physics can predict outcomes of some measurements carried out at B, or 2) quantum physics is incomplete in the sense that some elements of physical reality corresponding to B cannot be accounted for by quantum physics.

Einstein, Podolsky, and Rosen concluded that quantum theory must be incomplete, pointing out that it does not allow for elements of physical reality.[31] Chiao suggests that Bell's theorem offers a crucial insight into the EPR experiments.[32] Bell's theorem was designed to prove the incompleteness of quantum physics. In his paper, Bell started with essentially the same assumptions as EPR. From his assumptions, he derived an important result: Bell's inequality.

3. The Photon Tunneling Time Experiments at Berkeley

Regarding the non-locality in the phenomenon of quantum tunneling, Raymond Chiao, a professor at the University of California at Berkeley, raised the following question: "How long does it take for a particle to tunnel through a barrier?"[33] He pointed out that this question is very important because it states—precisely and at the very outset of the discussion—the operational definition of the quantity being measured.[34] His experiment proposed the following:

> Suppose . . . that a single parent particle (a photon) decays into two daughter particles (two photons). Suppose further that these two daughter particles have the same speed in the vacuum (i.e., c in our case), and that they were detected by means of two detectors placed at equal distances from the point of decay. . . . Now suppose we place a tunnel barrier in the path of one of the daughter photons. (The

30 Jammer, *Philosophy of Quantum Mechanics*, 170–71 and 230–32.
31 Chiao, "Quantum Nonlocalities," 22–23.
32 Ibid., 23.
33 Ibid., 29.
34. Ibid.

other daughter photon continues to travel unimpeded through the vacuum.) Of course, this would greatly diminish the coincidence count rate. However, whenever a tunneling event does occur, a single photon tunnels through the barrier as an indivisible unit, and the difference in the time of arrival of the two daughters, as measured by the difference in the time of the "clicks" of the two detectors, constitutes a precise definition for the tunneling time.[35]

From the results of the experiments above, Chiao points out that the superluminality of the tunneling process can have a "yes" or "no" resolution according to the interpretation of the experiment, even though there may be a question about whether or not relativistic causality is violated by the superluminality of the tunneling process.[36]

***

In this chapter, we have presented major issues in contemporary quantum physics. Contemporary quantum physics and the standard Christian, Islamic, and Judaic theologies move in different directions, since the standard religious theologies incorporate at least to some degree a Newtonian or even an early Greek understanding of the physical universe. Ordinary physical phenomena, such as winds, tides, earthquakes, rivers, etc., are described on the basis of a physics that was acceptable to an earlier century. Divine intervention in these physical phenomena is often presented as immediately operable. It was God who caused the ten plagues we read about in Exodus (7:14–11:10). Divine intervention is presented as taking place in an immediate way: in the birthing of a child, in human deception, in lightning, in rain, and in fire. At times, these are called "a Sign sent down to him for his Lord" (Surah 13:8, 27). Divine intervention takes place in Jesus's rebuking the storm, casting out demons, curing a woman with a long history of hemorrhages, and healing a distant young girl (Mk 4:35-41 and 5:1-43). Contemporary interpretation of these passages may soften or even eliminate a literal interpretation of the events, but the "new" interpretations do not address contemporary persons for whom quantum physics is a standard way of thinking.

The current physical differences are seen most strongly in the scientific implications of the uncertainty principles, complementarity, and quantum non-locality. Contemporary quantum physics describes a powerful interrelational form of the universe, while the three religions are centered on

35. Ibid.
36 Ibid.

The Major Issues in Quantum Physics

an immovable being, God, and on eternally valid truths about God and creation. When quantum physics is joined to the contemporary scientific age of the universe, the standard religious teachings by all three religions on divine intervention in the physical world are seriously challenged.

The challenge of quantum physics to the three religions can be summarized around the following two issues:

1. **The issue of relation:** In quantum physics, scientists continue to find new forms of interrelationship between microcosmic elements themselves (electrons, mesons, neutrinos, etc.). They do not find in the microcosm an individual or centering "substance" that provides a basic unity for all the other elements. Nor do they need to postulate a divine being who governs the relational activity of the microcosmic elements. Whenever the question of a first cause arises, the theme moves beyond the microcosm, since a first cause presented by religious scholars is the first cause not only of the microcosm but also of the macrocosm. Thus the issue of first cause moves beyond the boundaries of quantum physics. Quantum physics is not theological, in the sense that it is seeking a monotheistic first cause or a monotheistic God.

2. **The issue of a universal plan:** In quantum physics, there is no indication of a universal plan that ultimately governs all the relationships of the molecular world (electrons, mesons, neutrinos, etc.). The microcosmic elements do form certain patterns of interrelational change, which Kauffman describes in his book *The Origins of Order*.[37] Quantum physics has as yet not found a clear presence of a universal plan that governs the evolutionary activity of the microcosm. Physical changes take place, but these changes are not presented in quantum physics as factors in an overarching divine plan.

This chapter on quantum physics offers the religious leaders and scholars of the three religions a detailed meaning of this particular science. The relationship between quantum physics and religion needs to be more carefully stated by religious leaders. In chapter 5 we will point out some scientists and some religious leaders who are attempting to draw science and religion together. These men and women have a very deep understanding of science, especially quantum physics and the contemporary scientific age of the universe.

37. Kauffman, *Origin of Order*, 3–26.

4

CRITICAL ALTERNATIVES
The Three Religions and Contemporary Science

IN CHAPTER 4[1] WE reviewed the scientific position on quantum physics. In this chapter we will consider some major understandings of God in and through quantum theory. Hans Küng, in his book *Christianity: Essence, History, and Future*, states that Christianity is transformed by interacting with societies, cultures, and other religions.[2] The natural sciences could also be mentioned since the natural sciences have also affected the history and structure of the doctrines of Christianity in a strong way. Not only Christianity, but also Islam and Judaism have been transformed by their interacting with societies, cultures, other religions, and especially, for our purposes, the physical sciences.

Many contemporary theologians from the three religions have tried to harmonize their understandings of God with the natural sciences, especially evolutionary biology, neuroscience, stem cell research, cybernetics, chaos theory, and quantum theory. The discovery of quantum physics in particular has given theologians trouble. By and large, their theisms are based on Newtonian classical physics. To date, there have been several efforts to harmonize quantum physics to the contemporary religious world. The major theisms are as follows:

1. God as determiner of indeterminacies

---

1. Ki Wook Min is the major author of this chapter.
2. Küng, *Christianity*, xxi–xxv.

Critical Alternatives

2. God as communicator of information
3. The understanding of God through God's self-limitation
4. God as creative participant in a sort of process theism.
    Ian G. Barbour has supported or criticized all of these theisms from a fairly balanced viewpoint.[3] Barbour makes his criticisms on the basis of Christian thought, not on the basis of Islamic or Judaic thought. In the pages that follow, we will first present Barbour's position and later in this chapter turn our attention to the effects quantum physics has had and still has on Islam and Judaism.

Were there any problems with Barbour's view? Were there lost points due to his over-attempt or over-simplification to harmonize between Christian doctrines and natural sciences, especially between Christian religion and quantum theory? Can we generate some alternative understandings to overcome his theism or other theologian's theisms that have tried to harmonize and reconcile Christian doctrines and quantum theory?

In the present chapter the focus is on a number of criticisms of the theisms that Barbour has selected, introduced, supported, and criticized. Then, as an alternative, we will consider Robert John Russell's explanation of divine action, namely a "Non-Interventionist View of Objective Divine Action."[4] We will also consider a second alternative theism—one with a Trinitarian understanding—namely, the theism of Korean theologian Sang-Sung Lee. Lee formulates his theism through the analogy of physical forces existing in the universe, that is: gravity, electromagnetic force, the strong force, and the weak force. Lee's suggestion is a new attempt to overcome Barbour's weak points regarding the understanding of a Trinitarian God. In a third section we will consider the repercussions that quantum physics has had and continues to have on Islamic and Judaic religiosity.

---

3. See Ian G. Barbour, *Nature, Human Nature, and God*, 104–11. These four theisms were selected by Barbour rather than those that resonated with his own unique understanding of God based on a form of process philosophy. Even though Barbour had supported some process theisms, Robert John Russell points out that Barbour's more recent views are inclined to keep something of the *ex nihilo* position that process theologians have not accepted. In other words, Barbour's view has changed to some degree. In addition Russell insists that Barbour's position seems to lie somewhere between the positions of Peacocke and Peters regarding the *ex nihilo* doctrine of Christian faith and its relationship to quantum theory. See, Russell, "Finite Creation Without a Beginning," 298.

4. In Russell, *Cosmology*, 110–50.

Science and Religion: Fifty Years after Vatican II

PART ONE: CRITICAL RESPONSES TO IAN BARBOUR'S SELECTED THEISMS

There are four theisms that Barbour selected for his analysis. The four theisms are not from Barbour himself; rather, they are selected from other authors. Barbour's task is to analyze them and measure their acceptability. Consequently, it is not strange that Barbour critiques them, even though he suggested them. The four theisms are forms of analogy in which the authors have attempted to harmonize the relationship between theology and quantum physics. Barbour mentions a number of other theisms, but only four theisms focus in a central way on quantum theory.

F. LeRon Shults' book review of Barbour's book *When Science Meets Religion* provides a solid examination of Barbour's main points.[5] In his book review, Shults notes that Barbour utilizes his well-known taxonomy of the relationship between science and religion in five important case studies: astronomy, quantum physics, evolution, genetics, and neuroscience. These five case studies are then considered in their relationship to divine action. That is, Barbour's four theisms were selected on the basis of their relationship to quantum physics, and this interconnection comes from his taxonomy of "relationships between science and religion." Consequently, the "dialogue and integration" models are a part of Barbour's own taxonomy. According to Shults, Barbour's dialogue model focuses on "boundary questions that are at the limits of science, or on theological presuppositions (such as the doctrine of creation) that buttress scientific inquiry."[6] Also, Shults points out that "systematic synthesis" as an integration model involves "the pursuit of a metaphysics (such as process philosophy) that incorporates both science and religion."[7] In other words, "God as communicator of information" and "God's self-limitation" can be addressed in the dialogue model, and "God as determiner of indeterminacies" and "process theisms" can be addressed in the integration model. However, as Barbour points out, the integration model needs "a cautious use." Therefore, as Russell mentions, Barbour's standing on process theology seems to have shifted recently.[8]

---

5. Shults, review of Barbour, *When Science Meets Religion*, 434–35.
6. Ibid.
7. Ibid. 435.
8. Russell, "Finite Creation Without a Beginning," 298.

Critical Alternatives

McGrath points out in his book *Science & Religion* that "it is important to appreciate that Barbour has done more than encourage dialogue in this field."[9] McGrath estimates that Barbour has found his foundational ideas developed in what is known as process thought.[10] Also, he points out that Barbour uses the key aspect of process theology that has rejected the classic doctrine of God's omnipotence.[11] He often categorizes Barbour as a panentheist since Barbour's stand allows "God to be seen as present and active within nature, working within the limits and constraints of the natural order."[12] Yet, as mentioned above, Barbour indicates very clearly his criticism of process thought. In particular, in his book *Religion in an Age of Science* he offers his criticisms of process theology in the following chapters: "Christianity and Metaphysics," "God's Transcendence and Power," and "Criteria for Theological Reformulation."[13] However, even if there are some weaknesses in process thought, he estimates that process thought "can lead to the modification of classical religious models so that they more accurately reflect the experience of the Christian community as well as contemporary scientific understanding."[14]

Barbour's stance of evaluating theisms through quantum physics is related to the philosophical position of critical realism. He offers the following as a criticism of the views presented by instrumentalists.

> Critical realists are intermediate between classical realists and instrumentalists. They view theories as partial representations of limited aspects of the world as it interacts with us. Theories, they say, allow us to correlate diverse aspects of the world manifest in differing experimental situations. To the critical realist, models are abstract and selective but indispensable attempts to imagine the structures of the world that give rise to these interactions. The goal of science, in this view, is one of understanding, not control. The corroboration of predictions is one test for valid understanding (along with coherence and scope), but prediction is not in itself a goal of science. I have defended critical realism in my own writings.[15]

9. McGrath, *Science & Religion*, 208.
10. Ibid.
11. Ibid.
12. Ibid., 209.
13. Barbour, *Religion in an Age of Science*, 263–67.
14. Ibid., 267.
15. Barbour, *When Science Meets Religion*, 75.

He centers on "the Copenhagen interpretation [of] instrumentalism," and he compares three interpretations: classical realism, instrumentalism, and critical realism. For instrumentalists, according to Barbour, theories are only "practical tools for achieving technical control."[16] Also, Barbour points out that even though theories and models are useful intellectual tools for instrumentalists, they do not tell us anything about the world.[17] For Barbour, the worthiness of the instrumental model is temporary.

However, in his book *Scientists as Theologians*, John Polkinghorne criticizes Barbour's unclear distinction between model and metaphor.[18] According to Polkinghorne, although models are useful in science as exploratory devices, we do not have to treat models with ontological seriousness, since historically speaking, models are only pictures of a particular process.[19] Polkinghorne presents some other examples of temporal models: the quark model of matter, Einstein's discovery of general relativity, and Dirac's discovery of the relativistic equation of the electron.[20] According to Polkinghorne, metaphor is different from model. Metaphor is "not intrinsic to scientific discourse, but it certainly is to theological discourse."[21] Barbour might believe that models are aids to the discovery of theories.[22] However, Barbour's use of models is established on the basis of an unclear stance, since he does not distinguish clearly between critical realism and instrumentalism. Polkinghorne points out the following regarding the use of model and metaphor.

> The differences between Barbour, Peacocke and myself about how it is best to understand and use the concepts of model and metaphor in science are undoubtedly influenced by our differing experiences of doing science. . . . I would not call them models, because of their ontological seriousness, nor would I call them metaphors for it is a straightforward comparison that is being invoked in these cases.[23]

---

16. Ibid., 74.
17. Ibid., 75.
18. Polkinghorne, *Scientists as Theologians*, 18–19.
19. Ibid., 19.
20. Ibid., 19, 22.
21. Ibid., 20.
22. Ibid., 21.
23. Ibid., 22–23.

Critical Alternatives

Barbour's reckless use of models, analogies, and metaphors as represented in his books could easily confuse readers. Barbour is an open target and therefore he can receive strong criticism from scientists who have supported instrumentalism, since Barbour underestimates the positive points of instrumentalism.

In the above paragraphs, we have reviewed the positions of Shults, McGrath, and Polkinghorne. We have searched for any weaknesses in theisms selected by Barbour which attempt to harmonize the Christian perspective and quantum physics. We have seen that in his writings Barbour classifies the weaknesses in various explanations of God and the world as follows:

1. Theisms based based on process theology, which have been criticized often by many theologians and even by Barbour himself;
2. Theisms that recklessly use the terms "model," "analogy," and "metaphor";
3. Theisms that have received criticism from scientists because of an overly clear distinction between instrumentalism and critical realism.

In addition, there seems to be no discussion of the Trinitarian God in Barbour's selected theisms. Why did Barbour, as a Christian commentator, not explain the role of the Trinity in his discussion with scientists? Do we not need anything about the Trinitarian God in order to bridge the gap between science and Christianity? The theisms Barbour suggests might connote the Trinitarian perspective, but his theisms related to quantum theory seem to fail as regards the Trinity.

In the next section, we will consider two alternatives that seem to offer a better understanding of God's relationship to nature. Russell's "Non-Interventionist View of Objective Divine Action (NIODA)"[24] offers a remarkable understanding of divine action/providence in the world. Through his suggestion, we can understand divine action/providence in a better way today than the presentations on divine action/providence that are presented by Christian churches today. Russell's NIODA project seems to overcome other alternative theisms that have tried to harmonize the differences between divine action and contemporary natural science, including Barbour's selected theisms. A second alternative approach is a Trinitarian God approach that is based on a quantum world as an analogical understanding. This approach has been introduced by the Korean philosopher Sang-Sung Lee. This analogy uses in a new and unique way the similarities between the

---

24. In Russell, *Cosmology*, 110–50.

Trinitarian God and the physical forces in the universe. This analogy will help us to understand the Trinitarian God better than past understandings.

PART TWO: ALTERNATIVE THEISMS

a. Non-Interventionist View of Objective Divine Action (NIODA)

The NIODA project by Russell can overcome rather than reject Barbour's theisms. Russell developed Barbour's understanding of God by seeking a third option to solve the problem of divine providence that Barbour did not solve. On the question of divine action, Russell points out in his book *Cosmology: From Alpha to Omega* that under a "forced option" we should choose between the following two understandings of special providence:

1. The *objective* acts of God in nature and history to which we respond, where these acts are understood as divine *interventions* into the natural and historical world.

2. Our *subjective* response to God's acts, where these acts are understood as *uniformly the same* in all events.[25]

However, Russell argues that "this old assumption of a forced choice no longer holds."[26] Put simply, due to the development of natural sciences, we can begin to believe credibly in God really having done what the Bible speaks about and to overcome the split between theological liberals and conservatives.[27] Why does Russell state there is a split between them? And why does he insist on NIODA? Why is NIODA so important theologically?

Russell presents a historical background to the problem of divine action. According to him, the notion of divine action in the world is central in the Bible. Early Christians as well as the Hebrews thought of God as the creator of the world.[28] Therefore, divine action is the basis of all that happens in nature and in history. This point of view has continued throughout patristic and medieval times. The Reformers and Protestant orthodoxy, as well as the Roman Catholic Church, believed that God acts universally in all events and we act together with God in specific events. Furthermore, their faith in God the Creator was "articulated through two distinct but inter-

---

25. Ibid., 111.
26. Ibid.
27. Ibid., 111–12.
28. Ibid., 112–13.

woven doctrines: creation and providence."[29] However, the rise of modern science led many people "to reject the traditional views of divine action."[30] Even though there have been those like Isaac Newton and Pierre Simon Laplace who have tried to say something about God, their works have brought about "a causally closed [and] impersonal" mechanism that led to *interventionism*.[31] Via deism in the eighteenth century, Christian theology began to be faced with "a fundamental challenge not only to its content and structure, but even to its method."[32] Two groups appeared as responses against the challenge: liberals and conservatives. Briefly speaking, liberals have tried to accept and work within modernity, whereas conservatives still support traditional formulation and reject modernity. Liberals like Friedrich Schleiermacher considered religion as the ground of personal piety. Consequently, the distinction between creation and providence became blurry and universal divine immanence became characteristic of liberal Protestant theology.[33] On the other hand, religious conservatives with the rise of Darwinian evolution "rejected them all" or "gave [them] limited acceptance with the proviso that the objective acts of special providence constitute divine interventions in nature."[34] Russell points out that in the twentieth century, both Roman Catholicism and Barthian neo-orthodoxy faced the same theological problem: "Should special providence be understood entirely as our subjective response to God's uniform and undifferentiated action, or can it include an objective dimension of divine agency which grounds our response to special events?"[35] Russell distinguishes those who take a subjective view from those who take an objective view of special providence in the following:

> For those who take a subjective view, special providence tends to be absorbed into general providence and the latter is usually blended together with God's action in creation to give a single undifferentiated view of divine action. For those who hold to objective special providence, one's response to specific events or

29. Ibid., 113.
30. Ibid.
31. Ibid., 113–114.
32. Ibid., 114.
33. Ibid.
34. Ibid.
35. Ibid., 115.

experiences is based on God's special or particular action in these events and experiences.[36]

Russell reminds us why liberals and conservatives are divided. Also, he asks, "What initially led to this perceived linkage between objective divine action and interventionism?"[37] Russell points out that there is "the combination of *deterministic* physics and *reductionistic* philosophy." In this sense, we should choose either "objective special providence at the cost of an interventionist" or "abandonment of objective special providence at the cost of a scientifically irrelevant [option intended] to privatize and tame theology."[38] Under this circumstance, NIODA as a third option was required, explains Russell.[39] That is, we need both sides: "an intelligible concept of objectively special providence" and "the claim that God must not intervene in the laws of nature."[40] He insists that NIODA could serve as "a genuine *tertium quid* to conservative and liberal notions of special providence, combining strengths borrowed from each."[41]

Russell presents in his book *Cosmology* the following types of approaches to NIODA:

1. Lateral causality and chaos theory—John Polkinghorne
2. Top-down and whole-part causality, the mind/brain problem, and the universe-as-a-whole—Arthur Peacock
3. Bottom-up causality and quantum mechanics.
4. An alternative metaphysics: process philosophy and NIODA[42]

As we see above, Russell reviews the question whether or not the four types of approaches to NIODA have the ability to live and act, then concludes that we need "*a detailed exploration of quantum mechanics as the most viable basis for NIODA.*"[43] With this background, he suggests that quantum mechanics can meet the criteria for a successful proposal for NIODA,[44] pointing

---

36. Ibid., 116.
37. Ibid.
38. Ibid.
39. Ibid.
40. Ibid., 116–17.
41. Ibid., 117.
42. Ibid., 129–40.
43. Ibid., 140.
44. Ibid., 151–52.

Critical Alternatives

out that Barbour's claims are related to quantum mechanics.[45] Also, Russell argues that "a Trinitarian doctrine of God is the most suitable embedding context for the QM-NIODA"[46] as a linkage between quantum mechanics and NIODA or as the use of quantum mechanics for NIODA.[47] He suggests that "we locate the problem of divine action and quantum physics in an explicitly Trinitarian doctrine of God," utilizing Wolfhart Pannenberg's proleptic Trinitarian theology.[48] However, he seems to skip the Trinitarian part by jumping into Pannenberg's use of the concept of field. Why is a Trinitarian doctrine of God the most suitable embedding context for the QM-NIODA? At this point, we need something to understand better the Trinity, a central doctrine in Christian theology.

b. An Understanding of the Doctrine of the Trinity through the Metaphorical Application of Quantum Mechanics

Sang-Sung Lee's article, "Understanding of the Doctrine of Trinity through the Metaphorical Application of Postmodern Physics," can be accepted as an alternative model for harmonizing theology and quantum physics.[49] Lee suggests that we can have an understanding of the Trinitarian God through the metaphor of scientific language, even though there is some logical jump. He insists that the most significant problem in the Trinity is letting people understand that God is both one and three at the same time, not explaining that God is three persons—threeness of God.[50] Lee's starting point is that the existence of God appears from the center of "vibrating."[51] In Genesis 1, God was vibrating over the face of the waters when God created the universe. In the beginning the earth was "formless," which means that the

---

45. Ibid., 140.
46. Ibid., 152.
47. Ibid., 179.
48. Ibid., 192–93.

49. His essay is written in Korean except for the title. Lee in the Korean text of his book did not distinguish the two words metaphor and analogy. In this section of our volume, the term "metaphor" instead of "analogy" will be used in order to maintain consistency.

50 Ibid., Lee, "Understanding of the Doctrine of the Trinity," 207.

51 Lee says that he owes this insight to Hermann Gunkel, who expressed and translated "swept" into "vibrated" in *The New Interpreter's Bible*, vol. 1, 343.

earth was a chaotic situation, Lee says.[52] In ancient times water represented disorder. Therefore, according to the Hebrew Bible, God represents himself through vibration over the face of chaos or disorder. Lee points out that in modern physics vibration is the origin of distinction of every matter.[53] Every matter consists of quarks ultimately that have electric charge, color, spin, and mass. There are four fundamental forces in the universe: electromagnetic force, gravity, the strong force, and the weak force. Gravity is the force that all matter in the universe has. Electromagnetic force is the force that can interact only between matter that is charged electronically. The strong force and the weak force can be called the nuclear force, since these two forces bond sub-atomic particles together into nuclear components.[54] Therefore, the four fundamental forces can be seen as three forces, points out Lee. He believes that the classification of these three forces can give insight to understand the Trinitarian God in Christian theology.[55]

First of all, gravity is a phenomenon caused by gravitation (*graviton*). All matter in the universe emits gravity, and all matter in the universe absorbs gravity. And since gravity does not have any mass, gravity can travel even to the end of the universe. Lee thinks because gravity has these attributes it can be used for the expression of God's attributes.[56] Gravity itself can be immanent in everything, even though it is not matter itself. Also, gravity has an effect on all matter, including light, which is a sort of electromagnetic force. Nothing can be without gravity. Similarly, according to Lee, God the Father affects everything, even if God is not everything itself in the universe. This would speak to God's *omnipotence* and *omnipresence*.[57] Lee points out that Paul Tillich's theological language of "being-itself" as an attribute of God can support the simplicity of "gravity and God."[58] Also, Lee presents that we can translate God as being-itself into finite power through Tillich's eyes. Without gravity, the universe cannot be preserved. Therefore, Lee believes that at least gravity can be an element of God's *creatio continua*, and gravity can play a role as a metaphor for God continuously creating the world.[59]

52 Lee, "Understanding of the Doctrine of Trinity," 188.
53. Ibid.
54 Ibid., 189.
55 Ibid.
56 Ibid., 191.
57 Ibid.
58 Ibid., 192.
59 Ibid., 197.

Critical Alternatives

Secondly, Lee believes that the attribute of electromagnetic force is very similar to Jesus' character. Electromagnetic force can be said to be the force interacting selectively, even though it is immanent in everything. Lee points out that the selectiveness of electromagnetic force is similar to Jesus' power of salvation. Jesus' power for salvation wants to affect every *creature*; however, it depends on the condition of facing the creature. In other words, whereas the dynamic being-itself of God the Father can affect every creature, so that all people and other creatures are under the grace of the continuous creation of God, the grace of salvation offered by Jesus, the Son of God, can affect only the selected creature.[60] Due to electromagnetic force, an electron should lose its energy in order to be near the nucleus. Without losing energy, electromagnetic force cannot go near the nucleus. On the contrary, in order to get energy, an electron should orbit apart from the nuclear with a distance. Lee points out that these electromagnetic phenomena are similar to Jesus' dual nature of divinity and humanity. We cannot emphasize both. Lee criticizes that the decision of the Council of Chalcedon on whether Jesus is human or God remains ambiguous.[61]

Finally, Lee deals with nuclear force as a metaphor. Nuclear force is the strongest force in the universe, but it can be effective only in the nuclear dimension. Lee thinks that we can find a metaphor for the Spirit in the bonding power of strong nuclear force.[62] Divine providence happens via the Holy Spirit. Also, nuclear force is related to the forming of new matter. Creation is the Spirit's work absolutely. Similarly, we can say that creation in the universe comes from nuclear force.[63] Lee's expression seems to be naïve to us. Even though he speaks in scientific language, he uses the physical terms without exact correlation. However, there is something to learn from his insight. As Lee mentioned, the Christology of the Council of Chalcedon might have been affected by philosophies, cultures, political situations, and

---

60 Ibid., 199.

61 Ibid., 200. Lee's critique of the Council of Chalcedon seems to contain both a logical jump and an oversimplification.

62 Ibid. 203.

63. Lee's language on natural science or physics is, at times, somewhat naïve. On occasion, his language seems to be poetry. However, his metaphors are deeply insightful. Perhaps the union between the language of quantum physics and the language of the three religions can only take place if one can legitimately use poetic or metaphorical terms as well as strongly scientific terms. As long as there is no contradiction or exclusion of major scientific factors and major religious factors, such a linguistic union may be the only possible form of intercommunication.

social circumstances at that time. The expression "Father, Son, and Holy Spirit" might have been the best language for people at that time. If so, as Lee pointed out, the metaphorical application of physics based on quantum theory can give us insight and understanding for the doctrine of the Trinity, since we are living in a scientific era.

In this chapter, the theme has moved from an explanation of scientific data on quantum physics and the scientific computation of the age of the universe to the efforts of well-known scholars who are concerned about the relationship between science and religion. The positions on science and religion that are proposed by the men and women who have been mentioned in this chapter indicate that sincere efforts are already at work. There has been a determined effort to move away from a spirit of distrust between scientists and religious leaders. In the next chapter, we will analyze some of the ways in which distrust and trust have been expressed within the past few years.

5

SCIENCE AND RELIGION
Frequent Forms of Challenge and Response

THE PURPOSE OF THIS chapter is to indicate how extensive the contemporary science-religion discussions have become. Many of the discussions have been very insightful and helpful for both scientists and religious leaders. Through these discussions, both the scientific aspects and the religious aspects of the issues have become clearer and resolutions of the difficulties have become possible. Through these questions and challenges and through the varieties of responses, we are able to see how widespread and how serious the science-religion issue is for contemporary society. Today, neither the scientific world nor the religious world can avoid the issues that divide the two worlds. The science-religion The science-religion discussions have become a central theme for the leaders and the populace of the third millennium.

However, some of the ways in which the questions and challenges between science and religion have been formulated have resulted in stand-offs or, unfortunately, increased resentment. The examples mentioned in this chapter are not meant to be either all-encompassing or all-representative. Rather, the examples simply emphasize the diversity of responses and the diversity of occasions that have engendered a response. This chapter takes into account situations in which scientists have taken the initiative to respond to certain questions and challenges posed by contemporary religious leaders, and it also takes into account several frequent forms in which religious leaders and scholars have taken the initiative to respond to the scientific questions and challenges.

Since some of the differentiation stems from the diverse viewpoints of the three religions on which this volume centers, examples of response involving the three religions are highlighted. On the one hand, Christianity, Islam, and Judaism have different religious reactions to particular issues of science. On the other hand, some of the differences of responses arise from the personal views of scientists or from the inadequacy of the response given by the leaders and scholars of the three religions. Likewise, in the three religions, conservative groups have at times been the initiators of the exchange. Some of these religious conservative groups have exhibited a disdain for anything scientific that, in their view, "meddles" in religious matters. In the scientific field, a few scientists have expressed a disdain for religion generally.

With the above description of the multivalent science-religion atmosphere in our present time, let us reflect on a few examples of the interaction between the scientist and the religious leader.

PART ONE: SCIENCE AND RELIGION DISAGREEMENTS: SOME GENERAL CATEGORIES

Ted Peters, in his article "Contributions from Practical Theology and Ethics," describes four examples of the science-religion debate which he labels "Four Warfare Models." These include:

a. Scientism

Scientism is a naturalistic reductionism or a secular-humanistic position that states that science alone "provides the only trustworthy method for gaining knowledge about this material world. Science has an exhaustive monopoly on knowledge. It judges all claims by religion to have knowledge of supernatural realities as fictions or as pseudo-knowledge."[1]

b. Scientific Imperialism

Scientific imperialism does not dismiss religion in an outright way; rather it uses the materialist's reductionism to explain religious experience and to reassess theological claims. Briefly stated, scientific knowledge is superior to "supernatural knowledge." Some of these

---

1. Peters, "Contributions from Practical Theology and Ethics," 376.

men and women even grant the existence of God, but claim that science is able to discern eternal truth in ways that theology cannot. "Here religion is defeated in the war by being conquered and colonized."[2]

c. Ecclesiastical Authoritarianism

Ecclesiastical authoritarianism disproves scientific propositions "by ecclesiastical fiat, the Bible, or in Islam by the Qur'an." In this situation, "ecclesiastical authoritarianism wins the war over science through intellectual intimidation."[3] In this interplay, the religious side conquers and colonizes the scientific side.

d. The battle over Darwinian Evolution

Darwinian evolution has become a dominant focus in contemporary science-religion debate. Debates over this issue are found in churches, educational institutions, courts of law, national congresses, news media, and ordinary conversations in the general public. The issue of evolution and religion is found in a variety of formats: biological evolution is strictly a matter of science; biological evolution is connected to a materialistic ideology; biological evolution is baptized into a scientific creationism; biological evolution is a major part of intelligent design; and biological evolution is rethought through the form of a theistic evolution.[4] The battle over Darwinian evolution is in a class by itself.

Peters then moves to "Four Non-Warfare Models," which are intended to bring science and religion into a more peaceful form of communication. These four non-warfare models are the following:

a. The Two-Language Model

The two-language model states that science speaks in one form of language while religion speaks in a totally different form of language. Science centers on objective knowledge; religion centers on subjective knowledge. "Warfare is avoided by establishing a border and keeping science and faith in their respective territories."[5] This has been called the two-model form by the *Catechism of the Catholic Church*, as we shall see later in this chapter.

2. Ibid., 377.
3. Ibid.
4. Ibid., 378–79.
5. Ibid., 380.

b. The Hypothetical Consonance Model

The hypothetical consonance model moves slightly beyond the two-language model, since it assumes that there is an overlapping of religious and scientific data. An instance of this possible overlapping is the big bang theory on the part of the scientist and the theology of creation on the part of the religious person. The model is called hypothetical since it is meant to be only a preliminary dialogue, not a fully endorsed form of conversation.[6]

c. The Ethical Overlap Model

The ethical overlap model refers to a way in which the scientist and the religious person can be cooperative. This includes cooperation in issues of public policy, ecological crisis, human values, peace agendas, and medical research. All of these fields require creative cooperation.[7]

d. New Age Spirituality

New Age spirituality integrates and harmonizes science with religion. Evolution becomes a major concept in an attempt to incorporate ordinary time with global time, and this union of ordinary and global times brings about a global spiritual consciousness.[8]

The above models clearly indicate how wide the spectrum of science-religion discussion and debate has become. Peters has provided us with a litany of relationships between contemporary science and contemporary religious thinking. He does not go into detail vis-à-vis these eight issues, but he offers enough detail so that we can see how varied the contemporary interaction of science and religion truly is.

PART TWO: CASE STUDIES ON CONFLICTS BETWEEN SCIENCE AND RELIGION

Since this volume focuses on the three religions, we believe that a presentation of some science-religion conflicts involving all three denominations is helpful. There is, of course, negativity in these clashes of science and religion, but an insight into this negativity will help us in the later chapters when we try to bring some sort of unity into the relationship of the three religions to contemporary science.

6. Ibid., 381.
7. Ibid.
8. Ibid.

An Example in which the Jewish Religious Side Totally Rejected the Scientific Side on the Basis of Divine Revelation: The Case of Natan Slifkin

A recent example that received much attention in the media involved the written works of a Haredi Jewish author, Natan Slifkin. In 2005, twenty prominent Haredi rabbis in Israel and the United States not only rejected his positions but banned him from their jurisdiction. Among these rabbis were Yosef Sholom Eliashiv, Dovid Feinstein, Aharon Leib Shteinman, Chaim Pinchos Scheinberg, and Shmuel Auerbach. All of these rabbis belong to the Lithuanian stream of Haredi Judaism.

The basis for this total rejection included Slifkin's assertion that certain scientific issues in the Talmud may not be correct. In their condemnatory statement, the rabbis argued that the Holy Sages could not be wrong. To state "that *Chazal Hakedoshim* [Holy Sages] can err *chas vesholom* [heaven forbid] in worldly matters" is contrary to Jewish belief. Secondly, the rabbis took offense at the tone of Slifkin's work. They described Slifkin's tone as follows: "even what is not heretical is expressed in a way that only a heretic would speak."[9]

The ban and total rejection of Slifkin caused a major debate, particularly on the Internet, in which scholars and rabbis from around the world approved his condemnation or defended Slifkin's stance. Many rabbis and scholars were against the ban. On the other hand, many well-known rabbis defended the ban.

Sllifkin's writings dealt in depth with issues of biology, zoology, and natural history, but in many ways it was Slifkin's endorsement of evolution that created a major center of disdain on the part of the opposition. Another reason for the ban was his suggestion that the universe is billions of years old. Slifkin's endorsement of current scientific positions on the issues just mentioned was seen as a rejection of the scientific positions contained in the Talmud.

However, it would be an overstatement to say that Judaism itself totally rejected either Slifkin or his views that correspond to contemporary science. It would also be an overstatement to say that Judaism itself totally accepted either Slifkin personally or his views. Rather, it was a small but

---

9. Quoted from the Wikipedia page on Slifkin. In this latter reference, the authors present a detailed statement on Judaism and its considerations on evolution, particularly in post-1800 Kabbalistic views. See also "Jews and Evolution" at http://www.jewishvirtuallibrary.org/jsource/Judaism/jewsevolution.html.

significant group of very conservative Jewish rabbis who chose to reject certain positions of contemporary science that Slifkin endorsed, and they also chose not to have any open discussion of their position.[10]

This case is typical of a conservative religious group that totally rejects contemporary scientific positions. There have been and probably there will be again many cases of total rejection, not only by conservative Jewish leaders and scholars, but also by conservative Islamic and Christian leaders and scholars.

An Example in Which There Is a Positive Response by a Jewish Author to the Archaeological Complaints against a Literal and Historical Meaning of a Sacred Text, on the One Hand, but on the Other Hand the Spiritual Meaning of the Same Text Is Affirmed. However, the Author Continues to Use the Data of the Literal Sense as Though It Was Historically Valid.

A second example of the religious answering to the scientific questions is this: in the sacred scriptures of all three religions there is both a literal sense and a spiritual sense. The literal sense is, for some religious leaders and scholars, almost identical to the historical sense. In our example, a well-known Jewish scholar, Joel Rosenberg, regards the spiritual sense as the higher form of interpreting the sacred writings. However, when doing this, he also in a subsidiary way presumes that the historical data as found in the Sacred Scriptures can be used in a verified way.

This material is found in Rosenberg's essay "Biblical Tradition: Literature and Spirit in Ancient Israel." Rosenberg presents in an early part of his essay a description of the "modern reader," that is, a reader who is aware of the historical issues presented by contemporary scientific historians and archeologists.[11] In this section he distinguishes a "post-biblical reader" from a "modern Bible reader." Rosenberg carefully states the stages during which the Hebrew Bible was written and during which it was also accepted. His listing of seven stages of biblical development corresponds to contemporary biblical scholarship. Likewise, his description of the Torah in its written form and the Torah in its spiritual form is extremely helpful:

10. See the website for the Center for Islamic Sciences, www.cis-ca.org. The center has an abundance of Islamic books on Islam and science. See also www.judaismandscience.com, which also has a lengthy listing of books on Judaism and science.

11. Rosenberg, "Biblical Tradition," 89–91.

Science and Religion

> "Torah" in rabbinic parlance was more a process than a document: "engaging in Torah" meant teaching, interpreting, reciting, applying, and meditating on the words of Scripture, and, above all, transmitting one's deliberations [regarding the Torah] to a successor generation.[12]

Literally, the Torah does indeed express many historical issues, but Torah reading is an ongoing process. The Torah, he writes, is not simply a book to be read. Rather, it is a text to be read and reread. Who would want to reread the text? Rosenberg explains in detail how this rereading approach to the Torah has taken place from the Hellenistic period onward. What is written (and therefore the literal sense) is the soil that a reader reads and rereads again and again. In doing so, the readers fertilize the spiritual treasures in the Torah. The rereading, then, with its developed insights, engenders the spiritual sense.

Rosenberg acknowledges that the modern reader is confronted with scientific and historical details. He notes that there are "fragments" in the Torah, and other Jewish writings as well, that are like the fragments an archeologist finds. Questions arise when the fragments are discovered: What was x used for? How was it respected or disrespected? When did it start? Once again, Rosenberg reverts to a dual process: "Torah archized and Torah contemporized are two aspects of the same interpretive activity."[13]

He then moves on to a descriptive physiognomy of biblical tradition, which is the main part of his essay and also the lengthiest.[14] In this latter section on the physiognomy of the biblical tradition, he refers to many historical details as though they were acceptable as history. In this section, he does not address the problems that archeologists and historians have raised, even though he has clearly stated their problems early on in his essay when describing the "modern biblical reader." He describes the physiognomy of biblical tradition as follows:

> We can call this a "physiognomy," because it will at all times be rooted in specific features of the text, but it is traditionary, not specifically literary, processes that will be of special interest.[15]

---

12. Ibid., 85.
13. Ibid., 89.
14. Ibid., 91–107.
15. Ibid., 93.

What we see in Rosenberg' position is this: there is an acknowledgement of the veracity of scientific questions and there is an acknowledgement of legitimate historical challenges to various issues found in the Jewish sacred writings. Nonetheless, there is a way, he argues, to reread the text, namely a spiritual way. From page 91 to 107, he proceeds to reread certain texts, in which he names many people and also describes what they said and what they did. He calls this rereading a "physiognomy of biblical tradition."

These traditions, he writes, are best seen in a disproportionate way—who is mentioned more often and who is mentioned least often? "The greatest narrative space is lavished on the generations of Moses and David with Solomon, Saul, Samuel, Joshua, Joseph, Jacob, and Abraham as runners up."[16] This disproportionate gradation is textually very clear.

However, based on archaeological research and non-biblical writings in which some of these names are not even mentioned, and based on the interpretations of the Abraham-Moses data that one finds in a disparate way in the sacred writings of the three religions, which physiognomy are we looking for? Which Abraham, which Moses, which David, etc., are we looking for? There is a Christian Abraham, Moses, David, etc.; there is an Islamic Abraham, Moses, David, etc.; and there is a Jewish Abraham, Moses, David, etc. As a Jewish person, Rosenberg only sees the Jewish version, and most Jewish people would do the same. The question arises: is the Jewish version accurate or more accurate than the Christian and Islamic versions? Is there a subjective reading about Abraham, Moses, David, etc.?

One might even go further. What would one say if some of these people never existed? How could one use the details of the lives and the words of these people if they are interpreted in a non-historical way or only in a storyform? Once again, we have a format that is questionable, namely the "literal-spiritual" format. One knows the problems vis-à-vis historical verification of data in the sacred writings, but after one has explained these problems, can an author simply move on to describe the "spiritual sense" and at the same time and in a secondary way express no problems with his or her descriptions of historical biblical data as if the data actually happened, as if the words of these people are to be taken literally, or as if the very meaning of their lives is interpreted in very different ways?

The point of this description of Rosenberg's essay is this: if one *accepts* contemporary scientific questioning of certain data in the sacred writings

---

16. Ibid., 100.

Science and Religion

of the three religions, one cannot in the subsequent pages use the texts as though they were historically correct and as though they had a single interpretation. It seems that a non-acknowledgement of the historical verification of certain biblical material would require that the spiritual reading of the same texts would be done in a way that sees the textual material itself as a statement of stories and not a statement of history.

In his final chapter, Rosenberg in a very substantial and powerful way writes about the sacred texts of Judaism. "The Israelite traditionary venture [was] an experiment in literacy as such, in human continuity and reverence for God, which had its first fitful origins at least in the generation of Enosh: 'Then was begun [the custom of] calling upon the name of YHWH' (Gen. 4:26)."[17] In these final words, Rosenberg centers his thoughts on the religious and spiritual tradition of the Israelites. As we have seen in chapter 2, each religion has a spiritual beauty that calls people into its arms. The center of this spiritual beauty is not Judaism or Islam or Christianity. Rather, it is God. Rosenberg's final sentence reiterates this stance: "The gradual elaboration of the name and essence of the tradition's ultimate source, [leads to] the Sovereign whose majesty the world has not yet fully come to know."[18] No one religion has ever fully come to know the height and depth, and length and breadth, of an infinite God. Each religion, however, catches a glimpse of beauty divine, and this glimpse nourishes each and every member of that religion.

There are many excellent points in Rosenberg's essay, and his basic spiritual approach is deeply moving. However, it seems that there is an unresolved tension throughout the essay. If the contemporary archaeological data is even compelling in its questioning of the historical verification of Abraham, his descendants, and the entire Mosaic material, then the author in the latter part of the essay should have treated details on Abraham, his descendants, and the Mosaic material in a way that can only be labeled as "stories" and "narratives." It seems that Rosenberg wants to claim both the validation of the archaeological claims against historical verification of certain biblical texts and in the latter part use the historical data as the basis for the spiritual reading of the same texts. The archization and contemporization of the same texts do not seem to be valid. Rather, in the essay they seem to be merged together.

17. Ibid., 106.
18. Ibid., 107.

Many Christian and Islamic leaders and scholars follow this same way of responding to the contemporary questions and challenges of scientists, namely, they make a distinction between the literal and the spiritual meanings of biblical passages. These writers acknowledge the validity of the scientific findings, and then these Islamic and Christian scholars focus their attention on the spiritual meaning of the texts. In their description of the spiritual meaning of these texts they also at times refer to historical details as though they were verifiable historical details.[19]

An Example of Science and Religion within the Islamic Community: Its Historical Background and Issues Today in which There Are Controversies among Some Muslim Religious People and Contemporary Science

Islam has had a long history of discussion, debate, and questioning on the issue of science and religion. In order to understand the contemporary discussions between science and the Islamic faith, a few comments on the history of Islam and science will help us understand the current context regarding scientific issues and the Islamic communities. On the Internet, when one looks for details on Islam and science, almost all the websites provide some history of science and religion within the Arab countries. Obviously, this science-religion history shapes the way Muslims today, consciously or unconsciously, evaluate the issues between science and religion. Consequently, let us consider this Islamic history and it connections to science.

In the eighth to the tenth centuries, a major center of learning was located in the Arab world. During these centuries, the locus of scientific investigation far surpassed any other intellectual center in Europe, northern Africa, and the Near East generally.[20] Hourani notes that "virtually the whole of the Greek culture of the time, as it was preserved in the schools,

---

19. For Islamic-Christian relations, see Cragg, *Muhammad and the Christian Tradition*; Giulio Basetti-Sani, *Koran in the Light of Christ*; also Goddard, *History of Christian-Muslim Relations*; Endress, *Islam*.

20. Hourani may be overstating the situation, since in the ninth to eleventh centuries the status of civilization, including scientific factors, was well established in China under the Tang dynasty. See Shiao-yi, *Chronological Table of Chinese and World Cultures*: Tang Dynasty (618–907), the Five Dynasties (907–960) and Sung Dynasties (960–1279). See Latourette, *The Chinese*, 177–261.

Science and Religion

was assimilated into this expanded language (Arabic)."[21] As far as science is concerned, Hourani continues:

> Whatever its origins, science was accepted without difficulty in the culture and society which expressed themselves in Arabic: the astronomers became time-keepers, fixing the times of prayer and often ritual observances; doctors were generally respected and could have influence over rulers. Some of the sciences, however, raise question about the limits of human knowledge. . . . Above all, it was philosophy which posed questions, for in some ways the methods and conclusion of Greek philosophy seemed difficult to reconcile with the basic teachings of Islam.[22]

The struggle with the limits of human reason that Aristotle and other Greek philosophers described in their writings became a major issue for Islamic scholars. The Islamic scholars of the eighth, ninth, and tenth centuries struggled to maintain the Qur'an on the one hand and Greek philosophy on the other. The same issue became part and parcel of the Jewish world in the eleventh and twelfth centuries and in the Christian world from the twelfth century to the fifteenth century. For al-Farabi (d. 950), human intelligence could go far in its own way to understand the created universe, but not all human beings were philosophers.[23] Religion was a way to state truths through symbols. This gave rise to an intellectual elite on the one hand and the Arabic masses on the other.

In the nineteenth century, the Muslim world's encounter with modern science took the form of a double challenge, namely, a material challenge and an intellectual challenge. Western science at that time was part of Western colonization, and the Ottoman Empire was deeply threatened by Western colonization. Ernst Renan (1823–1892) gave an inaugural address entitled "Islam and Science." In this address, he mentioned the utter inability of Muslims to produce scientific discoveries since they had an inability to think rationally. The Muslim world was deeply offended by Renan's lecture.[24]

In the Qur'an, the term "knowledge" (*'ilm*) occurs more than four hundred times and the Islamic people were told that a "search for knowledge is a religious obligation," and that Muslims should "search for knowledge all

---

21. Hourani, *History of the Arab Peoples*, 76.
22. Ibid., 76.
23. Ibid., 78.
24. See Hourani, "Islam, Contemporary Issues in Science and Religion."

the way to China." 'Ilm has three connotations: religious knowledge found in the Qur'an; knowledge of the world that one acquires through investigation, study, and meditation; and knowledge of a spiritual nature, which Allah freely gives to individual people.[25]

Today, the Muslim world presents three different attitudes towards science.[26] The first approach is representative of the majority of Islamic women and men. In their view, contemporary science is an important and positive endeavor. Science presents us with factual issues that are religiously neutral. One of the more important Muslim scientists, Mohammad Abdus Salam (1916–1996), won a Nobel Prize in physics in 1997 for his work in electro-weak theory. He was a devout Muslim and said this about religion and science:

> The Holy Quran enjoins us on the verities of Allah's created laws of nature; however, that our generation has been privileged to glimpse a part of his design is a bounty and a grace for which I render thank with a humble heart.[27]

Salam, together with many other Islamic scientists and scholars, often spoke of the long list of Islamic scientists whom "history forgot." In one way or another, this represents the majority position of Islamic scholars today. For them, the West can be blamed only for its materialistic vision and its indifference to morals.

The second attitude focuses more on the social sciences than on the physical sciences. Isma'il Raji Al'Faruqi (1921–1986) was the founder of the International Institute of Islamic Thought (IIIT). Al'Faruqi was more a philosopher than a scientist and he can be associated with other philosophers such as Karl Popper, Thomas Kuhn, and Paul Feyerabend. He focused on the development of science and a religious vision of the world. In doing this, he opposed the Western approach of disseminating ideological, political, cultural, and economic interests through science but in a non-religious way.

The third attitude today is deeply metaphysical in nature. The main representative of this view is Seyyed Hossein Nasr (b. 1933). He is a renowned scholar in Persian religion as well as comparative religion. He is also skilled as a philosopher of science and metaphysics. He strongly calls

25. Ibid.
26. Ibid.
27. Quoted from the Abdus Salam biography page of *Rohama*, online: http://www.rohama.org/en/content/114.

Science and Religion

into question the Western approach that reduces reality to temporal issues alone. He advocates an "Islamic science" that preserves the harmony of creation with Allah. His books include *Islamic Life and Thought* (1981), *Muhammad, the Man of Allah* (1982), and *Ideals and Realities of Islam* (1985). He is also the editor of *Islamic Spirituality* (1987), and he contributed an essay, "Islam and Science," to *The Oxford Handbook of Religion and Science* (2006).

With this Islamic background regarding science and religion in mind, let us consider in some detail a few current instances of confrontation between Islam and science. Although the issue is not specifically a science-religion struggle, the Sunni-Shiite confrontation, which dates from the death of the fourth caliph, 'Ali ibn Abi Talib (656–661), has produced a long-lasting intrareligious conflict. When Mu'awiya (661–680) was chosen as the succeeding caliph, the Sunni-Shiite problem began. The dividing issue was based on heredity, and Mu'awiya marked the end of one hereditary regime and the beginning of a totally different family regime. After World War I, the Sunni Muslims, who represented nearly 90 percent of the Muslim world, lost their caliphate.[28] The Sunnis were devastated by this loss. In 1928, the Egyptian school teacher Hasan al-Banna founded the first Islamic fundamentalist movement in the Sunni world, namely the Muslim Brotherhood. Hasan al-Banna and his followers were appalled by the introduction of Western secularism into Egypt. The Egyptian schools were flooded with secular and immoral patterns of life. From this time onward, the Islamic world has been politically up and down, and the establishment of the independent state of Israel has further complicated the situation.

The recent killings between Sunnis and Shiites are based on political and religious issues, and science hardly plays a part in this issue. Nonetheless, the fact that one side kills members of the other side is indicative of the negative depth that religious belief can bring into critical issues.

An example of this death threat took place when Dr. Usama Hasan, a physicist at Middlesex University in London and an Imam at a local mosque, was giving a lecture at the mosque, in which he favored evolution. Forty hooded Muslims entered the building, distributing leaflets that condemned Hasan and shouting for his execution. Hasan had to cancel his lecture; subsequently he was dismissed from his position as Imam. In the

---

28. See Hourani, *History of the Arab Peoples*, 263–98.

news media that described this incident, he was also condemned for his belief that Muslim women should be allowed to uncover their hair in public.[29]

This is clearly a response to a religious issue by a conservative Muslim community in which there was a denunciation of a scientific position, namely evolution. The episode is similar to that of Natan Slifkin mentioned above.

Another example took place in Kuwait in 1983. A conference was being held in Kuwait for the rectors of seventeen Arab universities. The goal of the conference was to identify and remove bottlenecks in the development of science and technology in the Arab world. One topic was overriding, namely, is science Islamic? One of the Saudis was a member of the royal family and he was outspoken in his rejection of science. He and other Saudi members of the conference argued that pure science tends to produce "Mu'tazilite tendencies" potentially subversive of Islamic belief. Contemporary science, they argued, is totally secular and therefore against Muslim belief. Contemporary science, they argued, is totally secular and therefore against Muslim belief. In this argument, a representative of the Saudi royal family was trying to keep the Muslims away from science, because the royal family wanted to maintain its control of the national resources. In this science-religion argument, political power intervened to repress scientific learning and scientific development in the Arab countries.

We can conclude this section by citing a passage from Nasr. In his essay "Islam and Science," Nasr calls for a stop "to the worship-like attitude towards modern science and technology which is prevalent today in much of the Islamic world."[30] This worship of science has created tension between external piety and submission to scientism. "Only a science that issues from the source of all knowledge, from the Knower (al-'Alim), and that is cultivated in an intellectual universe in which the spiritual and the ethical are not mere subjectivisms but fundamental features of the cosmic, as well as the meta-cosmic Reality, can save humanity today from the mass suicide that parades as human progress."[31]

On the issue of science and the Islamic religion, there have been many diverse questions, challenges, and ways of responding. By and large, the Muslim religious world is open to such dialogues. Conservative groups of Islamic religion follow the pattern of conservative Christian and Jewish

29. See Coyne, "Islam and Science."
30. Nasr, "Islam and Science," 78.
31. Ibid., 85.

groups, namely, they are hostile towards contemporary science. These conservative groups, however, do not speak for the majority of Christians, Muslims, and Jews.

Science and Religion Disagreements within Some Christian Communities

At times, religious leaders and scholars acknowledge in a positive way the questions and challenges of contemporary science, but having done so, they immediately *change the subject* and consequently do not respond to the questions or to the challenges. Peters mentions this form of interrelatedness when he describes the two-language model and also the hypothetical consonance model.[32]

There is an excellent example of this positive affirmation of science followed by a changing of the subject in the *Catechism of the Catholic Church*. Since the *Catechism* is, today, a major textbook for the Catholic faith in many dioceses throughout the world, the way in which it acknowledges the positivity of science is highly important. The ways in which the *Catechism*, after such a positive acknowledgement of science, changes the subject and does not refer to science again until it touches on medical ethics clearly show that a Catechism of the Catholic Church can be stated without little to no reference at all to scientific thought.

Twice in the *Catechism* there is a brief and positive acknowledgment of scientific questions and problems. But after these two brief positive statements have been made, there is no other mention of science until, pages later, the theme of medical ethics is center stage. Ted Peters' two models mentioned above are present in the *Catechism*. The two-language model dominates the *Catechism* by its extended silence over scientific issues. The hypothetical consonance model finds it place, but only once, and this place is in the field of medical ethics.

The authors of the *Catechism* ask the question, "How Can We Speak about God?" In answer to this question, the authors immediately state:

> In defending the ability of human reason to know God, the Church is expressing her confidence in the possibility of speaking about him to all men and with all men, and therefore of dialogue with other religions, with philosophy and science, as well as with unbelievers and atheists. (39)

32. Peters, *Islam*, 380–81.

In this paragraph, the authors state two important issues. The first issue is that all men and women have the possibility to know God. The second issue is based on the first issue, namely, the human ability to know God. Therefore, the church is open to dialogue on this matter with many others including scientists. The use of the term "dialogue" indicates that the interchange should not be argumentative, accusatory, or condemnatory.

The next reference to science is found many pages later in n. 283. This reference appears in the *Catechism*'s presentation of the Christian Creed (nn. 185–267), in which there is a section entitled "I believe in God" and a second section entitled "The Father." This is the context in which the positive evaluation of science occurs.

In the opening paragraph of the section on the "Catechesis on Creation" (n. 282), two questions are posed which dominate the subsequent material. The first question centers on the origin of the universe, including the origin of men and women: "Where do we come from?" and "What is our origin?" The second question centers on the ultimate goal of creation and human life: "Where are we going?" and "What is our end?" These two questions, "Where does everything that exists come from?" and "Where is it going?," are considered inseparable.

After these basic orientating questions are stated, the authors mention contemporary science:

> The question about the origins of the world and of man has been the object of many scientific studies which have splendidly enriched our knowledge of the age and dimensions of the cosmos, the development of life-forms and the appearance of man. These discoveries invite us to even greater admiration for the greatness of the Creator, prompting us to give him thanks for all his works and for the understanding and wisdom he gives to scholars and researchers (283).[33]

There is more than a mere acknowledgement of contemporary scientific research is this paragraph, for the authors go out of their way to describe scientific findings. These findings, they write, have "splendidly enriched our knowledge" not only regarding the age of the universe, but also regarding the development of life forms, inclusive of human life. Moreover, the

---

33. In the prologue to the *Catechism*, we read, "The use of small print in certain passages indicates observations of an historical or apologetic nature, or supplementary doctrinal explanations" (n. 20). The citation in the text appears in small print, and is therefore considered simply as "supplementary."

authors continue, referring to the scientists who have painstakingly worked on this data. They are described as men and women of great "understanding and wisdom"—gifts that have been given to these scholars and researchers by the Creator God. A positive praise and admiration of scientists themselves and of the work that they have accomplished is clearly presented in this paragraph.

In the following paragraph, however, the authors of the *Catechism* clearly express a basic indifference toward scientific research.

> The great interest accorded to these studies is strongly stimulated by a question of another order, which goes beyond the proper domain of the natural sciences. It is not only a question of knowing when and how the universe arose physically, or when man appeared, but rather of discovering the meaning of such an origin: is the universe governed by chance, blind fate, anonymous necessity, or by a transcendent, intelligent, and good Being called "God"? (n. 284).

The authors state that there are two "orders:" the physical and scientific order on the one hand, and the transcendent and religious order on the other hand. The transcendent religious order "goes beyond the proper domain of the natural sciences." The religious order goes beyond the fundamental scientific questions, namely, "When and how did the universe arise physically?" or "When did man first appear?" In describing these scientific tasks, the authors specify the very nature and limits of the order of science. The higher order of religion and revelation provides us with the "meaning of such a [physical] origin." Only in and through the higher order can one see that the universe comes from "a transcendent, intelligent, and good Being called God." Only the religious order provides human beings with the overarching plan of history and time, with the basic reason for development and change, and with the meaning of the microcosm and of the macrocosm. The order of scientific research is limited to knowledge of when and how aspects of the universe physically arose.

In an earlier section of the *Catechism* that focused on the issues of faith and science, the authors cite a passage from a document of Vatican II, *Gaudium et Spes*, a "Pastoral Constitution on Church in the Modern World." In the *Catechism*, the citation is found in a single paragraph that centers on faith and science.

> Methodological research in all branches of knowledge, provided it is carried out in a truly scientific manner and does not override

moral laws, can never conflict with the faith, because the things of the world and the things of faith derive from the same God. The humble and persevering investigator of the secrets of nature is being led, as it were, by the hand of God in spite of himself, for it is God, the conserver of all things, who made them what they are (159).

The order of religious study alone offers us an overarching plan of creation. The revelation of creation is inseparable from the revelation of the covenant of the one God with his people (n. 287). The overarching plan of God for all creation—not just human life—is expressed as follows: "With creation, God . . . not only gives them [his creatures] being and existence, but also, and at every moment, upholds and sustains them in being, enables them to act, and brings them to their final end" (n. 301). These affirmations profess that the Catholic Church and contemporary physical sciences are not opposed to each other. The affirmation is made since a correct understanding of God is of great help to both the theologian and the scientist.

In a later section of the *Catechism* (nn. 2292–94), the authors focus on ethical issues and contemporary science and it is clearly stated in these three paragraphs that contemporary science must be "in conformity with the plan and the will of God." There are two orders, but the order of science is ultimately dependent on the order of revealed religion. This last sentence indicates that there is no "moral neutrality in scientific research and its applications" (n. 2294). Contemporary science is subject to the religious (here Catholic) teaching vis-à-vis ethical issues. It is one thing to claim that there are two orders and then disregard one order as if it were a different reality. It is another thing, in a later discussion, to maintain that the scientific order is subject to the religious order. One cannot simply make that statement of "subject to" if the two orders have been described as distinct. If some relationship of subjection of order A to order B is made, then where are the limits of this subjection of one order to another? The *Catechism* does not enter into this delicate issue of contemporary medical refinements; the *Catechism* simply says that one order is subject to the other order in ethical and medical matters. Modern medical science has presented very detailed and delicate issues that cannot be evaluated by a simple overarching statement: contemporary medical science is subject to the religious (here Catholic) teaching vis-à-vis ethical issues. There has to be a more profound dialogue by competent Christian scholars with the medical profession. If this does

Science and Religion

not happen, medical doctors will simply ignore what Christians might say about the ethical implications for medical research and practice.

***

In this chapter, it is obvious that the science-religion discussions or debates move in many directions and involve a multiplicity of elements. It is against this wide background of science-religion discussions that we have selected only four specific scientific issues and the responsive stances to these four issues by the three specific religions, Christianity, Islam, and Judaism. Even with this narrowing of the discussion, we have centered our material basically on the following components:

1. The *impact* from the findings of contemporary archaeology in the Near East on the Abrahamic-Mosaic material found in the Hebrew Scriptures, the Qur'an, and the New Testament. Can this Abrahamic-Mosaic material be used in a way that has *historical verification*?

2. The *impact* of contemporary scientific history as regards the *historical verification* on the same material as stated above. Can the Abrahamic-Mosaic material as found in the three religious sources be used in a history of Israel, Christianity, or Islam?

3. The *impact* from quantum physics for the microcosm and the *impact* from the contemporary scientific calculation regarding the age of the universe on the three plans for all finite reality as developed by the three religions. Can a plan for all creation be traced over a universe that is many billions of years old?

Before we draw any conclusions to these issues, another very important factor needs to be placed on our table of discourse. This issue is not an issue in which science is involved. It involves only the leaders and scholars of three religions. This intra-religion issue has major implications for any and every future science-religion dialogue. The problems in this intra-religion framework deal with the meaning of monotheism and secondly with the meaning of a divine plan for creation. These intra-religion issues need to be resolved at least to some degree. If this does not take place, then future science-religion discussions and debates are meaningless.

Chapter 6 addresses this situation in detail. Until the three religions (and hopefully other religions as well) resolve their own intra-religion issues, contemporary scientists may not have a clear presentation from the religious side of what a particular religion is claiming. Since the two issues confront the three religions in an intra-religious way, only the religions themselves can be called on for at least a beginning of a resolution.

6

TWO MAJOR INTRA-RELIGION COMPLICATIONS

THE GOAL OF THIS chapter is straightforward, namely, to review in detail two intra-religion complications that involve the faith-based teachings of the three religions. Although these two issues have been mentioned several times in the earlier chapters of this volume, this chapter presents the two issues in an in-depth way.

PART ONE: COMPLICATING FACTORS AS REGARDS MONOTHEISM AND THE DIVINE PLANS FOR THE UNIVERSE

A STANDARD DEFINITION OF monotheism can be stated as follows: "Monotheism is a belief in one, personal, transcendent deity as opposed to belief in and worship of many deities (polytheism), or worship of one deity without denying the existence of others (henotheism) or belief that the deity is indistinguishable from the world (pantheism)."[1] This definition is stated by a Roman Catholic Christian, namely Joseph Blenkinsopp, in his entry "Monotheism" in *The HarperCollins Encyclopedia of Catholicism*.

The Anglican scholar E. L. Mascall, in his volume *He Who Is: A Study in Traditional Theism*, begins with this statement: "Logically and essentially, the doctrine of God is the fundamental doctrine of the Christian Religion,

---

1. Blenkinsopp, "Monotheism," 889.

for according to its teaching, everything other than God depends upon him and exists for his glory."[2] Mascall goes on to say that in the middle of the twentieth century, at least in England, most Christians had a "knowledge of God which is practically non-existent." He states his position even more clearly in a later paragraph: "there is not just one uniform doctrine of God held without variation by all who profess and call themselves Christians."[3] For Mascall, the Christian doctrine of God has two main sources: the Jewish religion with its culmination in Jesus of Nazareth, and the philosophy of the Graeco-Roman world.[4] Mascall's understanding of a monotheistic God is clearly centered on the Christian God, not on Allah or Yahweh. However, he admits that Christians in the twentieth century had only a simplistic understanding of the Christian God.

Islamic and Jewish readers of Blekinsopp and Mascall would not agree that the monotheistic God they describe is the same as the monotheistic God who centers their respective religions, either Allah or Yahweh. Their disagreement indicates that in the three religions the term "monotheism" is not a univocally acceptable term.

In 1995, Jack Miles wrote a lengthy book entitled *God: A Biography*. In this book, Jewish monotheism is the theme Miles chose and which therefore appears repeatedly as he moves from pre-Israelite times to the heyday of Judaism as expressed in the Old Testament. The Jewish monotheistic God is described in his final page as follows: "The Lord God's character is contradictory, and he is trapped within his contradictions."[5] This entrapment is presented most strongly in a key section of his book, namely chapter 7, "Transformation."[6] In this chapter Miles analyzes Proto-Isaiah (Isaiah 1–19), in which God is portrayed as a king but also as the executioner of all who go against his kingdom (Isaiah 24:17–23). Then, in a section on Deutero Isaiah (Isaiah 40–66), God is no longer presented as the executioner but as the holy and compassionate one.[7] Is the Jewish monotheistic God a God of judgment and execution or a God of holiness and compassionate love? It is this transformation that Miles labels contradictory.

---

2. Mascall, *He Who Is*, 1.
3. Ibid., 2.
4. Ibid., 4.
5. Miles, *God*, 408.
6. Ibid., 195–236.
7. Ibid., 221. Miles presents five different changes in "Second Isaiah," through which he sees a radical change in the understanding of God from the "First Isaiah."

Two Major Intra-Religion Complications

Although the above definitions of monotheism vary and are seen more as descriptions of monotheism, the leaders and scholars of the three religions have emphasized again and again that there is a historical connection of each religion with the monotheism of Abraham. Woolley focuses on Abraham and the men and women "born in his house." He adds:

> What made the family was the cult of the common hearth, a tradition which found expression in the worship of the family god. And now, when the great gods were perforce left behind, the god who was the symbol and the essence of the natural link binding the clan together, the god who had protected Abraham from a child, as he had protected the father before him, was the one god not tied down to any one locality but able to be with him in the highlands of Palestine as well as in Haran or at Ur.[8]

In the sacred writings of Christianity, Islam, and Judaism, the "one God" of Abraham is referred to again and again. However, in the early history of Judaism, there is no clear and unambiguous denial of the existence of gods other than Yahweh prior to the sixth-century text of Deutero-Isaiah (Isaiah 40–66). Since Israelitic thought is neither discursive nor speculative, one does not find in the Hebrew Bible an intellectual approach to monotheism. Rather, in Deutero-Isaiah the emphasis is on Yahweh who alone is the God of the Jewish people. The Jews may have lived in an area where other people honored many Gods, but, as C. J. Labuschagne notes, for the Jewish people after the exile the emphasis was on the reality that for Israel there is only one Yahweh.[9] Yahweh is totally different from any and all other *elohim*. Mackenzie adds, "For the Israelites there is nothing they can ask from any other god and nothing to fear from any other god. This is not an explicit profession of monotheism, but it is to treat other gods as negligible."[10]

It is well known that in Islam, Allah is the one and only God. The *Shahabad* has two sections. The first and most important section honors the one and only Allah: "There is no divinity, but Allah alone." In the Qur'an, the second Surah, *The Cow*, repeats again and again the uniqueness of Allah: "Worship nothing but Allah."[11] This message is echoed throughout this chapter in a variety of ways. Allah is totally unique (monotheistic); all other gods should be treated as negligible.

8. Woolley, *Abraham*, 243.
9. See Labuschagne, *Incomparability of Yahweh*.
10. MacKenzie, "Aspects of Old Testament Thought," *NJBC*, 1287.
11. Ali, *Holy Qur'ān*, 83.

In Christian belief in the one God there are three emphases. First, there is only one God. Secondly, this one God is Trinitarian. Thirdly, this one Trinitarian God has been revealed in Jesus, who is the divine Logos made flesh. There is no other God than the God revealed in the humanity of Jesus. All other gods should be treated as negligible.[12]

With this quick overview of the term "monotheism" in Christianity, Islam, and Judaism, we can see that the standard definitions cited above have a major inadequacy. The standard definitions usually take into consideration all historical religions, and among all these religions there are a plethora of polytheistic religions and there are basically three monotheistic religions. Generally, the standard definitions imply that monotheism as found in the three religions is an identical form of monotheism as was cited above: "a belief in one, personal, transcendent deity as opposed to belief in and worship of many deities (polytheism)." The implication of a univocal monotheism is, however, questionable.

An overarching univocal definition for monotheism is common among scholars, but there is something "logical" about the common definition rather than actual. There are indeed three religions that can be identified as monotheistic. But the God of each religion (Trinity, Allah, and Yahweh) is in reality not the same God. The monotheistic Trinity is not identical to the monotheistic Yahweh or the monotheistic Allah. The monotheistic Allah is not identical to the monotheistic Yahweh or the monotheistic Trinity. The monotheistic Yahweh is not identical to the monotheistic Trinity or the monotheistic Allah.

When one leaves the logical world of thought and the rational definitions of monotheism in which monotheism is univocal, and moves to the actual world of human religious endeavor, one finds that the three "monotheistic" religions offer to their constituents three different theologies of God. The faith-based honoring of God in each of the three religions is an honoring of a different faith-based appreciation of God. Such an approach seems to eliminate any mutual discussion between the three religions regarding a monotheistic God.

The contemporary monotheism of the three religions has an intra-religion complication that involves the following foci.

---

12. See Eugene TeSelle, "Monotheism," in *The Cambridge Dictionary of Christianity*, 836–37.

Two Major Intra-Religion Complications

a. The Use of the Term "Monotheism" in Today's World

All three religions claim to be monotheistic, but the theology and faith-based understanding of God in each religion is essentially different in its Christian, Islamic, and Jewish form. As we have seen above, the Trinity, Allah, and Yahweh are not described and defined in a univocal way. Since the three religions do not share a univocal understanding of God, can the claim for monotheism, a claim which each of the three religions centrally affirms, be a valid claim? A Christian would not claim that the Trinity, Allah, and Yahweh are equivalent in their meaning. A Muslim would not claim that Allah, Yahweh, and the Trinity are equivalent in their meaning. A religious Jew would not claim that Yahweh, the Trinity, and Allah are equivalent in their meaning. The intra-religion problem, therefore, can be expressed in the following way:

> Each religion does indeed espouse only one God, but there can be no common monotheistic ground at all if the intra-religion complication of three different monotheisms is not resolved.

The primary issue of this intra-religion difficulty, then, is the internal incompatibility of the three monotheistic religions. This intra-religion complication on the issue of monotheism needs to be placed on the discussion table at which leaders and scholars of the three religions are at work. Contemporary scientists cannot resolve this issue. Whenever contemporary scientists claim that there is no God at all, many religious leaders and scholars have responded negatively to these scientists, claiming that science should at least see the need of a "first cause," or an "unmoved mover." In the argument against the "atheistic scientists" some scholars have centered on the need for a "first cause" of any and all created beings. The problem that arises is this: do these religious leaders and scholars admit that there is a univocal first cause called "God"? Do these religious scholars allow that Trinity, Allah, and Yahweh are simply three forms of the one God?

Until religious leaders and scholars resolve this complication, they cannot look to scientists for an answer to the question, is there a God? Rather, the religious leaders and scholars of the three religions must first come to a mutual understanding of the term "monotheism." Only then can they reply to any and every atheistic scientist. Moreover, contemporary scientists cannot be put in the position of arbiter. If a scientist says that there is a God and that this God corresponds to the Christian God, then the scholars of Islam and Judaism have every right to say that this particular scientist has gone beyond his/her scientific role since he/she favors Christianity. The same can be said if the scientist says there is a God who corresponds to either Allah or Yahweh. Their rejection is valid. Contemporary scientists cannot arbitrate which God—Trinity, Allah or Yahweh—is the one true God.

b. The Different Theologies of a Faith-Based Understanding of God That the Three Religions Present to Their Members

Over many centuries the three religions have developed an understanding of God that is the central beauty and wonder of each religion. God is the ultimate center for each of the three religions. Logically, one might speak of God in a univocal way, but in reality, the three religions profess a distinct and different faith in their specific "one God." In other words, the meaning of the term "God" *cannot be established* in a way that the following graph presents it.

GOD

a univocal term which is
equally applicable to the meaning of God
in the following three religions:

CHRISTIANITY   ISLAM   JUDAISM

None of the leaders and scholars of the three religions would accept this graph as a description of their respective belief in one God. For these leaders and scholars, there is no univocal God higher than the Trinity (in the Christian religion), or higher than Allah (in the Islamic religion), or higher than Yahweh (in the Jewish religion). For these leaders and scholars, a graph that indicates that there exists some sort of univocal God higher than the God of Christianity, or higher than the God of Islam, or higher than the God of Yahweh would be immediately rejected. This complication is the actuality of today's theological and faith-based understanding of God as professed in the three religions. An actual overriding and univocal God is not at all what their belief in the Trinity, in Allah, or in Yahweh might allow.

Can the three theological and faith-based understandings of God be unified to any degree? A univocal God might exist in someone's mind, but in reality such a univocal God seems to be unacceptable. Consequently, the issue of a univocal monotheism needs to be placed on the discussion table at which leaders and scholars of the three religions are at work, but the theological and faith-based belief in God must also be on the table. Divine univocity is logical but at times it has even been used theologically.

c. Each of the Three Religions Base Their Belief in God on Specific Historical Moments of Divine Revelation

The specific forms of monotheism that are present in the three religions are each based on three respectively different revelations from the monotheistic God. However, a major question immediately appears, namely, how can there be three different *divine revelations* of one and the same monotheistic God? The three religions base their belief in one God on divine revelation, and it is on the basis of divine revelation that each of the three religions is able to claim the righteousness of their belief in one God. The union of monotheism to divine revelation, as presented by the three religions, is a profoundly complicated intra-religion situation. The elements involved in this particular aspect of monotheism require a more lengthy evaluation. Let us move cautiously but clearly.

In the three religions, monotheism and the revelation of God go hand in hand. One without the other, that is religion without divine revelation, is unthinkable. Unless God reveals something of God's own nature to us, there can be no religious honoring of God. The religious honoring of a revealing God is clearly a major part of all three religions.

Each of the three religions, however, has its own distinctive approach to the relationship of monotheism to divine revelation. In all three religions, God has *historically revealed* both himself and his plan of creation. The precise form of God's historical revelation can be found in the sacred writings of each of the three religions, in the long-standing traditions of the three religions, and in the liturgical celebration of God's revelation that each religion has developed.

In Christianity, the divine revelation includes a revelation of the Trinitarian nature of the one God and also a revelation of the relation of the Logos-God to the incarnate Word. Jesus is both God and human. In the historical Jesus, God has revealed the foundational meaning of all creation, for with the incarnation of the Logos made flesh, creation has begun to move toward the final days when in Christ all created reality will have historically reached its fulfillment.

In Islam, the account of God's revelation is totally different. Allah has revealed his words in the Qur'an, and this revelation is the final historical revelation Allah will make before the end of the world. Those who abide by the revelation of Allah in the Qur'an will be saved. In Sūrah 2, *The Cow*, we read that the Torah and the Gospels were "sent down before you."[13] Both the Torah and the Gospels are acknowledged as earlier revelations of Allah. However, "the Gospel, meaning the revelation entrusted to Jesus, which the Qur'an refers to as the *Anjali*, is not considered exactly identical to the Christian New Testament as a whole, nor to the Four Gospels as they are now found in the Christian Bible."[14] On the other hand, "the Qur'an is the verbatim revelation of the Word of God, revealed in Arabic through the archangel Gabriel to the Prophet during the twenty-three-year period of his prophetic mission."[15] William C. Chittick, in his essay on "Eschatology," provides us with a detailed way in which the Qur'an and its major commentators present the end of the world. Those who attain the final resurrection do so because their lives have, for the most part, been in accord with the teachings of the Qur'an.[16]

In Judaism, the issue of divine revelation has gone through a massive reevaluation from the time of Benedict Spinoza down to the present. Spinoza temporalized any and all forms of divine revelation. Although Spinoza described statements and positions of many Jewish authors, including the Torah, as "divine revelation," they were in his view simply exemplifications of human thinking. From the time of Spinoza onward, revelation in Jewish thinking has become more and more secularized. Both in his book *Rethinking Modern Judaism: Ritual Commandment, Community* and in his essay "Secularization, 'Spirit,' and the Strategies of Modern Jewish Faith," Arnold Eisen has clearly demonstrated that divine revelation as found in the earlier centuries of Judaism has been secularized. Eisen studies the works of Jewish scholars from the nineteenth century onward, namely the

---

13. Ali, *Holy Qur'ān*, Surah 2:4: "And who believe in the Revelation sent to thee and sent before thy time and (in their hearts) have the assurance of the Hereafter." See the lengthy Appendix III in *The Meaning of the Holy Qur'ān*, 291–92. 'In these pages, 'AbdullanYūsuf 'Alī carefully explains the role of the gospel in the Qur'an. In Appendix II, 288–90, he carefully explains the role of the Torah in the Qur'an.

14. Cleary, *Essential Koran*, 167.

15. Nasr, "Quran as the Foundation of Islamic Spirituality," 3.

16. Chittick, "Eschatology." The details throughout this essay are numerous and the reader is generously given a thorough picture of Islamic eschatology. It is clear throughout the essay that the norm for risen life after death is the observance of the Qur'an.

works of such men as Abraham Geiger, Nahman Korchmal, and Asher Ginzburg. From the twentieth century onward, the list of names is longer: Ahad Ha'am, A. D. Gordon, Abraham Isaac Kook, Martin Buber, Abraham Heschel, and Mordecai Kaplan. What unites modern, secularized Judaism, Eisen concludes, is not a divine revelation but a "Jewish spirit" that provides an umbrella for Jews throughout the world. In many ways, this secularized Jewish spirit removes the Jewish community, except for those who are still religiously inclined, from the three religions that have centralized much of this present volume.

In the area of *contemporary religious Jews*, the revelation of Yahweh to Moses through the Torah is appreciated as the centering of Jewish faith. This revelation of Yahweh was not and is not coextensive with the revelation of a Trinitarian God to the Christian faith or with the revelation of Allah found in the Qur'an of the Islamic faith. In Judaism, revelation has become a major theme in the twentieth century and into the twenty-first century. Rivka Horwitz has documented this resurgence of the theme of revelation by contemporary leading Jewish scholars.[17]

From a religious point of view, divine revelation in all three religions is always relational. Divine revelation is an action of God *to* someone or *to* a group of men and women. God's revelation is, in these instances, limited to and molded by the recipients. In other words the term "revelation" itself implies both a sending and a reception.

On the issues of speaking and hearing, Jacques Lacan's analysis of human speech helps us understand that what is said by one person might have a different meaning by the person who hears. Revelation and reception, God speaking and humans hearing, is a relational event in a religious context. What God says and what is heard may not be identical.[18]

God's message is sent by God, but it is received in and through the existential abilities of the person or the group to whom God has made a self-revelation. Because of the reception factor, the three divine revelations mentioned above are intrinsically different. There is no univocal self-revelation of God that is then univocally heard by three different groups of men and women. Even in everyday life, what one person says does not always correspond to what another person has heard. This restructuring factor is an intrinsic part of a divine revelation, and therefore there are three highly different divine revelations. The difference is not simply based on the human

---

17. Horwitz, "Revelation and the Bible."
18. See the dissertation by Jürgen Braungart, "Creatures of Desire."

side. Rather, the act of divine revelation itself includes, as an intrinsic part of its reality, a reception that is diversely occurring. Thus, revelation in itself is relational and can only be understood as a relational interplay between the divine and the human. At one and the same time, it is a revelation *of* and a revelation *to*. In every revelatory event, these two dimensions (*of* and *to*) reciprocally shape the eventual meaning of divine revelation as presented by the three religions. This reciprocity raises the problem in an intense way: how can the one God (monotheism) reveal God's own self in three different and competing ways?

d. The Infinity of God, Namely, the Way in Which God's Infinitude Affects Any and All Divine Revelations of the Nature of God

In divine revelation, God remains an infinite God. Nothing and no one can limit God. At times, however, the infinity of God seems to be placed to one side whenever the issue under discussion is divine revelation. God has revealed, one group claims, God's own self to us. Therefore, we are the special recipients of a divine self-revelation. The members of this group could be Christian, Islamic, or Jewish. Because God has revealed himself to their group, their group is the privileged group.

If God is infinite and if we cannot limit God, then there may be a finite divine revelation to any of the three religions. Each religion has only a finite glimpse of the infinite God. No religion has a full understanding of God's own nature. In other words, each and every group that claims a revelation from one and the same God can feel blessed by God, but only if the group is willing to admit that God is infinite and that because of this no group will ever have a full revelation of God's nature.

In this volume, what is emphasized is the following: each group must see itself as honored since it has been given a glimpse of the infinite God. The approach of "glimpse" takes the competitive tone out of the three religions. Each of the three religions can legitimately claim to have received a limited revelation of God. The approach to revelation as a glimpse of God is theologically based on the infinitude of God.

The infinitude of God opens the doors of revelation even further. If the three religions only have a beautiful and awe-inspiring *glimpse* of God, then one might ask, are not all religions blessed with a glimpse of the one God? On hearing this question, someone is bound to raise the issue of relativity. Relativity implies that no one religion can be the final religion or the better

Two Major Intra-Religion Complications

religion, since in each religion God who is infinite provides only a small glimpse of his divinity. Since relativity undermines superiority, the three religions do not want to accept this form of revelation. On the other hand, when the leaders and scholars, as well as the members generally, of one religion claim that their religion is the only true religion, a major question arises: have these religious people set the infinity of God to one side so that the superiority of their individual religion can be maintained? This question and its answers by the three religions, each of which claim religious superiority, cannot be set to one side.

The issue that is fundamental here is this: since God is infinite, no human group will ever have a complete understanding of the nature of God. To claim otherwise is to deny the infinitude of God. God becomes domesticated in one small group of men and women. The immediate response to this situation is often the following claim: God has revealed to us that our religion is the only true religion. Our religion offers eternal salvation since we are the only true religion. This form of counterargument seems to be the standard position of Christianity, Islam, and Judaism.

In the many eons of human life, one has heard again and again that God reveals himself throughout the created world. Francis of Assisi is not the only person to see in nature his Brother Sun and his Sister Moon. Bonaventure is not the only person who teaches that in all things there is a *vestigium Dei*, a vestige of God himself. Jesus himself, in the Gospel of Matthew, not only cures the Canaanite woman, but he blesses the woman for her faith in God even though she is not Jewish (Matthew 15:21–28). Later in the same Gospel, the end of world and the gathering of the people at the last judgment are described (25:31–40). At the last judgment, the people who are blessed by Jesus have given food and drink to the hungry and the thirsty, have welcomed the stranger, have clothed the naked, and have visited those who were ill or in prison. To all of this, Jesus simply states that the people who have shared and helped others would be with God forever. In the New Testament there are many important passages in which non-Jews are praised for their faith and are promised life in heaven. There are also passages that castigate people who should have faith but do not act in a way blessed by God.

In Christian theology, based on the New Testament, there are three different theological positions on the forgiveness of sin in and through Jesus, and these three different positions indicate that our human theology is limited. The first theological position sees Jesus as Victor; the second sees

Jesus as Victim; the third sees Jesus as Revealer. The Catholic Church has never declared that only one of these theologies is a matter of faith. In other words, there has never been a dogmatic declaration by Catholic authorities that defines the meaning of redemption. This theological openness can be seen as an example of church authority honoring the infinitude of God. It is God who ultimately blesses someone with eternal life; it is not a church that proffers such a blessing.[19] God is infinitely free and no human group, not even a religious group, can set limits on God's infinity.

e. The Historical Verification of a Divine Plan for Creation

Leopold von Ranke (1795–1886) became a major historian during his lifetime. His famous citation, "Was eigntlich geschehen ist," has been cited again and again in the past one hundred years. For many, von Ranke's methodology meant that "what actually happened" at a given time can be restated in historical writings.[20] In the middle of the twentieth century there were several major scholars who wrote on the meaning of history, which included the notion of historical verification. Did something actually occur as it is described in a historical account? Or is the historical position simply a later reflection on what might have taken place? The door opened from the position of von Ranke, "Was eigntlich geschehen ist," to a variety of ways in and through which historical scholars can state that for a past action there is "historical verification."[21]

The question of historical verification and religious writings such as the sacred books of the three religions has become central today. The current Near East archaeological findings or non-findings have raised the issue of historical verification. So too, the critics of religiously biased histories have raised the issues of an acceptable format for historical verification. In this current discussion between scientific historians and religious historians, the scientific historians claim that religious historians utilize "divine revelation" as the basis for the historical veracity of the words and actions of Abraham, his descendants, and the Mosaic material. From a different standpoint one can say that the contemporary position that each of the three religions offers a divine plan for creation based on divine revelation,

---

19. See Osborne, *Theology of the Church for the Third Millennium*, 293–320.

20. Ranke himself did not use the phrase in such an overly literal way.

21. For an understanding of "historical verification" see the five-volume work edited by Daniel Woolf, *The Oxford History of Historical Writings*.

Two Major Intra-Religion Complications

and that these three plans are essentially different, has raised extensive and serious questions on the issue of historical verification. The three different plans for creation and a monotheistic and revealing God do not adequately coincide. The issue today does not require a religious historian to "prove" the actuality of what he or she has focused on. Rather, the issue today centers on the validity of using *only* a religious text, divinely inspired in one way or another, as the single criterion when making a judgment on historical verification. It was mentioned above that even the well-known scholar William Foxwell Albright judged his archaeological findings in ways that benefitted the Old Testament texts. In other words, for Albright, the sacred writings played a major role when it came to the verification or non-verification of archaeological work in the Near East.

A divine plan for the finite universe needs verification of some sort. If one says that revelation, and therefore God, provides this needed verification, then one can rightly ask, how is it possible for one and the same God to reveal three different plans for creation as expressed by the three religions? This is precisely the central complication of the second intra-religion complication. Only scholars and leaders of the three religions can face up to this complicating factor. If such a conversation does not take place, then any and every denial of God by contemporary scientists can be considered a valid position. There simply cannot be three different historical plans for creation, each of which has been revealed by the one God. This impossibility can only be resolved if and when some key scholars and leaders of the three religions enter into well-focused discussions.

Each of the three religions claims that its divine plan for creation is not only true, but also that it is *historically* true. These three plans, each in its own way, specifically refer to the historical actions and words of Noah, Abraham, his descendants, and Moses. That all of these people actually lived in past times is taken for granted. The actions and words of these people are also taken as historically self-evident. All of this has been called into question.

Contemporary Near East archaeology has raised serious conclusions from their findings and non-findings of the early Near Eastern world. Archaeological discoveries and their evaluation do not verify most of the Abrahamic-Mosaic material. Nonetheless, religious leaders and scholars of the three religions tend to ignore the archaeological data and its evaluation. Leaders and scholars of the three religions continue to explain the divine plan for creation even though the only place for historical verification of these plans is in the sacred books of Christianity, Islam, and Judaism. Many archaeologists today are not simply raising serious questions vis-à-vis this approach by religious scholars. Archaeologists *have challenged* the historical veracity of their presentations of God's plan for creation. Religious leaders and scholars cannot ignore these challenges. When they do ignore them, the veracity of the religious leaders and scholars themselves is called into question.

The existence of Noah, Abraham, his descendants as well as Moses can be tentatively affirmed. By the use of the term "tentatively," there is an acknowledgement that the archaeological data has brought serious questioning on the historical existence of these people but not enough to deny their existence. Thus, that these people actually existed can be "tentatively" accepted, and only in that tentative degree can the acceptance be validly maintained.

The major focus, however, is not on the existence of the religious leaders. Rather, the major focus is the claim for historical verification of the words and actions of these people as presented in the sacred writings of the three religions. Did Abraham say *x*? Did Isaac make this or that statement? Did Moses express himself in these or those exact words? These are major questions and they are unsettling questions. If their only verification is their inclusion in the sacred writing—and this is true for almost all the Abrahamic-Mosaic material—then the argument for validity ends up in an unending circle centered on the phrase: God has revealed these "historical" situations.

Today, scholars whose focus is on the sacred texts of the three religions are called on to read the Abrahamic-Mosaic material in a "sacred story" form rather than in a historical form. At times, when one hears the phrase "story form," one thinks of fairy tales and other descriptive literature. However, stories can be found throughout the history of the human race, and these stories contain precious data on the ways that earlier generations thought, judged, and even lived.

In a common way, the scholars and leaders of the three religions state that the universe, from the time of creation onward, has been directed by God (that is by the Trinity, by Allah, or by Yahweh) and that the universe is moving historically in a direction that has a final conclusion. Each of the three religions teaches that God has revealed the plan for creation. Therefore, so it is argued, this plan is not a plan that has its basic origin in and

Two Major Intra-Religion Complications

through human construction. Rather, the historical unfolding of the plan of creation is God's plan and God has revealed this plan to human beings.

The difficulty is this: since each religion presents its own revealed plan of creation, there are three different revealed plans for creation. For the Jewish people, the plan of creation ultimately centers on the chosen people who have continued to live out their covenant with God down to the present day. For the Christian people, Jesus is both the goal of all creation and its centerpiece. Human history after the time of Jesus is a continuation of Jesus history, for God's ultimate plan for all creation began in Jesus and will climax in Jesus at the end of time. For the Islamic people, the Qur'an, given by Allah to Mohammad, is the final revelation prior to the end of the world. From the time when the Qur'an was revealed down to the present, the entire world is living within Qur'anic history and this will continue down to the end of the world.

Many individual components of these three plans are accepted by the three religions, such as the patriarchal role of Abraham and his descendants; the role of Moses in his connection to God's plan of the universe; and the role of Adam and Eve and the role of Noah in God's plan for the universe. These common areas, however, are fairly generalized. The descendants of Abraham include not only early leaders in the Jewish world, such as Isaac, Jacob, Joseph, Moses, and Aaron, but also they slowly but surely became the ancestors of the Islamic religion. Abraham's descendants include Hagar and Ishmael and their journey to Mecca; Abraham and Ishmael built the Casaba. All of this was reiterated in the revelations of Allah to Mohammad. These are all parts of the Abrahamic ancestry of the Islamic religion. Likewise, Abraham's descendants include Joseph, who is mentioned in the opening verse of Matthew's Gospel: "The book of the genealogy of Jesus Christ, the son of David, the son of Abraham" (Matthew 1:1). In the Gospel of Luke, it is Jesus' mother, Mary, who says, "[God] has helped Israel his servant, remembering his mercy, according to his promise to our fathers, to Abraham and to his descendants forever" (Luke 1:34–35). Jesus is the historical fulfillment of the covenant made to Abraham.

The Jewish plan historically centers on the Jewish religion; the Islamic plan historically centers on the Qur'an, which was revealed through Mohammad; the Christian plan historically reaches its apex in Jesus, the Christ. Each plan claims that its beginning centers on the patriarch Abraham. After this common claim, the recounting of the Abrahamic and Mosaic material is interpreted in three non-compatible formats. Moreover, all three plans, each in its own way, move further back in history through Abraham to the covenant that God (Yahweh, Allah, Trinity) made with Noah and even to the supposed covenant that God (Yahweh, Allah, Trinity) made to Adam and Eve. The world itself was initially created with an intermediate goal, the creation of human beings: "God [Yahweh, Allah, or Trinity] made man in his image; in the divine image he created man" (Genesis 1:27). Jewish scholars read this passage from Genesis with the image of Yahweh in mind; Muslims read this passage with the image of Allah in mind; and Christians read this passage with the image of the Trinity in mind.

A major value for these initial discussions is the clarification of the term "religion" in the phrase "science and religion." In the first chapter of this volume, we mentioned that the term "science" was used in a variety of ways in the book *The Oxford Handbook of Science and Religion*. In this book the term "science" is used at times as an overarching term. However, in sections of the book that center on religion in the light of contemporary sciences, specific sciences, not just "science," were mentioned and these specific sciences raised specific questions and challenges to religious leaders and scholars of the three religions.

The term "religion" also became specific in the section entitled "Religion and Science across the World's Traditions." However, no mention is made in the Oxford volume that the term God had different meanings in the three religions we have studied—Christianity, Islam, and Judaism. When the authors use the term "God" is this Yahweh, or Allah, or the Trinity? Who are the scientists addressing when they say something directed to a person who believes in "God"?

Likewise, no mention is made in the Oxford volume that these same three religions present three distinct divine plans for finite reality. Rather, the terms "God" and "God's plan for finite reality" are used as if these three religions in particular had a common understanding of God and a common understanding of a divine plan for finite reality.

The God honored in Judaism is not the same God who is honored in Islam or Christianity. The God honored in Islam is not the same as the God who is honored in Judaism or Christianity. And the God honored in Christianity is not the same as the God honored in Islam or Judaism. Rather, the theological understanding of God in each of these three religions and the faith-based confession of one God in each of these three religions are ultimately incompatible with each other. As a result, there has been and there remain three differing religions which each claim to be monotheistic and which claim to be the rightful heir of the God who appeared to Abraham.

f. The Resolution of the Complications within the Intra-Religion Conversations

The conflicting issues on monotheism and on God's plan for all creation have at present only a limited number of ways in which the problems and complications can be resolved. The three more important resolutions can be stated as follows:

a. Only one of the three religions worships the one true God and follows the one true plan for creation.

b. The membership of the three religions honors one univocal God, while the individual adherents of each religion honor one and the same God in three different and secondary ways.

c. The issue of monotheism is dated; polytheism should reclaim its former integrity.

Let us consider each of these resolutions.

g. Only One of the Three Religions Worships the One True God.

The first answer is a blunt statement: only one of the three religions can claim that "our" understanding of the one God is the only true understanding of the one God. In the history of these three religions, this position has often been selected, for over the centuries there have been strongly stated positions that "our" religion is better, truer, and more perfect than "your" religion. In this view, only one of the three religions can be considered the true religion; the other two religions are false, blasphemous, and not blessed by God.

Arthur Hertzberg, in his volume *Judaism* (1991), presents a lengthy chapter on the Jewish theological and faith-based understanding of God.[22]

22. Hertzberg, *Judaism*, 63–84. Throughout this chapter, Hertzberg simply states that the Jewish faith honors one God and does so in a deeply spiritual way. He writes about the Jewish belief in God without mentioning that there are different views about "one true God" in Christian and Islamic religious literature. The impression one has from Hertzberg's text is this: there is only one God and Jewish religious people honor the Jewish theological and faith-based understanding of God. Therefore, they are monotheists. Since Christians and Muslims also honor the one true God in their respective

In his chapter, he emphasizes that the Jews honor only one God and he does so in a deeply spiritual way. Hertzberg's description of Yahweh is eloquent, prayerful, and deeply moving. Throughout this chapter, however, he writes about the Jewish belief in one God without mentioning that there are different views about the "one true God" in Christian and Islamic religious literature. The impression one has from Hertzberg's text is this: there is only one God and Jewish religious people honor the Jewish theological and faith-based understanding of this one God. Therefore, they are monotheists. Since Christians and Muslims also honor the one true God in their respective communities, there is a challenge to Herzberg's position, but he makes no mention of this. Hertzberg's presentation of Jewish faith in Yahweh is typical of today's discussion of God. Authors from each of the three religions simply present in a non-competitive way the view that their respective religion believes in one God. Their religion is monotheistic.

In the Middle Ages, Saadoa Gaon composed *The Book of Belief and Opinions*, in which he argues that the Torah must be divine revelation because the children of Israel saw it and it is unlikely that they would agree to a lie.[23] Rivka Horwitz comments:

> In the Middle Ages an appeal was often made to the enormous number of witnesses, the six hundred thousand Israelites who heard the voice at Sinai. This argument seemed very appealing and was used in disputations with Christians, one form being the claim that since the number of witnesses to the Israelite revelation was far greater than those who attested to Jesus, their religion was the more reliable.[24]

From the late eighteenth century on, the Jewish community tended to become secular. Many Jews chose to live outside of the traditional patterns of Judaism. The disaffection of many Jews with their religious past and the eagerness of the "new Jews" to assimilate into Western society led to a massive desertion of Jewish religious traditions. The question of the superiority of the Jewish faith over the faith of Christians and Muslims was set to one side. In this new atmosphere of Jewish secularism and liberalism, a host of contemporary Jewish writers have tried to reunite modern Jews with their faith. Asher Ginzburg, Martin Buber, Mordecai Kaplan, and

---

communities, there is a challenge to Herzberg's position, but he makes no mention of this.

23. See Gaon, *Book of Beliefs and Opinions*, 31.
24. Horwitz, "'Revelation and the Bible," 351.

Two Major Intra-Religion Complications

Gerhom Scholem have been leaders in this renewal. Even more contemporary are the voices of Arthur Green, Arnold Eisen, Paul Mendes-Flohr, Rivka Horwitz, and Laurence Silverstein. All of these authors are well aware of contemporary relativization, a situation in which nothing seems to be absolute. Nonetheless, their efforts are not directed at a relativized goal, in which one religion is as good as another. The effort of these Jewish scholars and leaders is to revitalize Jewish faith with it center in the Jewish belief in one God, Yahweh.

Not one of these scholars focuses directly on the problematic meaning of monotheism. Rather, they tend to focus on the meaning of revelation to the Jewish people. Martin Buber, Hermann Cohen, Franz Rosenzweig, Eugen Rosenstock-Heusy, Abraham Heschel and others have centered their renewal on Yahweh who is personally addressing contemporary Jews. "Personally addressing" is a phrase that, in their view, includes the ways in which Yahweh personally reveals himself to contemporary Jewish women and men.

Nonetheless, some secularized Jewish women and men have reacted negatively to the efforts of authors such as Buber and Cohen. They have raised such issues as: why is Yahweh the center of my life? Why are Jewish customs and worship necessary? Why is there only a revelation that centers on Jewish issues? With no overwhelming answer to these issues, many Jews even today have remained secular.

If we turn to Christianity, and more pointedly to Roman Catholicism, the supremacy of the Catholic Church over all other religions and over all other forms of Christianity has been officially standard from the Tridentine period onward. A very thorough analysis of this standard Roman Catholic view appeared in the lengthy essay by the Jesuit Joachim Salaverri, entitled "De Ecclesia Christi," which was published in 1962. Salaverri states clearly that outside the Roman Catholic Church there is no salvation.[25] In paragraph 1108 of his essay, he states that a non-Roman Catholic can be saved only if he or she prior to death has the desire, at least virtually and

---

25. Salaverri, "De Ecclesia Christi." He maintains that outside the Roman Catholic Church, there is no salvation for any man or woman. Non-Roman Catholics can be saved only if the following takes place: "Actu perfectae caritatis homo iustificatur et salvatur, quatenus in tali actu, saltem virtualiter et implicite, votum pertinendi ad Ecclesiam includitur." If a person does not have such a desire, at least *virtualiter et implicite*, he or she will never be saved. In these pages, Salaverri presents the common and official teaching of the Roman Catholic Church, which one can abundantly document from the post-Reformation time down to the Second Vatican Council.

implicitly, of joining the Roman Catholic Church. If a man or woman does not have such a desire, they can in no way be saved. Salaverri presents in an accurate way the official position of the Roman Catholic Church just prior to the Second Vatican Council.[26]

Salaverri's position of the Roman Catholic Church calls into question the belief of non-Roman Catholics, Jews, and Muslims and also of all who belong to other world religions or those who are atheistic. Non-Catholics, in this Catholic view, are basically considered non-redeemed. These women and men do not truly believe in the one God, the Trinity, and therefore they are not able to be saved. This standard Catholic position on "non-believers" is harsh and exclusive. Roman Catholics believed and still believe in only one God, but in Salaverri's presentation only Catholics have the correct understanding of monotheism. All other religions are unacceptable.

Since Vatican II, a different approach has begun to take place in the Catholic Church regarding the salvation of non-Catholics. The Declaration on Religious Liberty, *Nostra Aetate*, promulgated on October 28, 1965, was a milestone vis-à-vis contemporary interreligious dialogues. The bishops wanted to "examine more carefully its relations with non-Christian religions."[27] In section two, the text focuses on the history of religions, and in these religions there has been recognition of a hidden power, of a supreme being, of a divine father, of a divine mystery (nn. 1–2). After this litany of "divine presences," the bishops state, "The Catholic Church rejects nothing of what is true and holy in these religions" (n. 2). In a special way, the bishops honor Islam (n. 3) and Judaism (n. 4). In their concluding section (n.5), we read, "We cannot truly pray to God the Father of all if we treat any people as other than sisters and brothers, for all are created in the God's image." In this final section, the bishops focus on religious discrimination and condemn any form of such discrimination. However, there is one statement in this document that makes the entire document questionable. We read:

> The church [Roman Catholic Church] held and continues to hold that Christ out of infinite love freely underwent suffering and death because of the sins of all, so that all might attain salvation. It is the duty of the church, therefore, in its preaching to proclaim

---

26. See Part III in Madges, *Vatican II*, 247–367; and Phan, *Evangelization and Interreligious Dialogue*.

27. *Nostra Aetate*, n. 2, quoted in Flannery, *Basic Documents of Vatican II*, 570.

Two Major Intra-Religion Complications

the cross of Christ as the sign of God's universal love and the source of all grace.[28]

In this paragraph, the death of Jesus is God's sign of universal love and the source of all grace. Other religions may have holy people, but these women and men possess their holiness because of the death of Jesus. At Vatican II, the conservative bishops again and again required such statements as the one cited above. Consequently, in many stances, as in the above instance, there are in the Vatican documents contradictory positions. This combination of conservative bishop and more open-minded bishop needs to be kept in mind as one reads the documents of Vatican II.

Since the close of Vatican II, a few important Catholic theologians have begun to change this theological position. They argue that salvation can be found in all religions and salvation is not necessarily tied to any virtual or implicit desire to be a Christian or a Catholic.[29]

Islam has also faced the issue of monotheism. Albert Hourani, in his volume *A History of the Arab Peoples*, describes a fairly peaceful time when Islamic people lived rather serenely with Christians and Jews.[30] From the eighth century down to the thirteenth century, Iraq and Iran were the centers of religious intellectual life. Gradually, other main centers developed in Cairo and Spain. At first, Christians in Spain formed the majority of the population, and there were centers of Jewish people as well. Slowly but surely, the Muslim minority throughout the Western world became the dominant intellectual majority. Muslims formed a strong and autonomous self-confidence as well as a profound intellectual and spiritual life.[31] Muslim intellectual centers gradually dominated the academic world in the areas of present-day Iraq and Iran. There was a major transmission of Greek scientific and philosophical literature into Arabic. The presence of Islam improved the position of the Nestorian and Monophysite churches, since the Arabic government removed the leaders of these churches from Byzantine rule.

In spite of this mutual living together within an Arabic world, Hourani describes the relationship of Islam, Christianity, and Judaism in these early centuries in the following way.

---

28. *Nostra Aetate*, n. 4, quoted in ibid., 573–74.

29. See for instance "Understanding Christian-Muslim Dialogue in South East Asia: Summary Report and Reflections," in Eilers, *For All the Peoples of Asia*, vol. 4, 77–87.

30. See Hourani, *History of the Arab Peoples*, 186–88.

31. Ibid., 187.

> However easy and close relations between Muslims, Jews and Christian might be, there remained a gulf of ignorance and prejudice between them. They worshipped separately and had their own high places of worship and pilgrimage: Jerusalem for the Jews; another Jerusalem for the Christians.[32]

Little by little, however, antagonism between Islam and Christianity as well as Islam and Judaism began to take over. When the Crusades began to take place (1096–1221), the goal of these wars moved from a Christian recovery of Jerusalem to the destruction of the Islamic religion in the Near East. Peters describes the sacking of Jerusalem by the crusaders in a bloody way:

> The Western knights, most of them French, took Jerusalem in 1099, slew the Muslim defenders down to the women and children—the fate of the Jewish community is less clear; some were doubtless killed but many others were ransomed by their coreligionists in Egypt—and so they (the Crusaders) found themselves in a possession of city that was filled with holy places but had no inhabitants other than themselves.... Some Eastern Christian were lured back into the city, and eventually too a few Jews and Muslims made their tentative and modest reappearance in Jerusalem.[33]

In Spain, the Muslims gained control of most of the country in 711, but Ferdinand of Aragon, with his wife, Isabella of Castile, forcibly took over northern Spain and eventually conquered the last Muslim-controlled area, Granada, in 1492. One can hardly say that there was a peaceful acceptance by the Christian community of either the Muslims or the Jews from 1096 to 1492. The Catholic European communities believed that they and they alone truly believed in the one true God. Muslims and Jews were seen as heretics and infidels. However, in the Qur'an one finds an openness to some initial form of ecumenism.

> Those who believe (in the Qur'ān),
> And those who follow the Jewish (scriptures),
> And the Christians or Sabians—
> Any who believe in Allah
> And the Last Day
> and work righteousness
> Shall have their reward

---

32. Ibid., 188.
33. Peters, *Islam*, 231.

Two Major Intra-Religion Complications

With the Lord; on them
Shall be no fear, nor shall they grieve. (Qur'an, *The Heifer*, 62)

In the Ottoman Empire, the period after the Crusades down to the nineteenth and twentieth centuries, the Muslim people experienced a life-changing situation. Religious cooperation was no longer a major part of Muslim life. The official and sometimes only permitted religion was Islam. Allah was the only true God. Any other God (read: Christian or Jewish) was not considered sacred. Nonetheless, Muslims who lived outside the frontiers of the Ottoman Empire and who professed faith in Allah lived their religion through the medium of the Arabic language. Their connection to Islam was deeper than political allegiance or shared interests. Among these Muslims beyond the Ottoman boundaries, common languages also helped, namely, Arabic, Turkish, and Persian. For these people, they lived communally since they professed an enduring and unshaken faith in the final revelation of God through the prophet Mohammad, namely, through the Qur'an.[34]

Today, the three religions live together in a fairly open way, but there are many deep-seated misgivings on the part of each religion vis-à-vis the correct understanding of God. The three religions still maintain, although not in an openly war-strewn way, that their respective God, Yahweh, Allah, and the Trinity, is the only true God. The leaders and scholars of the three religions continue, for the most part, to present a theological and faith-based understanding of God that is respectively Yahweh or Allah or the Trinity. In actuality, the leaders and scholars implicitly acknowledge the value of each other's religion but they have not as yet focused formally on the issue of monotheism, which all three religions claim. Implicitly, there is no acknowledgement of three monotheistic Gods. Rather, but again implicitly, there is a strong faith-based position that only "our God" is the "one and true God." What is needed is an honest review and discussion of monotheism by some key leaders and scholars of the three religions. In such a discussion, the basic question is this: how can our three religions claim to be monotheistic? How can there be three differing monotheistic Gods?

---

34. Hourani, *History of the Arab Peoples*, 256–57.

h. The Membership of the Three Religions Honors One Univocal God While the Individual Adherents of Each of the Three Religions Honor One and the Same God in Three Different and Secondary Ways.

Basically, this approach is only logical. The approach logically posits one univocal God. The honoring of this one univocal God is a secondary yet deeply important factor. At the secondary level there is Jewish worship, Islamic worship, and Christian worship. Probably no theologian in any of the three religions would accept this position. This position is mentioned only because it is a logically possible solution.

However, its presence in these pages makes the question of a univocal God for all three religions very clear. Unless the one God in the three religions is a univocal God in some way or another, then members of the three religions are not honoring one and the same God. Allah, Trinity, and Yahweh, in this approach, are not and cannot be interpreted as one and the same God. Nonetheless, each of the three religions strongly states that their religion respectively is monotheistic. If each of the three religions is monotheistic, then one and same God must be present in each of the three religions. This is the logical view mentioned above, but it is only within a logical framework that "monotheism" can actually be a univocal term.

What this option offers is a strange way of eliminating the current difficulties connected to monotheism. The integrity of each religion is seriously endangered if one holds that the religious worship of God is ultimately a worship of a single monotheistic God present equally and univocally in each of the three religions. Logically one might argue that this acceptance of a common, univocal monotheistic God is viable. In practice, however, it is not viable since such a position denies the actual reality of Christianity, Islam, and Judaism.

If this logical view would be a possible solution, one might as well consider the Gods of Hinduism and the transcendence within Buddhism, as well as the Gods of all other cultures and groupings to be valid. Throughout the human world people are "logically" worshipping one univocal monotheistic God. If three religions can be united in this cerebral way, then there is no reason why all other religions should be left out of this worship of one logically and univocally monotheistic deity.

i. The Issue of Monotheism Is Dated; Polytheism Should Reclaim Its Former Integrity.

An outright acceptance of polytheism over monotheism has in the history of religions been an accepted form of religious worship. Polytheism is still part of our present religious situation, although it is not prevalent. Even today, medicine men, shamans, and other totems are routinely attractive to a large number of men and women. Their divine power may be the power of lesser gods, but they are in some way or another connected to the divine. No one today has advocated that the three religions should become openly polytheistic.

At times, outsiders have judged that the powers of medicine men, shamans, and other totems come from polytheism. This may only be an outsider's view. A given group of men and women may believe in the divine and belong to a distinct religion, and at the same time they ask for help from shamans or reverence totems. In their religious thinking, however, these intermediate divine persons and things might only be, in their view, a manifestation of one God. In Christianity, Islam, and Judaism there are saints, imams, and prophets. These holy people are not gods but they often present a strong spiritual power. When discussing polytheism, it might be more exact to say that some seemingly polytheistic religious groups are basically monotheistic.

PART TWO: A FRAMEWORK FOR RESOLVING THE INTRA-RELIGION COMPLICATIONS

With this summation of the intra-religion complication, we ask once again that key leaders and scholars within Christianity, Islam, and Judaism meet together and face the difficult issues of monotheism that each of the three religions claim. Indirectly their monotheistic claims seem to allow three different theological and faith-based understandings of God. If this is so, then the focus is not directly on monotheism but on a pluri-theism that disguises itself as monotheism. One might even call this *proprio-theism*, that is, "our own proper theism," namely, a belief in a communal God that no other religious community has.

Eventually, one may have to acknowledge that the three religions are not monotheistically identical, for each of the three religions in actuality worships a different God. If this is true, then no one religion can claim exclusive monotheism. The faith structures of the three religions, however, seem to disallow such a step, since Yahweh, Allah, and the Trinitarian God are not three names of one and the same divine being.

The Yahweh-Allah-Trinity distinctions of God profoundly complicate any and every science and religion discussions. Some scientists do believe in God, but depending on their religion they may believe in the Yahweh God or they may believe in the Allah God or they may believe in the Trinitarian God. Some scientists, however, do not believe in any God at all, and these are often the scientists who have raised the science-religion issue over the existence of God, such as Richard Dawkins, Peter Atkins, Michel Onfray, and Christopher Hitchens.

As regards the three monotheistic religions, the respective leaders and scholars cannot argue with non-believing scientists over the existence of God before they themselves have come to some common understanding of what "monotheism" means. Each of the three religions has a differently defined understanding of God. Consequently, scientists cannot be expected to show from the standpoint of science that Yahweh or Allah or the Trinitarian God actually exists. Since many contemporary scientists have disclaimed the existence of God and since generally this disclaiming of God has been most often challenged by Christians, Muslims, and Jews, no satisfactory resolution can be established until the leaders and scholars of the three religions come to some agreement on the understanding of monotheism. No scientist who denies the existence God will resolve the issue by saying that Allah truly does exist or that Yahweh truly does exist or that the Trinitarian God truly does exist. Since there is no common God for these three Abrahamic religions, there can be no scientific answer that will satisfy the leaders and scholars of the three religions. Thus, the issue of monotheism falls back to an intra-religion setting.

The issue of the three monotheistic religions is historically and essentially connected to the three divine plans regarding the history of the created universe. Each of the three religions proposes a different historical plan of God for created reality. This problem is further complicated since the leaders and scholars of all three religions claim that a divine revelation has provided the validity of the three plans. Once again, there arises a major problem, since a monotheistic God could not have revealed three different historical plans for creation.

Scientists, who have been confronted by religious leaders on the issue of a divine plan for finite reality, are incapable of resolving the situation as

Two Major Intra-Religion Complications

long as the three religions maintain separate divine plans of created reality. Only an intra-religion discussion on the issue can help resolve the fundamental problems inherent in the divine plans for creation. If the religious leaders and scholars do not communally discuss the problematic of these three divine plans, the scientific world remains baffled. Which divine plan of an individual religion are they supposed to corroborate?

Moreover, the issues of divine revelation and of *historical verification* have moved beyond a *questioning stage*. Today, the scientific material on the history of human development within the ancient Near East has *challenged* in a very overarching way the material on Abraham, on his descendants, and on the Mosaic material as well, all of which are found to some extent within the Jewish Scriptures, the Christian Scriptures, and the Qur'an. Can the material in these sacred writings regarding Abraham and Moses be accepted as verified history? Or is this same material presented in a literary way, that is, in a story-focused way? Near Eastern archaeologists and scientific historians have confronted religious leaders and scholars with data that seriously questions and challenges the three divine plans for created reality.

Historically, one can say that Abraham did exist, but one cannot say that the material on Abraham as presented in these writings has any historical verification. One can say that Abraham had descendants, but again the material in the sacred writings cannot be established as historically verified. One can also say that a man named Moses might have existed, but the material on Moses in the sacred writings cannot be historically verified.

Since these problems are central to the three religions, some form of intra-religion discussion seems to be the only way in which a resolution of the problems can be made. Without some form of intra-religion activity on these issues, the issues themselves will not disappear and the tension between science and religion will deepen. The initiative for this discussion lies with the leaders and scholars of the three religions; the initiative does not lie with scientists.

At the end of 2011, the world population registered at 7 billion. Christians were registered at 2.1 billion, Islam was registered at 1.5 billion, and Judaism registered at only 14 million. In 2010, the world population was established at 6,840,507,000. These figures are important since in the teachings of the three religions, God has created all human beings. Clearly, the majority of human beings have no personal affiliation with the three religions. Over the centuries, statistics such as these have raised the issue of salvation after death. The major writings in Christianity and Islam contain an abundance of passages on salvation and life after death. The sacred writings of Judaism have only a few comments on the afterlife and these comments appear in the later books of the sacred writings and the Pseudopigraphy (Daniel and Maccabees). We have seen above that Salaverri's presentation of the official teaching on redemption in the pre-Vatican II Catholic Church was very limited for those outside Christian faith. A person must have an implicit and virtual belief in Jesus if that person wants to gain salvation. The question cannot help but be asked: if most human beings are not saved in the afterlife, why do the three religions teach that God created every human being? Is it not strange that such a God creates human beings who will have no life after death or who will be in hell forever after death?

In chapter 2, we already saw that there is an overwhelming beauty in each of the three religions and that this beauty can be called a "glimpse of God." The presence of God in each of the three religions is the fundamental reason why each religion has its legitimacy. By using the phrase "glimpse of God," we are stressing that God is infinite and no matter what clarity each of the three religions brings to the understanding of God, God, as infinite, moves and lives beyond the limited views of each religion. This is not saying that each religion offers a biased view of God; rather, it is saying that each religion offers a very true and beautiful glimpse of God, but no human group can ever describe an infinite God. If we say that God is infinite, are we not also saying that God is infinitely free? God is not confined by denominational limits.

Leaders and scholars of the three religions have, over the centuries, reacted negatively to any and all divine presence beyond their respective religion. They have found ingenious ways to unite the freedom of the Holy Spirit to their own denomination and only because of this link with their own denomination is the Holy Spirit able to work beyond the limits of their religion. In these efforts of Christian, Islamic, and Jewish leaders and scholars, the infinitude of God seems to be compromised. No created person in any religious group can tell the Spirit what the Spirit can and cannot do. Unfortunately, in all three religions the infinitude of God has at times been limited again and again.

The title of this volume is *Science and Religion: Fifty Years after Vatican II: A Time of Peace and Reconciliation*. The complex series of issues detailed in this chapter need a peaceful discussion by scholars and leaders of the three religions and eventually in a discussion with contemporary scientists. We cannot expect that those in the top brackets of either religion or science will take the first steps toward a peaceful discussion. Top-bracket scholars and leaders tend to have a sense of being the guardians of their field of study. Nor can we expect that the first steps will be taken by the membership of the three religions or the general public who are interested in science. For these two groups of people, there is generally a need of some "green light" or at least a blinking "cautionary light." Thus, the leadership of any and every peaceful discussion group will be those. These women and men should have a strong background on the questions and challenges established by either science or religion. They also should not have a self-identity of guardianship. Nor should they await a green light. Hopefully, some of these leaders and scholars in the middle from all three religions will sit down at the same table and in a peaceful way discuss the questions and challenges outlined in this volume. If in the future several such discussion groups would arise, the relationship of the three religions to contemporary science would move to a more focused and insightful level.

7

CONCLUSIONS
A New Dimension in Science and Religion
A Time of Peace and Reconciliation

THIS VOLUME HAS FOCUSED on four specific issues of contemporary science, namely, the findings of contemporary Near East archaeology, the emphasis on scientific history, quantum mechanics, and the contemporary scientific age of the universe. These scientific issues have had serious repercussions on the religious world of the twentieth and twenty-first centuries. In this final chapter, we will present conclusions that can be drawn from this tension between science and religion.

This volume has also focused on two issues that are present in the three Abrahamic religions: the meaning of monotheism on the one hand and, on the other hand, the meaning of a divine plan for all creation. The three religions not only claim to be monotheistic but each of them presents a distinctive historical plan for God's creation. The three religions have a common originating patriarch in Abraham and his descendants, and the three religions honor the Mosaic tradition. In their three divine plans for creation, the Arbrahamic-Mosaic material is presented as if it has historical verification. In this final chapter, we will present conclusions that can be drawn from these tensions found in the Abrahamic religions.

Conclusions

CONCLUSIONS BASED ON THE FINDINGS OF NON-FINDINGS OF CONTEMPORARY MIDDLE EAST ARCHAEOLOGY

There are two conclusions that are based on the findings and non-findings of contemporary archaeologists who have studied early Near Eastern cultures.

First Conclusion

Contemporary Near East archaeologists, during the twentieth century, questioned the historical verification of the Abrahamic-Mosaic material that the three religions, in three differing ways, presented to their constituents. In the twenty-first century, however, contemporary Near East archaeologists have challenged the leaders and scholars of the three religions on the issue of historical verification of their respective presentations regarding the Abrahamic-Mosaic material. The first conclusion, therefore, focuses on the scientific change that have moved from questioning to challenging. Religious leaders and scholars of the three religions need to take this challenge in a far more serious way than they have in the past.

Since the beginning of the twentieth century, Near East archaeology has enriched the current understanding of the times and places in which Christianity, Islam, and Judaism originated. From 1960 to 2000, early Near East archaeological findings became a major factor vis-à-vis the religious claims of historical verification for the Abrahamic-Mosaic material. However, it became a negative factor rather than a positive factor, since early Near East archaeological findings, particularly early Egyptian findings, did not offer references to the historical verification of Abraham, his descendants, and Moses in Egypt and in the Sinai.

Archaeological studies that have focused on B.C.E. became one of the most dominant sources of historical knowledge regarding the ancient Near East. Archaeological studies that have focused on times from 3000 B.C.E. onward have been enriched because of emerging historical writings and new archaeological findings. All of this material has provided a more comprehensive view of ancient Near Eastern politics, religion, and economics.[1]

---

1. See Kenyon, *Archaeology in the Holy Land*, 3. For a Jewish positive response to the questions on the historical verification of the exodus, see the Society of Humanistic

Science and Religion: Fifty Years after Vatican II

The major base for the move from questioning to challenging the stance of the three religions on the historicity of the Abrahamic-Mosaic material is not simply archaeological findings, but in a more challenging way the *non-findings of archaeological evidence*. The non-findings of archaeological material on Abraham, on Moses, and on the exodus have raised serious questions regarding the historical verification of the relevant material in the sacred writings of the three religions. One can only conclude that, as of today, the leaders and scholars of the three religions have not adequately responded to this challenge, namely, the lack of archaeological findings regarding Abraham, his descendants, Moses, and the exodus.

Second Conclusion

The findings and non-findings of Near East archaeology have been complicated by the lack of clarity regarding the issue of monotheism as presented by the three religions as well as the lack of historical unity in the three divine plans for the finite universe as presented by the three religions. The findings and non-findings of contemporary Near East archaeology have at times been used to "prove" a respective monotheism of one of the three religions. However, since the three religions cannot agree on the meaning of monotheism, no archaeological finding can be used to validate understanding God as Trinity or as Allah or as Yahweh. Archaeology is not and cannot be the adjudicator of an in-house religious issue such as the meaning of monotheism.

This second conclusion seriously complicates the challenging as expressed in the first conclusion. The two conclusions need to be taken together. The second conclusion centers on Near East archaeological data that reflects or mentions a term for God. As regards the three religions, however, the very term "God" is fundamentally unclear. Does "God" mean Trinity or Allah or Yahweh?

The Hebrew Bible, for example, is cited by all three religions, but when the leaders and scholars of these three religions use passages that refer to God, they do so with a different meaning. Christians interpret passages in the Hebrew Bible that mention God, but this God is the God who became incarnate in Jesus of Nazareth. Muslims interpret passages in the Hebrew

---

Judaism (shj.org). These views are more often than not disregarded or minimized by conservative Jewish intellectual leaders and scholars.

Conclusions

Bible that mention God, but this God is Allah who also speaks in the Qur'an. Jewish scholars interpret this God as Yahweh who, through Moses, made a covenant with the Jewish people and called this people his chosen ones.

Consequently, archaeologists might find material dating from the ancient Near East in which a term for God appears or a picture of God appears, but is this God the Christian God, the Islamic God, or the Jewish God? Even if mention of God is made in the Hebrew Bible, the Bible itself can be read in a Christian way, in an Islamic way, and in a Jewish way.

Because of this interpretive factor, the second conclusion centers of the issue of monotheism. The three religions claim to be monotheistic and they further claim that their respective monotheistic God is the God of Abraham, the God of his descendants, and the God of Moses. Archaeologists cannot and should not be called on to settle this issue. The meaning of monotheism needs to be seen as a major intra-religion problem, and the leaders and scholars of the three religions need to come together and resolve this monotheistic dilemma. Based on the writings of the three religions, one can only conclude that it is impossible that three different monotheistic Gods, as worshipped by the three religions, actually exist. Archaeologists cannot and should not be the scholars who prove that only one God exists. A clarification of the monotheistic impasse is the responsibility of the leaders and scholars of these communities. Only the religious leaders can ultimately resolve the monotheism problem.

CONCLUSIONS BASED ON CONTEMPORARY SCIENTIFIC HISTORY

There are two conclusions based on the findings of contemporary scientific historians that center on the issue on historical verification.

First Conclusion

Since the time of von Ranke (1795–1886), the issue of historical verification has become a major issue for the science of historiography. Whenever historical details are based exclusively on their inclusion in the sacred writings of the three religions, then their verification does not meet contemporary standards of scientific historiography. Almost all of the Abrahamic-Mosaic material lacks verification from sources outside of the sacred writings.

Science and Religion: Fifty Years after Vatican II

Consequently, the historical veracity of this material has been both *questioned* and *challenged* by scholars of the ancient Near East (e.g., historians, Assyriologists, Egyptologists, etc.). As of now, the leaders and scholars of the three religions have not adequately responded to these questions and challenges regarding historical verification.

In this volume, we have seen that religious history has been questioned by some major contemporary historians. These historians can be called "scientific historians" since they view the writing of history as a matter of science in which historical verification is essential. Contemporary religious historians have, on many occasions, been criticized by scientific historians, since the religious writers are primarily intent on maintaining religious teaching and only secondarily on honoring historical verification. For their part, the religious historians often consider that historical data cited only in the sacred writings of the three religions can and must be considered historically verified solely on the basis that God has revealed *what truly happened at various historical moments of time*. Since God has revealed these happenings, they must be verifiable history.

From the earliest historical writings, circa 3000 B.C.E. onward, religious history has been an honored and respected study. Today, however, some of the earliest historical writings on religious issues are often described as legends, mythologies, fictional writings, mythopoetics, symbolic writings, and non-historical narratives.[2] One can legitimately argue that parts of the sacred writings of Christianity, Islam, and Judaism should today be labeled as mythological, legendary, mythopoetic, etc.[3] One should note that many biblical scholars from the three religions are not opposed to such nomenclature.[4] Many contemporary biblical scholars apply the "story approach" (*māšāl*) to the books of Judith, Esther, Jonah, Tobit, and Ruth. These books are not presenting historical material. Rather, they are telling a story that has a profound religious meaning.

However, there are also many mythological elements in the Torah. There are also mythological elements in the Historical Books of the Hebrew

---

2. See Albrektson, *History and the Gods*; Jacobsen, *Treasures of Darkness*; Starr, *History of the Ancient World*; Campbell, *Mask of God*; Schwartz, *Tree of Souls*; Leeming, *Oxford Companion to World Mythology*.

3. See McKenzie, "Aspects of Old Testament Thought." See also Cassirer, *Language and Myth*.

4. See Rudolf Bultmann, *Jesus Christ and Mythology*. Bultmann began a major study of biblical material that could be called in one way or another "mythology."

Conclusions

Bible (Samuel, Kings, Chronicles), and in the Prophetic Books of the Hebrew Bible (Isaiah, Jeremiah, Ezekiel, Daniel and the Minor Prophets). In the New Testament there are also instances of "storytelling." These can be found in all four Gospels, in Acts, and in the letters of various authors. In these writings, the authors portray the actions and the preaching of Jesus by means of stories. They also portray the actions and preaching of early Christian leaders such as Peter and Paul by means of stories. Since there were no tape recorders or video equipment in the first century C.E., oral traditions were the first expressions of what Jesus and others said or how he acted. Over time, some of these oral traditions were accepted and others were not accepted. The latter have generally been called the Pseudepigrapha or Apocrypha. These two terms imply that such written material does not have historical verification. However, there is a growing number of contemporary Christian, Islamic, and Jewish scholars who argue that many passages in the sacred writings of the three religions are historically non-verifiable as, for instance, the exact words of Jesus, of Yahweh, or of Allah. These authors claim that the Christian, Islamic, and Jewish authors use a story form to convey spiritual issues (e.g., parables, "historical" narratives, physical happenings, etc.). Religious issues are expressed not in verifiable historical statements but in mythopoetic ways.

Robert J. Alter, in his volume *The Art of Biblical Narrative*, states that a historical reading of the Old Testament is not what many biblical authors intended. Rather, many authors used literary methods such as the play of ideas, the tone, the imagery, etc. to convey their message. Consequently, when historical questions are asked of a given sacred text, these texts do not immediately yield historical answers, since the historical aspect depends on the norms for historical verification. When literary questions are asked of a text, the text generally yields a literary answer. Both the literary and the historical forms of questions have profound meaning.[5]

In chapter 5, we saw how the leaders of the Roman Catholic Church have reacted to a non-literal understanding of the sacred writings. The Vatican II document *Dei Verbum* carefully and even hesitantly expresses an acceptance of some non-literal reading of Scripture. The *Catechism of the Catholic Church* (nn. 109–141) presents a major outline for interpreting scriptural texts, but on the basis that "All other senses of Sacred Scripture

---

5. See Alter, *Art of Biblical Narrative*. See also Galvin, *Egypt as a Place of Refuge*. Both of these authors offer a bibliography that indicates that a "story form" interpretation of sacred literature has become acceptable today.

are based on the literal [sense]" (n. 115). In both instances, the leaders of the Catholic Church do not want to engage in an open and honest way with the issues of historical verification. Both documents seem to reject any serious questioning of the standard Catholic interpretation of the Scriptures, and the authors do not seem to acknowledge that new data on the issue of historical verification has taken place.

Today, there is an acceptable "story form" for many parts of the sacred books. Today, there is also a position that religious histories should be evaluated by acceptable standards of historical verification. Even if the sacred writings of the three religions are ultimately based on divine revelation, historical details must be separated from faith details. Only when sources outside of the sacred writings are also found that provide adequate historical verification can a given scriptural passage be accepted as a historical detail rather than a faith detail.[6]

Second Conclusion

A second conclusion as regards scientific history is this: one should offer a full presentation of the historical picture in order to understand the historical material itself. A full historical picture includes the major facets of life and activity that took place alongside the religious account as found in the sacred writings of the three religions. These facets include the political and economic factors that were in play at the time referred to. These facets also include the sociological as well as the wide range of religious factors of the given time.

---

6. The history of Egypt has been researched enormously in the past fifty years. Two issues stand out: first of all, during the time of Moses, the Egyptian government at almost all levels kept meticulous records; secondly, the Egyptian government at the time of Moses maintained a strong military presence along its frontiers. The Egyptian records at the time of Moses evidence a major lack as far as the Jewish presence in Egypt is concerned. There are no Egyptian records regarding the Mosaic material as found in the Torah. Thus, it is not only the "minimalists" who question the presence of Abraham, his descendants and Moses in Egypt. The lack of any historical records in Egypt for the presence Abraham, his descendants, and Moses raises major obstacles for the verification of the sacred text that "historically" describes Abraham, his descendants and Moses as active individuals in Egyptian society. Contemporary scriptural scholars who are mainline Christian, Muslim, and Jewish experts have also raised questions on the historical veracity of many parts of the Abrahamitic-Mosaic material.

Conclusions

A current example of this full historical picture might explain what this conclusion is all about. In 2010, Philip Jenkins' book *Jesus Wars* was published. Its subtitle reads: "How Four Patriarchs, Three Queens, and Two Emperors Decided What Christians Would Believe for the Next 1,500 Years." In most volumes of Christian church history, the first early councils of the Christian church have been historically explained in a way that favors the winners. Once the bishops, political leaders, etc. had voted for a given text, the issue was presented as the official teaching of the church at that period of time, and subsequent church leadership continued to honor the official teaching.

Jenkins, however, has gathered together numerous historical details that are not generally mentioned: namely, the intrigue and machinations of an imperial-sponsored, militia-wielding group of bishops. The negative response to the early councils of the Christian church brought about a much larger development of alternate Christian churches than the sixteenth-century Reformation had done. The historical activity that led up to the Council of Chalcedon in 451, as well as the effects of the council itself, divided the Christian world into several alternate Christian entities. This schism has never been healed. If the separation was based simply on solid theological data, there could be an acceptable basis for this division. However, before, during, and after the council, all sides engaged in political, military, and economic activities to further their respective positions.[7] These activities included murder, maiming, denunciation reputations, exile, etc. From a religious standpoint, such atrocities raise serious questions about a proclaimed integrity and univocal interpretation of a religious or theological teaching.

In a similar way, there is a need for a more thorough documentation when interpreting the historical data about the Abrahamic-Mosaic material. The new criteria for historical verification cannot be dismissed as though it had no legitimacy. Rather, some form of mutual discussion between current historians and current scriptural scholars needs to be encouraged. This discussion would involve Christian, Islamic, and Jewish scholars.

CONCLUSIONS BASED ON QUANTUM PHYSICS

There is one major conclusion in which contemporary quantum physics challenges the three religions, namely, the challenge to the three divine plans for creation respectively formulated by Christianity, Islam, and Judaism.

---

7. See Jenkins, *Jesus Wars*, 229–78.

First Conclusion

In quantum physics there are a number of plans, processes, orders, interrelationships, etc., but there is no overarching plan that directs all of the microcosmic activity within the universe. The complexity of these various plans, processes, etc., challenge the religious formation of a divine plan for all finite reality. Moreover, the complexity of these various plans, processes, etc., has been taking place for billions of years, and this extensive timeline complicates any effort to formulate an overarching plan for the microcosmic world. Scientists, therefore, see the current religious plans as oversimplified, and as a result the scientific world does not question these plans. Rather, the quantum scientific world today challenges the veracity of the religious plans.

Because of the major position that quantum physics has attained within today's scientific field, the above conclusion must be seen as a *challenge* and not simply as a *question*. To date, the leaders and scholars of the three religions have not adequately faced the implications of this challenge insofar as it affects their respective divine plans for finite reality that they continue to profess.

More specifically, quantum physics has shown that the microcosmic world is replete with a variety of programs, orders, plans, interconnections, and relationships. Mesons, neutrons, electrons, neutrinos, etc. are all interrelated and the energy within these relationships is continually changing. Because of this interrelational structure of the microcosm, four factors arise:

1. There is no overarching plan for all the microcosmic orders, interconnections, and relationships, plans, etc. Rather, there are numerous competing or interacting relational interconnections, which indicate that some form of mass-energy is at work. If there were a divine plan or even a scientific finite plan for all finite reality, some indications of an overarching plan would as of now be evident. However, in the framework of all the relationships in the microcosm, there is no evidence of an overarching plan that governs the activities of the multiple mesons, neutrons, electrons, neutrinos, etc.

2. The microcosmic interrelational world offers no indication whatsoever that all these programs, orders, plans, interconnections, and relationships have as their ultimate goal the production of human life.

Conclusions

In the divine plans of the three religions, human life is seen as the apex of creation. Such a view finds no echo in the microcosmic world of quantum physics. Human life is simply one of the many atomic and subatomic developments within the universe.

3. The microcosmic, interrelational world is totally different from the world as understood by Galileo and Newton. For Galileo and Newton, at the base of all finite change there was a reality that one can call "substance," namely, a form of finite being that, in its Aristotelian form, has no underlying conditions or connections. Quantum physics is not a substance-centered explanation. Rather, quantum physics indicates that all finite reality is relational, or more carefully stated, interrelational.

4. Relation, or even more carefully stated, interrelation, is the ultimate basis of mass-energy. Many scientific experiments and conclusions lead to this interrelational understanding of the universe, such as: the dual slit experiment and buckyballs, the dual nature of light, De Broglie's matter-wave position which Erwin Schrödinger refined in a mathematical way, Werner Heisenberg's uncertainty principle, superposition or two-slit experimentation, the data from particle interferometers which involves non-locality, and the EPR paradox in conjunction with John Bell's inequality theorem. All of these issues in quantum physics stress relationship over substance as the basic structure of finite reality.

From a microcosmic point of view, the sun in our solar system is gradually moving towards self-destruction, and microcosmic factors in the solar system are also moving towards eventual self-destruction. At a certain point in this process of self-destruction, the gravitational solar power, which affects human life as well as the various energy levels of human existence provided by the sun, will diminish to such a point that human life is no longer viable on Earth. However, this stage of self-destruction of the sun does not indicate that the universe itself has reached its ultimate "culmination." As with many stars, the sun will indeed become self-destructive, but the remainder of the vast universe will continue on. The universe, therefore, will continue to exist without human life and without the solar system within which human life had lived. For the scientist today, a plan for the universe cannot be one that culminates in human life.

Science and Religion: Fifty Years after Vatican II

The above material has been dealt with in this volume, and it leads to a conclusion regarding quantum physics and the religious position of a divine plan, namely, that human life is not the final goal of the processes and plans that are found throughout the microcosmic world. Because of this decentering of human life as the summit of creation, the three divine plans for creation offered by Christian, Islamic, and Jewish leaders and scholars have been called into question. Quantum physics, however, does not *question* these religious plans. Rather, quantum physics *challenges* all three of these religious plans.

The challenge, however, does not mean that contemporary science provides the answers to all our human questioning. George Ellis, in his essay "Physics, Complexity, and the Science-Religion Debate," outlines the radical understanding of relationality in physics in a thorough way. The physical sciences do deal with relational structures both in the microcosm and in the macrocosm. Ellis, however, notes that there are boundaries to the physical sciences. Quantum physics, for instance, cannot be seen as the ultimate structure of the cosmos, but it can be seen as the relational way in which the microcosm has developed to date. He also states that scientific fundamentalism shares the same problematic as those found in religious fundamentalism, namely, a quick answer to an overwhelming and universal question.[8]

Quantum physics is not anti-religion. However, it does not support a divine plan for finite reality as proposed by the three religions. This lack of support is not based on an atheistic stance. Rather, it is based on quantum physics itself, which disallows, at least to date, any and every form of an overarching plan. Since there is no evidence of an overarching scientific plan for finite reality, a religious-historical plan is simply a negation of the factual data that quantum physics has disclosed. Divine plans for creation may have been in sync with the physics of Galileo and Newton, but they are essentially not in sync with quantum physics today. Today, quantum physics dominates the physical sciences.

---

8. G. Ellis, "Physics, Complexity," 751–65. Ellis cites the works of George Monbiot that reflect Monbiot's total denial of religion. He refers to George Montbiot, 759–60.

CONCLUSIONS BASED ON THE AGE OF THE UNIVERSE AS COMPUTED BY CONTEMPORARY SCIENCE

There are two conclusions that are based on the age of the universe as computed by today's scientific investigations. The first conclusion is really a *challenge* to the leaders and scholars of the three religions because the contemporary findings regarding the age of the universe completely undermine the current religious presentations of a divine plan for all creation. The second conclusion is also a *challenge*, but it is a challenge to both contemporary science and to the standard teachings of the three religions.

First Conclusion

The age of the universe as computed by contemporary science places the beginning of the universe somewhere between fourteen to eighteen or even twenty billion years ago. Given this enormous length of time, contemporary scientists realize that any and every pinpointing of time, including the beginning of the universe or the establishment of a given reality or process, is very difficult. Consequently, whenever scientists claim that x began at such and such a time, other scientists generally question such specific computation. The same inability to establish a particular time affects religious leaders and scholars as well. In other words, to say that the history of the entire universe, from creation down to the present, fits into a plan that religious scholars have developed is not only questioned; it is profoundly challenged.

Christians, Muslims, and Jewish people believe that the universe began in and through a divine act of creation. This position has dominated the Euro-American and the Arabic world for centuries. Prior to creation, nothing other than God existed. In earlier centuries, many religious scholars also computed when the Earth was created and also when human life began. Faced with a contemporary scientific approach to the age of the universe, many religious leaders and scholars have adapted these computations. However, there is still a basic claim by religious leaders and scholars that God has *de facto* a historical plan for all creation, and that this historical plan is evident even today. As we have seen above in chapter 6, there are three different plans: the Christian plan, the Islamic plan, and the Jewish plan.⁹ Contemporary scientists not only call into *question* all three plans; they also *challenge* all three plans as totally non-verifiable.

The data on the age of the universe no longer questions the religious plans for creation presented by the three religions; it challenges them in a profound and all-encompassing way. Scientists have found no trace of such a universal and overarching plan in the macrocosm. Scientists generally judge the religious plans as simplistic and unfounded. To date, leaders and scholars from all three religions have not offered a strong response.¹⁰

In many ways, it would be far more acceptable if the leaders and scholars of the three religions as well as leaders in science simply dropped all discussion of an overarching plan. When one is face with billions of years, it is almost impossible for both scientists and religious persons to claim historical verification for any cosmic dating. That a divine being can be

---

9. In the Asian world, the book called the *Huai-nan-tzu* explains the Chinese view of the origin of the universe more clearly than any earlier philosophical writings. Cosmological interest became popular in the Chinese world only at the beginning of the Han Dynasty (201 B.C.E. to 220 C.E.). Chinese cosmology is non-religious and profoundly interrelational.

See J. P. Leahy, *Infinity and Eternity in the Universe*, www:jb.man.acuk/~jpl/cosmo/infinity.html. Aristotle, for his part, favored durational infinity, which means that there was no beginning to the finite universe(s) nor will there ever be an ending to the finite universe(s). Over the centuries, some scientists have favored durational infinity. A large number of Western scholars over the past three thousand years have expressed in one way or another a first cause for all finite reality. This first cause at times has not been a divine being but some other transcendent form of power. Contemporary science on the age of the universe challenges these views as well.

10. Eisen attempts to meet this challenge in his essay "Strategies of Modern Jewish Faith." Eisen presents some of the ways by which contemporary Jews are able to live with scientific challenges such as quantum mechanics and the scientific age of the universe. Eisen explains that Peter Berger had one way of facing scientific challenges. Berger took issue with efforts to debunk scientific claims to absolute truth. He called these efforts a "relativizing of the relativizers." Thomas Kuhn, Eisen writes, urged people to realize that science is merely one way of looking at things among others. The scientific account "of creation or the solar system, therefore, is no more entitled to our prima facie assent than that of Genesis or its medieval interpreters." Eisen continues by writing: "Space, time, objectivity, subject-object knowledge, all lay with the limits of the 'It-it' world. Lived immediacy and relationships, including our relation the Eternal You, occurred in the other world of 'I-Thou.'" Eisen's view is similar to the position found in the *Catechism of the Catholic Church*, which stresses that there are two distinct orders. It should be noticed, however, that in the "It-it" world and the "I-Thou" world, as also in the *Catechism*'s two orders, there is still a divine plan for human life and for human life on planet earth and in our universe. Complete duality may not be the best way to challenge contemporary science, since complete duality means that religion and science should simply walk in different directions and leave each other alone.

Conclusions

considered as the creator or first cause of all being is a possible religious position. That we are able to comprehend this divine being's overarching plan for all finite reality is, today, a chimera.

Second Conclusion

Given the age of the universe, contemporary scientists cannot and should not enter into the non-scientific question of whether God exists. Not only is the issue of God not a scientific issue and therefore remains outside the authentic ambit of scientific endeavor; it is also an issue that, as noted several times in this volume, leaves the scientist as an arbiter vis-à-vis the three religions. No scientist should or can say that there is a God and this God is the Christian God, or the Islamic Allah, or the Jewish Yahweh. The issue of which God is the true God is a problem among the three religions. The scientific world is focused on the microcosm, the macrocosm, and perhaps on multiverses as well. The scientific world is not focused on issues of faith.

Scientists cannot be put into the position arbiter on which of the three divine plans for creation can be substantiated by scientific study. A scientist is not meant to be the arbiter between these three religious groups. Thus, the three religious groups need to understand that the issue is an intra-religion complication, and the respective leaders and scholars of the three religions need to begin a peaceful but competent intra-religion "trialogue" on the issue of a possible single divine plan for all creation.

CONCLUSIONS BASED ON THE INTRA-RELIGION ISSUE OF MONOTHEISM

There is one conclusion based on the intra-religion issue of monotheism, and it can be stated in a very simple and forthright way.

First Conclusion

Even though the material on monotheism is abundant, too often an author simply states that there are three religions that are formally monotheistic:

Christianity, Islam, and Judaism. There is little material on how these three religions can be monotheistic if by "monotheism" an author means that there is only one possible God. A univocal God with three differing forms of worship has not been nor is it today an accepted resolution of the issue of one monotheistic God. Since the one God is also the *infinite* God, no limits can be placed on God. A Christian cannot say, "Our God is the one and only God," nor can a Muslim or a Jewish person make a similar claim for the Islamic or Jewish God. The leaders of the three religions cannot limit an infinite God. Today, given globalization, ecumenism, multiculturalism, and a gigantic growth in human population, monotheism needs to be restudied by the three religions in an open and honest way. Otherwise, none of the three religions should claim to be monotheistic. The basic key to this restudying is a foundational acknowledgement by the three religions that the monotheistic God is infinite.

The formation of an intra-religion dialogue is the beginning for this most basic conclusion. A group of leaders and scholars from all three religions needs to meet in a peaceful and scholarly way to discuss how all three religions can claim monotheism even though the individual understanding of God in each of the three religions is, in many ways, radically different from the understanding of God found in the other two religions. The only thing that can bring monotheism honestly into all three religions is a profound acknowledgment of the infinitude of God.

With the acceptance of an infinite God, the leaders and scholars of each religion can conclude that their respective understanding of a monotheistic God is limited. No leader and no scholar of any religion can claim that our human mind can comprehend the infinitude of God. Consequently, we are urging that each religion accept the fact that it has only a *glimpse* of the infinite God. Each religion maintains its center and core, namely, the beauty and power of its glimpse of God, but at the same time the leaders and scholars of each religion humbly acknowledge that the divine beauty that lies at the core of their faith is only a partial glimpse since God is infinite. There is no univocal beauty that centers each religion, for Christians, Muslims, and Jews see each in their own way something uniquely special in this overwhelming beauty of God. However, by humbly admitting that God is infinite, these same leaders and scholars have to admit that their glimpse of the divine beauty is partial and limited. When this happens, then these

Conclusions

leaders and scholars can acknowledge a monotheistic God whose infinite beauty is appreciated and honored in many finite ways.[11]

Until this is done, the conversations and debates over contemporary science and religion issues cannot go forward. In these conversations and debates by religious leaders and scholars, the interrelationship of God and science is secondary. However, if there is no common understanding of the term "infinite God," then conversations and dialogues between religions and science are meaningless. Scientists will rightfully ask, "Which God are you religious people talking about?" The scientists will also say, "Science cannot be called on to verify the existence of a Christian God or an Islamic God or a Jewish God." Until the meaning of a monotheistic God can apply to these three religions (and to other world religions as well), scientists can rightfully reject any dialogue between God talk and science talk. God talk and scientific talk can go together only if the term "God" is the same for all three major religions.

In a straightforward way, the intra-religion discussion on the meaning of monotheism needs to take up the following issues:

1. Can the term "monotheism" be univocally used by all three religions that are based on the monotheism of Abraham?

2. If "monotheism" is not a univocal term, can any of the three religions maintain its position on monotheism and, at the same time, not negate the validity of the monotheistic God in the other two religions? Such a negation destroys any and every ecumenical discussion.

3. Does the claim by one religion about its monotheistic God in any way limit the infinitude of God? Since the infinite God cannot be limited by any human being or human group, can a single religion claim a theology of God that basically denies the role of an infinite God active in all other religions? This question is foundational to any and every claim of a "monotheistic religion."

4. Is it possible to say that each religion has a wondrous and holy glimpse of God but not a total understanding of God? Would a "glimpse of God" monotheistically satisfy the religious status of Christianity, Islam, and Judaism?

---

11. A strong academic help on the matter of divine infinity can be found in the writings of John Duns Scotus. He presented in his final years a fairly well-formed understanding of God's infinity. See Osborne, *Theology of Church for the New Millennium*, 165–80.

Other issues will certainly arise for the members of these discussion groups, but there needs to be some resolution regarding the term "monotheism," since it is applied to a Trinitarian God and Jesus for Christianity, and since it is also applied to the divine Allah as presented in the Qur'an, and since it is also applied to the Jewish Yahweh with its Mosaic and Davidic traditions.

CONCLUSIONS REGARDING THE ISSUE OF GOD'S PLAN FOR ALL CREATION

Each of the three religions has developed its own divine plan for all creation. These three plans are so different that they cannot be melded into a unified divine plan. For the issue of God's plan for all creation, there is only one specific conclusion that is presented in this volume.

First Conclusion

The age of the universe that contemporary physical sciences have calculated is computed in billions of years. Some scientific calculations posit that the universe is about seventeen billion years old. A majority of scientists posit a universe that is fifteen billion years old. There is no way that either scientists or theologians can determine with accuracy when changes in the universe took place. The three religious plans for the history of creation are not merely called into question by this scientific data. Rather, such theological plans are negated and invalidated by contemporary science. Moreover, within the microcosm and the macrocosm of today's scientific worldview, no overarching "plan" has as yet been established. All of this challenges the three religions vis-à-vis their divine plans for creation in a very negative way. Consequently, the leaders and scholars of the three religions need to acknowledge the findings of contemporary science by disclaiming their religious presentations of a divine plan for all finite reality.

Religious leaders and scholars have been clearly challenged by contemporary science in and through the scientific data on the age of the universe. Their individual divine plans are not compatible to this data on the age of the universe. This incompatibility needs to be recognized and acknowledged by the leaders and scholars of the three religions.

Conclusions

With an acknowledgement of the scientific material on the age of the universe, the same religious leaders and scholars have to reassess their claims that God has revealed a historical plan for creation. Two competing factors need to be assessed. First of all, each of the three religions base their historical plan for all creation on God's revelation, but each of the three religions claim a different presentation of these divine revelations. Science cannot be the arbiter to determine which religion has the correct format. Rather, the leaders and scholars of the three religions have to face the issue that God cannot be presented as a divine being who reveals competing plans for the history of creation.

Perhaps, the religious issue of a divine plan should not begin today with the origin of the universe but only with the origin of human life. This position is simply stated as a possible way for the three religions to arrive at an acceptable format for a divine plan. On this reduction of a divine plan to the issues of human life, there will be a total reinterpretation not only of the current scientific data of the age of the universe, but also of the findings of current Near East archaeology. A human-only focus helps us face in an honest way the call for scientific history and the call for religious history.

***

To all of the above, the authors of this volume conclude with this hope. Science today is a marvelous enterprise, but religion is also a marvelous experience. It is our hope and our prayer that this volume is a help to bring these two marvelous aspects of human life into a closer unity and respect. This objective can take place only if and when the leaders of the three religions confront in an honest way the issue of monotheism and the issue of a divine plan for a universe that is many billions of years old. This objective can also take place only if the four areas of archaeology, scientific history, quantum mechanics, and the age of the universe remain within their scientific dimensions and do not attempt to disprove religion. Peaceful discussions between science and religion are needed at this juncture of time. There will, of course, be questions and challenges from both sides, but questions and challenges can be made and even resolved in a peaceful way. We have focused on only three religions and on only four scientific issues. Hopefully, the conversations will eventually include other world religions as well as other scientific projects.

BIBLIOGRAPHY

Albrektson, Bertil. *History and the Gods: An Essay on the Idea of Historical Events as Divine Manifestation in the Ancient Near East and in Israel.* Lund: Gleerup, 1967.
Albright, William F. *The Archaeology of Palestine and the Bible.* Cambridge, MA: American Schools of Oriental Research, 1974.
Albright, William F. "The Impact of Archaeology on Biblical Research—1966." In *New Directions in Biblical Archaeology*, edited by David Noel Freedman and Jonas Greenfield, 1–14. Garden City, NY: Doubleday, 1969.
'Alī, 'Abdullah Yūsuf. *The Holy Qur'ān: Text and Translation.* Kuala Lampur, Malaysia: Islamic Book Trust, 1996.
———. *The Meaning of the Holy Qur'ān.* New ed. with rev. translation. Beltsville, MD: Amana, 1996.
Ali Ashraf, Syed. "The Inner Meaning of the Islamic Rites: Prayer, Pilgrimage, Fasting, Jihad." In *Islamic Spirituality: Foundations*, edited by Seyyed Hossein Nasr, 111–30. New York: Crossroad, 1987.
Al-Kahili, Jim. *Quantum: A Guide for the Perplexed.* London: Weidenfeld & Nicolson, 2003.
Alter, Robert J. *The Art of Biblical Narrative.* New York: Basic Books, 2011.
Andrae, Tor. *Mohammed—The Man and His Faith.* New York: Dover, 2000.
Atkins, Peter. "Atheism and Science." In *The Oxford Handbook of Religion and Science*, edited by Philip Clayton and Zachary Simpson, 124–36. Oxford: Oxford University Press, 2006.
Auvray, P. *Richard Simon, 1638–1712.* Paris: Presses universitaires de France, 1974.
Barbour, Ian G. *Nature, Human Nature, and God.* Minneapolis, MN: Fortress, 2002.
———. *Religion in an Age of Science: The Gifford Lectures 1989–1991.* San Francisco: Harper & Row, 1990.
———. *When Science Meets Religion.* San Francisco: HarperSanFrancisco, 2000.
Barrows, J. D., and F. J. Tipler. *The Anthropic Cosmological Principle.* Oxford: Oxford University Press, 1986.
Basetti-Sani, Giulio. *The Koran in the Light of Christ.* Translated by W. Russell Carrol and Bede Dauphinee. Chicago: Franciscan Herald Press, 1977.
Bell, Richard. *The Qur'ān: Translated, with a Critical Re-Arrangement of the Surahs.* 2 vols. Edinburgh: T. & T. Clark, 1937–1939.
Bhattacharyya, Kalidas. "Vedanta as Philosophy of Spiritual Life." In *Hindu Spirituality: Vedas through Vedanta*, edited by Krishna Sivaraman. New York: Crossroad, 1989.
Blachère, Régis. *Le Problème de Mahomet.* Paris: Presses Universitaires de France, 1952.

Bibliography

Blenkinsopp, Joseph. *A History of Prophecy in Israel*. Philadelphia: Westminster, 1983.

———. "Monotheism." In *The Harper Collins Encyclopedia of Catholicism*, edited by Richard McBrien. New York: HarperCollins, 1989.

Boff, Leonardo. *Passion of Christ: Passion of the World*. Translated by Robert R. Barr. Maryknoll, NY: Orbis, 1987.

Bohr, Niels. "The Quantum Postulate and the Recent Development of Atomic Theory." *Nature* 121 (April 14, 1928) 580–90.

Bonnefoy, Jean-Francois. *Christ and the Cosmos*. Patterson, NJ: St. Anthony Guild Press, 1965.

Bornkamm, Günther. *Jesus of Nazareth*. New York: Harper & Row, 1956.

Braungart, Jürgen. "Creatures of Desire: The Psychonalytic View of Religion in Freud and Lacan. A Philosophical Analysis." PhD diss., Graduate Theological Union, Berkeley, CA, 2000.

Bright, John. *A History of Israel*. Philadelphia: Westminster, 1981.

Brohi, Allahbakhsh K. "The Spiritual Significance of the Quran." In *Islamic Spirituality: Foundations*, edited by Seyyed Hossein Nasr. New York: Crossroad, 1987.

Brown, Raymond, Carolyn Osiek, and Pheme Perkins. "Early Church." In *The New Jerome Biblical Commentary*, edited by Raymond Brown, Joseph Fitzmyer, and Roland Murphy. Englewoods Cliffs, NJ: Prentice Hall, 1990.

Brown, Raymond, and Sandra Schneiders."Hermeneutics." In *The New Jerome Biblical Commentary*, edited by Raymond Brown, Joseph Fitzmyer, and Roland Murphy. Englewoods Cliffs, NJ: Prentice Hall, 1990.

Bultmann, Rudolf. *Jesus Christ and Mythology*. New Jersey: Prentice Hall, 1997.

Cajes, Prisco. *Anitism and Perichoresis: Towards a Filipino Christian Eco-Theology of Nature*. Bagbag, Novaliches, PH: Our Lady of the Angel Seminary, 2002.

Campbell, Joseph. *The Mask of God: Occidental Mythology*. New York: Penguin, 1991.

Carr, Bernard. "Cosmology and Religion." In *The Oxford Handbook of Religion and Science*, edited by Philip Clayton and Zachary Simpson, 139–55. Oxford: Oxford University Press, 2006.

Cassirer, Ernst. *Language and Myth*. Translated by Susanne K. Langer. New York: Dover, 1953.

Catholic Church. *Catechism of the Catholic Church*. Vatican City: Libreria Editrice Vaticana, 1994.

Cheah, Joseph. *Race and Religion in American Buddhism: White Supremacy and Immigrant Adaptation*. New York: Oxford University Press, 2011.

Chiao, Raymond Y. "Quantum Nonlocalities: Experimental Evidence." In *Quantum Mechanics: Scientific Perspectives on Divine Action*, by Robert J. Russell et al. Vatican: Vatican Observatory, 2001.

Chishti, Saadia Khawar Khan. "Female Spirituality in Islam." In *Islamic Spirituality: Foundations*, edited by Seyyed Hossein Nasr, 199–219. New York: Crossroad, 1987.

Chittick, William H. "Eschatology." In *Islamic Spirituality: Foundations*, edited by Seyyed Hossein Nasr, 378–409. New York: Crossroad, 1987.

Clayton, Philip, and Zachary Simpson, editors. *The Oxford Handbook of Religion and Science*. Oxford: Oxford University Press, 2006.

Cleary, Thomas. *The Essential Koran: The Heart of Islam*. Edison, NJ: Castle Books, 1998.

Coyne, Jerry. "Islam and science: cowed Muslim physicist cancels lecture on evolution." *Why Evolution Is True*. Online: http://whyevolutionistrue.wordpress.com/2011/03/06/islam-and-evolution-cowed-muslim-scientist-cancels-lecture-on-evolution/.

Bibliography

Cragg, Kenneth. *Muhammad and the Christian Tradition*. London: Darton, Longman and Todd, 1984.

Davies, Paul. *The Mind of God: The Scientific Basis for a Rational World*. New York: Touchstone, 1993.

———. *Superforce: The Search for a Grand Unified Theory of Nature*. New York: Simon & Schuster, 1984.

Davies, Paul, and J. R. Brown. *The Ghost in the Atom: A Discussion of the Mysteries of Quantum Physics*. Cambridge, MA: Cambridge University Press, 1986.

Dawkins, Richard. *The Blind Watchmaker*. New York: Norton, 1986.

Denzinger, H., and A. Schönmetzer. *Enchiridion symbolorum, definitionum et declarationum de rebus fidei et morum*. New York: Herder, 1974.

Diaz, Jonathan Blas. *Towards a Theology of the Chamoru*. Quezon City, PH: Claretian, 2010.

Doi, Abdur-Rahman Ibrahim. "Sunnism." In *Islamic Spirituality: Foundations*, edited by Seyyed Hossein Nasr. New York: Crossroad, 1987.

Dunn, Marcia. "Astronomers shed light on early stars in cosmos." November 10, 2011. Online: http://www.boston.com/news/science/articles/2011/11/10/astronomers_shed_light_on_early_stars_in_cosmos/.

Eilers, Franz-Josef, editor. *For All the Peoples of Asia*. 4 vols. Quezon City, Philippines: Claretian, 2007.

Einstein, Albert. "Über die einen Erzeugen und Verwandlung des Lichtes betreffenden heuristischen Gesichtspunkt."*Annalen der Physik* 17 (1905) 132–48. Online: http://www.physik.uni-augsburg.de/annalen/history/papers/1905_17_132-148.pdf.

Eisen, Arnold. *Rethinking Modern Judaism. Ritual, Commandment, Community*. Chicago: University of Chicago Press, 1998.

———. "Secularization, 'Spirit,' and the Strategies of Modern Judaism." In *Jewish Spirituality from the Sixteenth Century Revival to the Present*, edited by Arthur Green. New York: Crossroad, 1987.

Ellis, George. "Physics, Complexity, and the Science-Religion Debate." In *The Oxford Handbook of Religion and Science*, edited by Philip Clayton and Zachary Simpson, 751–66. Oxford: Oxford University Press, 2006.

Ellis, George, and Stephen Hawking. *The Large Scale Structure of Space-Time*. Cambridge, MA: Cambridge University Press, 1973.

Endress, Gerhardt. *Islam: An Historical Introduction*. New York: Columbia University Press, 2002.

Ferris, Timothy. *Coming of Age in the Milky Way*. New York: Harper, 1988.

Finkelstein, Israel and Neil Asher Silberman. *The Bible Unearthed: Archaeology's New Vision of Ancient Israel and the Origin of Its Sacred Texts*. New York: Free Press, 2001.

Flannery, Austin, editor. *The Basic Documents of Vatican II*. Northport, NY: Costello, 1996.

Freedman, David Noel, and Jonas C. Greenfield, editors. *New Directions in Biblical Archaeology*. Garden City, NY: Doubleday, 1969.

Fung Yu-Lan. *A History of Chinese Philosophy*. Translated by Derk Bodde. Princeton, NJ: Princeton University Press, 1983.

Galvin, Garrett. *Egypt as a Place of Refuge*. Tübingen: Mohr Siebeck, 2011.

Gaon, Saadian. *The Book of Beliefs and Opinions*. Translated by Samuel Rosenblast. New Haven, CT: Yale University Press, 1948.

Geiger, Abraham. *Das Judenthum und seine Geschichte von der Zerstörung des zweiten Tempels bis zum Ende des zwölften Jahrhunderts. In zwölf Vorlesungen. Nebst einem*

Bibliography

Anhänge: Offenes Sendschreiben an Herrn Professor Dr. Holtzmann. Breslau: Schletter, 1865–71. ET: *Judaism and Its History: In Two Parts*. Lanham, MD: University Press of America, 1985

———. *Was hat Mohammed aus dem Judentum aufgenommen?* Bonn, 1833. ET: *Judaism and Islam*. Translated by F. M. Young. New York: Ktav, 1970.

Gibbs, Wayt. "Profile: George F. R. Ellis." *Scientific American* (1955).

Goddard, Hugh. *A History of Christian-Muslim Relations*. Edinburgh: Edinburgh University Press, 2000.

Goswami, Amit. *Quantum Mechanics*. Dubuque, IA: Wm. C. Brown, 1997.

Green, Arthur. "Introduction." In *Jewish Spirituality from the Bible through the Middle Ages*. New York: Crossroad, 1987.

Haught, John F. *Christianity and Science: Toward a Theology of Nature*. Maryknoll, NY: Orbis, 2007.

Hawking, Stephen. *A Brief History of Time*. New York: Bantam, 1988.

Hawking, Stephen. *Black Holes and Baby Universes and other Essays*. New York: Bantam, 1993.

Hawking, Stephen, and Leonard Mlodinow. *The Grand Design*. New York: Random House, 2010.

Heisenberg, Werner. *Physics and Philosophy: The Revolution of Modern Science*. New York: Harper & Row, 1958.

Hertzberg, Arthur. *Judaism: The Key Spiritual Writings of the Jewish Tradition*. New York: Free Press, 1991.

Hessler, Bertram. *Die Bibel in Spannungsfeld der Modernen Naturwissenschaft*. Werl im Westfallen: Dietrich Coelde, 1957. ET: *The Bible in the Light of Modern Science*. Translated by Sylvester Saller. Chicago: Franciscan Herald, 1960.

Horwitz, Rivka. "Revelation and the Bible according to Twentieth-Century Jewish Philosophy." In *Jewish Spirituality from the Sixteenth Century Revival to the Present*, edited by Arthur Green, 346–70. New York: Crossroad, 1987.

Hourani, Albert. *A History of the Arab Peoples*. New York: Warner, 1991.

———. "Islam, Contemporary Issues in Science and Religion." In *Encyclopedia of Science and Religion*, edited by J. Wentzel Vrede van Huyssteen, vol. 1. Gale Cengage, 2003. Online: http://www.enotes.com/topics/islam-contemporary-issues-science-religion.

Jacobson, Thorkild. *The Treasures of Darkness: A History of Mesopotamian Religion*. New Haven, CT: Yale University Press, 1976.

Jammer, Max. *The Philosophy of Quantum Mechanics: The Interpretations of Quantum Mechanics in Historical Perspective*. New York: Wiley & Sons, 1974.

Jenkins, Philip. *Jesus Wars: How Four Patriarchs, Three Queens, and Two Emperors Decided What Christians Would Believe for the next 1,500 Years*. New York: HarperOne, 2010.

Jeremias, Joachim. *Neutestamentaliche Theologie*. Gütersloh: Gütersloher Verlagshaus Gerd Mohn, 1971. ET: *New Testament Theology: The Proclamation of Jesus*. Translated by John Bowden. New York: Scribners, 1971.

Jomier, Jacques. *Introduction à l'Islam actuel*. Paris: Éditions du Cerf, 1964.

Karris, Robert. "The Gospel According to Luke." In *The New Jerome Biblical Commentary*, edited by Raymond Brown, Joseph Fitzmyer, and Roland Murphy. Englewood Cliffs, NJ: Prentice Hall, 1990.

Karsh, Efraim. *Islamic Imperialism: A History*. New Haven, CT: Yale University Press, 2007.

Bibliography

Kato, Julius-Kei. *How Immigrant Christians Living in Mixed Cultures Interpret Their Religion: Asian-American Diasporic Hybridity and Its Implications for Hermeneutics*. Lewiston, NY: Edwin Mellen, 2012.

Kauffman, Stuart A. *The Origin of Order: Self Organization and Selection in Evolution*. Princeton, NJ: Princeton University Press, 1993.

Kenyon, Kathleen Mary. *Archaeology in the Holy Land*. New York: Frederick A. Praeger, 1960.

———. *Digging Up Jerusalem*. London: Benn, 1974.

Kilpatrick, G. D. *The Origin of the Gospel According to St. Matthew*. Oxford: Oxford University Press, 1946.

Kloppenburg, Bonaventure. *A Ecclesiololgia do Vatican II*. Petropolis, Brazil: Vozes Limitada, 1971. ET: *The Ecclesiology of Vatican II*. Translated by Matthew J. O'Connell. Chicago: Franciscan Herald, 1974.

Knitter, Paul. "Bridge or Boundary? Vatican II and Other Religions." *Vatican II: Forty Years Later*, edited by William Madges, 261–82. Maryknoll, NY: Orbis, 2006.

Köchler, Hans, editor. *The Concept of Monotheism in Islam and Christianity*. Vienna: Wilhelm Brautmüller, 1982.

Kosowsky, Arthur. "The Cosmic Microwave Background." Online: http://ned.ipac.caltech.edu/level5/Kosowsky2/frames.html.

Kugel, James. "Topics in the History of the Spirituality of the Psalms." In *Jewish Spirituality from the Bible through the Middle Ages*, edited by Arthur Green, 113–44. New York: Crossroad, 1987.

Kumar, Manjit. *Quantum: Einstein, Bohr and the Great Debate about the Nature of Reality*. New York: Norton, 2010.

Küng, Hans. *Christianity: Essence, History, and Future*. New York: Continuum, 1996.

———. *Trinitätslehre im Dialog mit dem Islam*. Gütersloh: Gütersloher Verlagshaus Gerd Mohn, 2006.

Kutner, Marc. *Astronomy: A Physical Perspective*. New York: Cambridge University Press, 2003.

Labuschagne, C. J. *The Incomparability of Yahweh in the Old Testament*. Leiden: Brill, 1966.

Latourette, Kenneth Scott. *The Chinese: Their History and Culture*. New York: Macmillan, 1946.

Ledit, Charles J. *Mahomet, Israel et le Christ*. Paris: Éditions du Vieux Columbiere, 1956.

Lee, Sang-Sung. "Understanding of the Doctrine of Trinity through the Metaphorical Application of Postmodern Physics." *Sinhaknondan* 30 (2002) 187–210.

Leeming, David Adams. *The Oxford Companion to World Mythology*. New York: Oxford University Press, 2005.

Levenson, Jon. "The Jerusalem Temple in Devotion and Visionary Experience." In *Jewish Spirituality from the Bible through the Middle Ages*, edited by Arthur Green, 32–61. New York: Crossroad, 1987.

Liverani, Mario. *Israel's History and the History of Israel*. London: Equinox, 2003.

Lombard, Peter. *Summa Theologica—Libri IV Sententiarum*. Quaracchi-Florence, Italy: Typographia Collegii S. Bonaventurae, 1924.

Madges, William, editor. *Vatican II: Forty Years Later*. Maryknoll, NY: Orbis, 2006.

Maloney, Francis. "Johannine Theology." In *The New Jerome Biblical Commentary*, edited by Raymond Brown, Joseph Fitzmyer, and Roland Murphy, 1417–20. Englewoods Cliffs, NJ: Prentice Hall, 1990.

Bibliography

Mangalith, Othniel. "On the Origin and Antiquity of the Name Israel." *Zeitschrift für die Alttestamentliche Wissenschaft* 102/2 (October 2009) 225–37.

Mascall, Eric Lionel. *He Who Is: A Study in Traditional Theism*. London: Longmans, Green, 1958.

Massignon, Louis. *Essai sur les origines du lexique technique de la mystique musulmane*. Paris: J. Vrin, 1954.

McKenzie, John. "Aspects of Old Testament Thought." In *The New Jerome Biblical Commentary*, edited by Raymond Brown, Joseph Fitzmyer, and Roland Murphy, 1288–90. Englewood Cliffs, NJ: Prentice Hall, 1990.

McGrath, Alister. E. *Science & Religion: An Introduction*. London: Blackwell, 1999.

Meier, John P. "Jesus." In *The New Jerome Biblical Commentary*, edited by Raymond Brown, Joseph Fitzmyer, and Roland Murphy. Englewood Cliffs, NJ: Prentice Hall, 1990.

Meyers, Eric M., editor. *The Oxford Encyclopedia of Archaeology in the Near East*. 5 vols. New York: Oxford University Press, 1997.

Menon, Sangeetha. "Hinduism and Science." In *The Oxford Handbook of Religion and Science*, edited by Philip Clayton and Zachary Simpson. Oxford: Oxford University Press, 2006.

Michon, Jean-Louis. "The Spiritual Practices of Sufism." In *Islamic Spirituality: Foundations*, edited by Seyyed Hossein Nasr. New York: Crossroad, 1987.

Miles, Jack. *God: A Bibliography*. New York: Alfred A. Knopf, 1995.

Moubarac, Youakim. *Abraham dans le Coran—L'Histoire d'Abraham dans le Coran et la naissance de l'Islam*. Paris: J. Vrin, 1958.

Mombarac, Youakim. *La Pensée Chretienne et l'Islam*. Beirut: Université Libanaise, 1986.

Nasr, Seyyed Hossein. "God." In *Islamic Spirituality: Foundations*, edited by Seyyed Hossein Nasr, 311–23. New York: Crossroad, 1987.

———. "Islam and Science." In *The Oxford Handbook of Religion and Science*, edited by, hilip Clayton and Zachary Simpson. Oxford: Oxford University Press, 2006.

———, editor. *Islamic Spirituality: Foundations*. New York: Crossroad, 1987.

———. "The Quran as the Foundation of Islamic Spirituality. In *Islamic Spirituality: Foundations*, edited by Seyyed Hossein Nasr. New York: Crossroad, 1987.

Neusner, Jacob. *Formative Judaism: Religious, Historical, and Literary Studies*. Chico, CA: Scholars, 1982.

———. "Varieties of Judaism in the Formative Age." In *Jewish Spirituality from the Bible through the Middle Ages*, edited by Arthur Green, 171–97. New York: Crossroad, 1987.

Neusner, Jacob, Bruce Chilton, and William Graham. *Three Faiths, One God: The Formative Faith and Practice of Judaism, Christianity, and Islam*. Leiden: Brill, 2002.

North, Robert, and Philip J. King. "Biblical Archaeology." In *The New Jerome Biblical Commentary*, edited by Raymond Brown, Joseph Fitzmyer, and Roland Murphy, 1196–1218. Englewood Cliffs, NJ: Prentice Hall, 1988.

Noth, Martin. *The History of Israel*. Edinburgh: T. & T. Clark, 1960.

Omnès. Roland. *Philosophie de la science contemporaine*. Paris: Éditions Gallimard, 1994. ET: *Quantum Philosophy: Understanding and Interpreting Contemporary Science*. Translated by Arturo Sangali. Princeton, NJ: Princeton University Press, 1999.

O'Murchu, Diarmuid. *Quantum Theology: Spiritual Implications of the New Physics*. New York: Crossroad, 2004.

Osborne, Kenan, editor. *The History of Franciscan Theology*. St. Bonaventure, NY: The Franciscan Institute, 1994.

Bibliography

———. *A Theology of Church for the Third Millennium: A Franciscan Approach.* Leiden: Brill, 2009.
Palakeel, Joseph. *The Use of Analogy in Theological Discourse: An Investigation in Ecumenical Perspective.* Rome: Gregorian University Press, 1995.
Parkes, James. *The Conflict of the Church and the Synagogue: A Study in the Origins of Anti-Semitism.* London: Soncino, 1961.
Patte, Daniel, editor. *The Cambridge Dictionary of Christianity.* Cambridge: Cambridge University Press, 2010.
Peacocke, A. R. *Creation and the World of Science.* Oxford: Oxford University Press, 1986.
Penrose, Roger. *Cycles of Time: An Extraordinary New View of the Universe.* London: Vintage, 2012.
Perkins, Pheme. "The Gospel According to John." In *The New Jerome Biblical Commentary,* edited by Raymond Brown, Joseph Fitzmyer, and Roland Murphy, 942–50. Englewood Cliffs, NJ: Prentice Hall, 1990.
Peters, Francis E. *Islam: A Guide for Jews and Christians.* Princeton, NJ: Princeton University Press, 2003.
Peters, Ted. "Contributions from Practical Theology and Ethics." In *The Oxford Handbook of Religion and Science,* edited by Philip Clayton and Zachary Simpson. Oxford: Oxford University Press, 2006.
Phan, Peter. *Being Religious Interreligiously: Asian Perspectives on Interfaith Dialogue.* Maryknoll, NY: Orbis, 2004.
———. *Evangelization and Interreligious Dialogue: Compatible Parts of Christian Mission?* Santa Clara, CA: Ignatian Center for Jesuit Education, Santa Clara University, 2010.
Polkinghorne, William G. *Reason and Reality: The Relationship between Science and Theology.* Philadelphia: Trinity, 1991.
———. *Scientists as Theologians: A Comparison of the Writings of Ian Barbour, Arthur Peacocke and John Polkinghorne.* London: SPCK, 1996.
Popper, Karl R., and W. W. Bartley. *Quantum Theory and the Schism in Physics.* Totowa, NJ: Rowman and Littlefield, 1982.
Prigogine, Ilya. *From Being to Becoming: Time and Complexity in the Physical Sciences.* San Francisco: W. H. Freeman, 1980.
Ratzsch, Delvin. *The Battle of Beginnings: Why Neither Side Is Winning the Creation-Evolution Debate.* Downers Grove, IL: InterVarsity, 1979.
Rees, Martin. *Our Cosmic Habitat.* Princeton, NJ: Princeton University Press, 2001.
Redford, Donald B. *Egypt, Canaan and Israel in Ancient Times.* Princeton, NJ: Princeton University Press, 1992.
Rosenberg, Joel. "Biblical Tradition: Literature and Spirit in Ancient Israel." In *Jewish Spirituality from the Bible through the Middle Ages,* edited by Arthur Green, 82–111. New York: Crossroad, 1987.
Rosenberg, Matt. "Current World Population." Online: http://geography.about.com/od/obtainpopulationdata/a/worldpopulation.htm.
Russell, Robert J. *Cosmology: From Alpha to Omega: The Creative Mutual Interaction of Theology and Science.* Minneapolis: Fortress, 2008.
———. "Finite Creation Without a Beginning: The Doctrine of Creation in Relation to the Big Bang and Quantum Cosmologies." In *Quantum Cosmology and the Laws of Nature: Scientific Perspectives on Divine Action,* edited by Robert J. Russell, Nancy C. Murphy, and C. J. Isham. Vatican City: Vatican Observatory Pub., 1993.

Bibliography

Russell, Robert J, Philip Clayton, Kirk Wegter-McNelly, and John Polkinghorne, editors. *Quantum Physics: Scientific Perspectives on Divine Action.* Vatican City: Vatican Observatory Pub., 2001.

Salaverri, Joachim. "De Ecclesia Christi." In *Sacrae Theologiae Summa*, by Miguel Nicolau and Joachim Salaverri, vol. 1, 487–976. Madrid: Biblioteca de Autores Cristianos, 1962.

Sayous, Edouard. *Jesus Christ d'apres Mahomet ou les notions et les doctrine musulmanes sur le Christianisme.* Paris: Ernest Leroux, 1880.

Schloss, Jeffrey P. "Evolutionary Theory and Religious Belief." In *The Oxford Handbook of Religion and Science*, edited by Philip Clayton and Zachary Simpson, 187–206. Oxford: Oxford University Press, 2006.

Schmidt, Helmut. *Religion in der Verantwortung: Gefährdungen des Friedens im Zeitalter der Globalisierung.* Berlin: Porpyläen-Ullstein Buchverlag, 2011.

Schoeps, Hans Joachim. *Theologie und Geschichte des Judenchristentum.* Tübingen: Hildesheim, 1949.

Schwartz, Howard. *Tree of Souls: The Mythology of Judaism.* Oxford: Oxford University Press, 2004.

Shiao-yi, Chin. *Chronological Table of Chinese and World Cultures.* Taipei, Taiwan: National Palace Museum Publications, 1985.

Shults, LeRon F., Review of *When Science Meets Religion: Enemies, Strangers or Partners*, by Ian G. Barbour. *Theology Today* 58/3 (October 2001) 434–35.

Sivaraman, Krishna, editor. *Hindu Spirituality: Vedas through Vedanta.* New York: Crossroad, 1989.

Smolin, Lee. *The Life of the Cosmos.* London: Weidenfeld & Nicolson, 1997.

Sperling, David. "Israel's Religion in the Ancient Near East." In *Jewish Spirituality from the Bible through the Middle Ages*, edited by Arthur Green, 5–31. New York: Crossroad, 1987.

Starr, Chester. *A History of the Ancient World.* New York: Oxford University Press, 1983.

Steinmann, Richard. *Richard Simon et les origenes de l'exégèse biblique.* Bruges: 1960.

Sweeney, Marvin A. "A Reassessment of the Masoretic and Septuagint Versions of the Jeroboam Narratives in 1 Kings/3 Kingdoms 11–14." *Journal for the Study of Judaism in the Persian, Hellenistic and Roman Periods* 38 (2007) 165–95.

Thompson, Thomas L. *The Bible in History.* London: Jonathan Cape, 1999.

———. *The Historicity of the Patriarchal Narratives: The Quest for the Historical Abraham.* Berlin: W. de Gruyter, 2002.

Trigano, Schmuel, Gregory Baum, and Salah Sétié. *Le Monotheisme: Un Dieu, Trois Religions.* Montreal: Fides, 2003.

Trinh, Xuan Thuan. *The Birth of the Universe: The Big Bang and Beyond.* New York: H. N. Abrams, 1993.

Van Seters, John. *The Edited Bible: The Curious History of the 'Editor" in Biblical Criticism.* Winona Lake, IN: Eisenbrauns, 2006.

Vaux, Roland de. *Ancient Israel: Its Life and Institutions.* Translated by John McHugh. New York: McGraw-Hill, 1965.

Viviano, Benedict. "The Gospel According to Matthew." In *The New Jerome Biblical Commentary*, edited by Raymond Brown, Joseph Fitzmyer, and Roland Murphy, 6306–74. Englewood Cliffs, NJ: Prentice Hall, 1990.

Widengren, George. *Muhammad, the Apostle of God, and His Ascension.* Uppsala: Lundeauistska Bokhandeln, 1955.

Williams, Walter George. *Archaeology in Biblical Research*. New York: Abingdon, 1965.
Willis, T. "The Text of 1 Kings 11:43—12:3." *Catholic Biblical Quarterly* 53/1 (1991) 37–44.
Wilson, Edward O. *Consilience: The Unity of Knowledge*. New York: Knopf, 1988.
Woods, Richard. "Angels." In *The New Dictionary of Theology*, edited by Joseph A. Komonchak, Mary Collins, and Dermot A. Lane, 18–19. Wilmington, DE: M. Glazier, 1987.
Woolf, Daniel, editor. *The Oxford History of Historical Writings*. Oxford: Oxford University Press, 2011–2012.
Woolley, Leonard. *Abraham: Recent Discoveries and Hebrew Origins*. London: Faber, 1935.
World Council of Churches. "Lima Document" ("Baptism, Eucharist and Ministry"). Faith and Order Paper 111. Geneva: WCC, 1982. Online: http://www.oikoumene.org/en/resources/documents/wcc-commissions/faith-and-order-commission/i-unity-the-church-and-its-mission/
Wright, George Ernest, editor. *The Bible and the Ancient Near East: Essays in Honor of William Foxwell Albright*. Garden City, NY: Doubleday, 1961.
Wright, G. Ernest. "Biblical Archaeology Today." In *New Directions in Biblical Archaeology*, edited by David Noel Freedman and Jonas Greenfield. Garden City, NY: Doubleday, 1969.

INDEX OF AUTHORS

Albrektson, Bertil, 164
Albright, William F., 16, 39, 40, 143
'Ali, 'Abdullah Yūsuf, 61, 66
Ali Ashraf, Syed, 179
Alter, Robert J., 165
Andrae, Tor, 11
Aristotle, 4, 172
Atkins, Peter, 20, 80, 156
Auvray, Paul, 42

Barbour, Ian G., 99, 100, 101, 102, 103, 104
Barrow, J. D., 80
Barth, Karl, 105
Basetti-Sani, Giulio, 120
Berger, Peter, 172
Bhattacharyya, Kalidas, 19
Blenkinsopp, Joseph, 131
Boff, Leonardo, 55
Bohr, Niels, 89–92
Boling, Robert, 40
Bornkamm, Günther, 55
Braungart, Jürgen, 139
Brohi, Allahbakhsh, 48, 61, 64
Brown, Raymond, 10, 43
Bultmann, Rudolph, 43, 164
Buber, Martin, 139, 148, 149

Cajes, Prisco A., 5
Campbell, Joseph, 164
Capellus, L, 42
Carr, Bernard, 20, 29
Cassirer, Ernst, 164
Cheah, Joseph, 5
Chiao, Raymond Y., 92, 93, 94, 95, 96

Chittick, William C., 138
Clayton, Philip and Zachary Simpson, 18, 146
Cleary, Thomas, 62, 63, 74, 138
Cohen, Hermann, 149
Copernicus, Nicolaus, 27
Coyne, Jerry, 124
Cragg, Kenneth, 120
Cross, Frank Moore, 40
Crossan, Dominic, 43

Darwin, Charles, 105, 113
Davies, Paul, 80, 82
Davies, Paul and J. R. Brown, 82
Dawkins, Richard, 80, 156
de Vaux, Roland, 40
Diaz, Jonathan Blas, 5
Dickie, Robert, 31
Dirac, Paul, 102
Dunn, Marcia, 28

Ebeling, Gerhardt, 43
Eilers, Franz Joseph, 151
Einstein, Albert, 83, 92, 94, 95, 102
Eisen, Arnold, 67, 68, 73, 74, 138, 139, 149, 172
Ellis, George, 33, 34, 170

Ferris, Timothy, 29
Feyerabend, Paul, 122
Filson, Floyd, 40
Finkelstein. Israel, 16, 18, 38, 39, 40
Fuchs, Emile, 43
Funk, Robert, 43
Freedman, David Noel, 40

Index of Authors

Gadamer, Hans-Georg, 43
Galileo, Galilei, 27
Galvin, Garret, 42, 43, 165
Gaon, Saadian, 148
Garfinkle, Yosef, 40
Geiger, Abraham, 11, 139
Gibbs, Wayt, 29
Ginzburg, Asher, 139, 148
Goddard, Hugh, 120
Gordon, A. D., 139
Goswami, Amit, 82, 83
Green, Arthur, 70, 71, 149
Greenfield, Jonas, 40
Grotius, Hugo, 42
Gunkel, Hermann, 107

Ha'am, Ahad, 139
Hasan, Usama, 123, 124
Haught, John F., 16
Hawking, Steven, 33, 34
Heisenberg, Werner, 83, 84, 85, 86–88
Hertzberg, Arthur, 147
Heschel, Abraham, 139, 149
Hewlett, Martinez, 20
Hitchens, Christopher, 156
Horwitz, Rivka, 139, 148, 149
Hourani, Albert, 18, 63, 120, 121, 122, 123, 151, 152, 153
Hoyle, Fred, 31

Ilam, David, 40
Jammer, Max, 89, 93, 95

Jenkins, Philip, 54, 167
Jeremias, Joachim, 55, 56

Kaplan, Mordecai, 139, 148
Karris, Robert, 58
Kato, Julius K., 5
Kauffman, Stuart, 26, 27, 97
Kennicott, B. F., 42
Kenyon, Kathleen, 16, 18, 38, 39, 40, 161
Kilpatrick, G.D., 52
King, Philip J., 16, 18, 40
Kloppenburg, Bonaventure, 59
Kook, Abraham Isaac, 139
Korchmall, Nahman, 139

Kosowsky, Arthur, 32
Kugel, James, 72, 73
Kuhn, Thomas, 122, 172
Kumar, Manjit, 84, 85
Küng, Hans, 98
Kutner, Marc, 30

Laplace, Pierre Simon, 105
Latourette, Kenneth Scott, 121
Labuschagne, C. J., 133
Leahy, J. P., 172
Leclerc, Jean, 42
Lee, San Sung, 99, 103, 107, 108, 109, 110
Leeming, David Adams, 164
Levenson, Jon, 71, 72
Levy, Thomas, 40
Liverani, Mario, 16, 43, 44
Lombard, Peter, 75

Madges, William, 150
Madin, Ygael, 40
Maloney, Francis, 54
Mangalith, Othoniel, 39
Marriotini, Claude, 43
Mascall, Eric Lionel, 131, 132
Mazar, Amihai, 40
Mazar, Eliat, 40
McGrath, Alister, 89, 90, 101, 103
McKellar, Andrew, 31
McKenzie, John, 133, 164
Meier, John P., 10, 55
Mendes-Flor, Paul, 149
Menon Sangeetha, 18, 19
Meyers, E. M., 18
Michon, Jean-Louis, 64, 65
Miles, Jack, 132
Min, Ki Wook, 13, also chapters 3 and 4
Morinus, J, 42

Nasr, Seyyed Hossein, 18, 60, 61, 64, 123, 124, 138
Newton, Isaac, 105
North, Robert, 16, 18, 40

Omnès, Roland, 16, 27
O'Murchu, Diarmuid, 16
Onfray, Michel, 156

190

Index of Authors

Osborne, Kenan B., 13, 54, 58, 142, 175
Osiek, Carolyn, 10

Palakeel, Joseph, 89
Pannenberg, Wolfhart, 107
Peacock, A. R., 17
Peebles, Philip James, 31
Penrose, Roger, 33, 34
Penzias, Arno, 31
Perkins, Pheme, 10, 54
Perrin, Norman, 43
Peters, Francis E., 63, 64, 125, 152
Peters, Ted, 14, 112, 113, 114
Phan, Peter C., 5
Planck, Max, 31
Plato, 4.
Polkinghorne, John, 16, 27, 102, 103
Popper, Karl R., 122
Popper, Karl R. and W. W. Bartley, 84
Prigogine, Ilya, 17
Prochaska, J. Xavier, 28

Ratzch, Delvin, 17
Redford, Donald, 16, 43
Rees, Martin, 29
Renan, Ernst, 121
Rosenberg, Joel, 6, 72, 77, 116, 117, 118, 119, 120, 149
Rosenstock-Heusy, Eugen, 149
Russell, Robert J., 14, 27, 99, 100, 103, 104, 105, 106, 107

Salam, Mohammad Abdus, 122
Salaverri, Joachim, 149
Samuelson, Norbert, 20
Sayous, Edward, 11
Schleiermacher, Friedrich, 105
Schloss, Jeffrey P., 17
Schmidt, Helmut, 5

Schneiders, Sandra, 43
Scholem, Gerhom, 149
Schults, LeRon F., 100, 103
Schwartz, Howard, 164
Shiao-yi, Chin, 120
Silberman, Neil Asher, 16, 18, 38, 39
Silverstein, Laurence, 149
Simon, Richard, 42
Sivaraman, Krishna, 19
Simpson, Zachary, 18
Skehan, Patrick, 40
Slifkin, Natan, 113, 114
Sperling, David, 71
Spinoza, Benedict, 138
Starr, Chester, 164
Steinman, Jean, 42
Sweeney, Marvin, A., 42

TeSelle, Eugene, 134
Thompson, Thomas L., 16, 43
Trinh, Xuan Thuan, 29

Van Seters, John, 43
Viviano, Benedict, 52
Von Ranke, Leopold, 142, 163

Wallace, B. Allan, 20
Wegter-McNelly, Kirk, 20
Wilder, A. N., 43
Wilkinson, Marc, 31
Williams, Walter, 36, 39, 40
Willis, John T., 42
Wilson, Edward, 80
Wilson, Robert, 31
Windengren, George, 11
Woods, Richard, 213
Woolf, Daniel, 142
Woolley, Leonard, 16, 37, 38, 39, 133
Wright, G. Ernest, 37, 40

www.ingramcontent.com/pod-product-compliance
Lightning Source LLC
Chambersburg PA
CBHW062001220426
43662CB00027B/1633